FLY FISHING FOR TROUT

FLY FISHING FOR TROUT

THE NEXT LEVEL

Tom Rosenbauer

STACKPOLE
BOOKS
Guilford, Connecticut

Published by Stackpole Books
An imprint of Globe Pequot
Trade Division of The Rowman & Littlefield Publishing Group, Inc.
4501 Forbes Boulevard, Suite 200, Lanham, Maryland 20706

Distributed by
NATIONAL BOOK NETWORK
800-462-6420

Photography by Tom Rosenbauer
Animations by Josh Lokan

British Library Cataloguing in Publication Information Available

Library of Congress Cataloging-in-Publication Data

ISBN 978-0-8117-1346-7 (paperback)
ISBN 978-0-8117-6557-2 (e-book)

∞™ The paper used in this publication meets the minimum requirements of American National Standard for Information Sciences—Permanence of Paper for Printed Library Materials, ANSI/NISO Z39.48-1992.

To my kids, the two Bs

VIDEOS

You can access the videos included in this book by scanning the codes with your phone or by opening the link stackpolebooks.com/videos/9780811713467/001.

CONTENTS

ACKNOWLEDGMENTS

There are many more people than those listed here who have shared their perceptive knowledge about trout behavior and trout fishing over the years, and I know I have left many of them out. This was not intentional but can be blamed on my onset of senior moments. In particular, for this book I would like to thank Chris Alexopoulos, Lewis Coleman, Shawn Combs, George Daniel, Kirk Deeter, John Herzer, Kurt Herzer, Spencer Higa, Dave Jensen, Amelia Jensen, Kory Kapaloski, Jeremy Kennedy, Colin McKeown, Sam Orvis, John Packer, Mark Raisler, and Paul Roos.

Fishing images and videos aren't very compelling without people in them. Many of the people listed here didn't realize they were models, but I hope they realize the companionship and laughs they've given me over the past few years on trout water: John Arlotta, Kelly Bastone, Monte Burke, Jeremy Cameron, Adam Cook, Buzz Cox, Marshall Cutchin, Tim Daughton, Joe Fucci, Bob Gotshall, Dave Grossman, Steve Hemkens, Tim Johnson, Joel Johnson, Robin Kadet, Dave Karczynski, Jeff Karczynski, Pete Kutzer, Tim Linehan, Joey Maxim, Joe Sr. Maxim, Cole Paschen, Steve Seinberg, Todd Tanner, Patrick Timmins, Patrick Jr. Timmins, and Melanie Timmins.

Thanks to Josh Lokan for putting far more work into the animations than either of us ever envisioned.

Thanks to Judith Schnell for believing we could put together a book combining words, images, charts, animations, and videos, and especially for being so patient and understanding when I delivered the final product over two years later than we agreed upon. And to her assistant Stephanie Otto for making sense of all the elements I threw at them.

My wife, Robin, and children, Brooke and Brett, have put up with me spending many weekend days and late nights either fishing or pounding a keyboard. Thank you from the bottom of my heart for putting up with my obsession.

Finally, I would like to thank the roughly 40,000 people who download my podcasts and offer up questions on fishing techniques. One of the most frequent requests goes something like this: "I have been fly fishing for a year with moderate success. How do I take my fly fishing to the next level?" In this book I hope to cover techniques and tidbits to help people who want to feel a bit more comfortable on trout streams. Although I try never to forget what it was like in my early days of fly fishing, the generous suggestions from podcast listeners have made my job that much easier.

INTRODUCTION

"How can I take my fly fishing to the next level?" That's a question I'm often asked, and it's a question I hope to answer in this book. Why do we want to take our fly fishing to the next level? Why can't we be happy where we are? Some of us will be, but for most of us the appeal of fly fishing is that we are constantly learning. We will never know half of what's involved; most of us will never even know one-quarter of it. But we enjoy, even thrive on, making discoveries and connections and solving puzzles—and the natural world introduces a dizzying array of variables. Our minds are in constant search of novelty and answers—it's hard-wired into us. Being able to satisfy our intellectual urges while being immersed in the natural world is a combination that's hard to beat.

Still, to be somewhat comfortable in the middle of a cacophony of moving water and having some idea where to begin your search for a trout are prerequisites for really having fun. Frustration is not an aspect of fly fishing we enjoy. And by frustration I don't mean getting your fly caught in trees. That is going to happen every time you go out. I mean feeling helpless when faced with a moving river at your feet.

Fly-fishing schools and clinics do a decent job of teaching people how to cast, showing the basics of the equipment you need, and demonstrating how to tie a few basic knots. If you are at that level, a recent graduate of a fishing school with perhaps a season under your belt, I think this book will be valuable. Those of us who depend on the fly-fishing world for our livelihood know that one of the biggest obstacles we face is the "leaky bucket" phenomenon. In other words, lots of people take introductory fly-fishing classes each year, but more give up after a month or two than stick with it.

There are many reasons for dropping out of the fly-fishing world. Some people were dragged to a class by a friend or spouse and just have no interest in it. Others find that it takes too much of their time away from family, a job, or yard work (although I have never understood the appeal of recreational lawn mowing). But I suspect a significant percentage of these dropouts just don't know how to take the next step, they never feel comfortable with a fly rod in their hands, and thus give up.

If you don't like fly fishing, I can't help you. If it takes too much of your free time, I can't help you either. There is always something more important in life than sticking a hook in a trout's mouth, and you just have to prioritize fly fishing as something you do for yourself, to recharge your batteries. But I think I can give you some ideas on how to understand what's going on in a trout's world, what makes them feed (or not), and how to feel more proficient at this addicting pastime.

Some other things I can't help you with either: You must practice your casting. There is no shortcut to this. You must be able to place a fly 40 feet away with a reasonable amount of accuracy and delicacy. You must be comfortable stripping line and shooting line on your cast. You must practice a few basic knots. I would advise you to practice your casting on a lawn or in water that has no fish in it, and practice your knots at home where there is good light and you are relaxed and can take some time. If you save these drills for your fishing trips, you will be wasting a lot of your free time.

And you must get out there and fish. If you don't have a trout stream near your house, find a pond or lake with sunfish in it and practice casting, setting the hook, and playing and releasing fish. If you do have a trout stream within a reasonable distance, go there as much as you can. If you want to learn, it is better to spend eight hours on a not-so-good stream than to drive three hours to fish for two hours. I know this is common sense, but it's amazing how many novice fly fishers feel they have to drive many hours to famous rivers, forgoing a nice little stream near where they live. That nice little stream may only have small stocked trout instead of big wild ones, but it will be the best classroom you'll ever find.

You may decide to fish on your own. It's the way I learned as a kid because I did not know anyone else who fished with a fly rod. It's satisfying but definitely the hard way to go. So if you want to shortcut your learning, it's best to team up with someone. Probably the best way to shortcut your learning curve is to fish with a guide. The level of professionalism of trout guides in North America is very high, and most guides are terrific teachers providing you establish up front that you would rather catch fewer fish and learn some skills as opposed to catching many fish. If a guide suspects you just want to catch a lot of fish, he or she will probably have you repeat the same technique by rote all day long. It's fun for fish-counters, but if you want to take your fishing to the next level, give up on getting bragging rights.

Not everyone can afford to fish with guides all the time. In that case, one approach is to find someone who is both a better fly fisher than you and very patient. If you don't know the person well, make sure you are up front with your skills and don't try to oversell your abilities. Not everyone appreciates fishing with a novice and, believe me, if you are not as experienced as you make yourself out to be, your fishing buddy will know in five minutes. Additionally, if you are lucky enough to fish with an experienced hand, do him or her a huge favor and practice your casting before you go, and make sure you are capable of tying on your own flies and tippets. It's inconsiderate to expect someone to tie on your flies or fix your leader when he or she had planned on a nice day on the water. Everyone's time is valuable these days.

Another approach, which can sometimes be as effective as fishing with an expert, is fishing with someone who is at the same level as you. Sure, you will both muddle through many things, but discovering them together, or sharing discoveries, can be even more satisfying than having someone else show you the way. Whether this works for you probably depends on the chemistry between the two of you and the way you best learn things. Once I got over my initial bewilderment with fly fishing and could at least muddle my way through, I met another kid in my Boy Scout troop who was at about the same level as me. Throughout our teenage years we learned together, and some of the lessons I learned are the most poignant in all my years of discovery.

So what exactly will this book do for you? You can't always fish and you can't always practice, and sometimes just reading or watching a video on the trout stream environment and techniques used there fill in the hours or months when you can't do anything else. If nothing else, I think the book will give you new cues on what to look for in the confusing array of currents in a river, how trout feed and what they feed on, how the game changes with the seasons, how to develop a philosophy of fly selection, and what to do when you first hit the river. I've also included some casting and rigging techniques that are beyond the basic level taught in fly-fishing schools but are essential if you want to be more successful.

Because fly fishing is so dynamic, I also wanted to include animations and video where still photos just will not do the job. Most of us still like to curl up with a book, but the technology is there to offer up both still photos and moving ones, and I didn't want to shortchange your learning.

Above all, remember three things:

- This is supposed to be fun. Sometimes fly fishing is challenging, sometimes frustrating, but at the end of the day, if you don't feel better than when you started, you are missing the point. In that case you might want to reevaluate your expectations about fly fishing and not set your sights so high.
- Share what you learn with others—if they ask for advice. Don't preach, but be free with what you've discovered once you become more proficient.
- Protect the resource. Trout streams cannot be totally overfished, and as long as the habitat is intact, even a completely poisoned trout stream can be restored in a matter of a few short years, because there are always surviving fish in the headwaters or tributaries of a river. But if we lose the habitat to overdevelopment, poor logging practices, roads that are not constructed properly, or global warming, no amount of catch-and-release fishing or stocking can restore what is lost. You need to be an advocate for both habitat protection and public access, and you have to scream loud about anything that threatens our ability to have cold, clean waters available to everyone.

CHAPTER 1

How Trout Feed

HOW DO DRIFT-FEEDING TROUT BEHAVE?

In your first successful trout-fishing trip, you might have cast a Woolly Bugger randomly in all directions until, wondrously, you felt the electrifying jolt of the line straining in the opposite direction, and you held your breath until you could actually touch the fish and count it as your first. Or maybe you threw a Prince nymph under an indicator to the spot a guide told you to hit and stared at the bobber like it was a high fly ball into center field, until it twitched against the current and you felt the weight of a fish beneath your rod tip. You probably didn't think about what the fish was doing underwater and how it took your fly. You probably didn't care.

Was your first trout purely luck? Probably.

Most of the trout we catch in our early days on the water are aggressive feeders. Optimum water temperatures put their metabolism into high gear, and they feed almost constantly during daylight hours. The more often they feed, the better the chance that your random cast puts a fly in their face. So are these early fish more luck than skill? Of course they are. You had not really developed into an efficient predator. You didn't understand why fish live in certain places in a river and not others. You hadn't developed the skills to make an educated guess as to what kind of food they might be eating. And most of all, you probably did not suspect that most trout stay put, letting the current bring the food to them. You probably thought they swam around looking for stuff to eat, which is why many novices spend so much time fishing for hours in unproductive water.

Under some conditions, and with certain individuals in a trout population, fish do roam around like lake or ocean fish, ambushing prey when they find it. But in a typical trout stream, under the conditions we most often fish (daylight hours, relatively clear water, moderate current depth and speed), the trout that are feeding utilize a strategy called drift feeding. And never forget that it's fish that want to feed that we must find. A big trout that is an ambush feeder, preferring minnows and crayfish to insects and smaller crustaceans, might be right in front of you but that fish does not feed as often as the drift feeders, and it feeds at times of its own choosing, when light levels, water clarity, or turbulence favor its feeding method. We'll discuss those shortly.

But for now let's observe a typical drift-feeding trout and then explore some variations on this behavior. A fish lies in 2 feet of relatively slow water, with an edge or seam of faster water 6 inches from its right-hand side. The fish rests its head on the trailing edge of a small flat rock, using the rock just like a pillow. The fish sways from side to side, gently enough that it appears to use almost no energy to remain stationary. It's not swimming, just holding its position by using the streamlined shape of its body. The gentle current actually helps the fish

This trout drift-feeding to tiny spent mayflies has merely been hovering below the surface.

stay in position, because without at least a little current, the fish might drift out of place.

The fish's body tenses faintly, its eyes swivel to the right, and the fish quickly eases 6 inches to the right and slightly above its position, and then returns to its original spot. You wouldn't really call it swimming because the fish merely used its fins to take advantage of the current, gliding like a seagull on an ocean breeze. What just happened is that the fish spotted a piece of drifting food, intercepted it (or rejected it when it got closer), and then returned to stand guard for the next morsel. If you had seen the white of the trout's mouth as it reached the end of its slide, the fish ate something. If it kept its mouth closed, the trout rejected a bit of drifting debris (or perhaps your fly!) because at the last instant it did not look like or behave like drifting food.

If the light is right and you're lucky enough to spot a feeding trout, you'll see the fish hovering on station like this one just behind the trailing edge of a rock.

Next the fish stiffens again, but this time its eyes look up. The trout slides backward and upward in the current, tips its snout up slightly above the surface of the water, porpoises so that its dorsal fin creases the surface, and then tips down to the bottom. This time, it has to swim a foot or so back to its original position by wiggling its tail and body. It's now back in the original position, waiting for the next victim. It all looks so calm and casual, but this fish is preying on animals just as much as a wolf taking down a deer, and it's every bit as serious to the trout.

But how often does this fish feed from the same spot? Does it swim around looking for good spots to feed? Most trout don't move around much, as they have defined places in a pool or run where they feed and rest, sometimes as many as three or four spots but sometimes only one. As Dr. Robert Bachman in his landmark study of brown trout feeding behavior found, not only would a single brown trout feed from the same location in a pool all season long, but it would be in the same place year after year.

If you carefully observed a trout's feeding spots in a pool, each spot might look distinctly different, but they would all share some common elements. The micro-environment where the trout's body rests would have a current speed somewhere around 1 foot per second. It would also be close to a place where the current was slightly faster, because the amount a drift-feeding trout can eat in a given hour is based on the num-

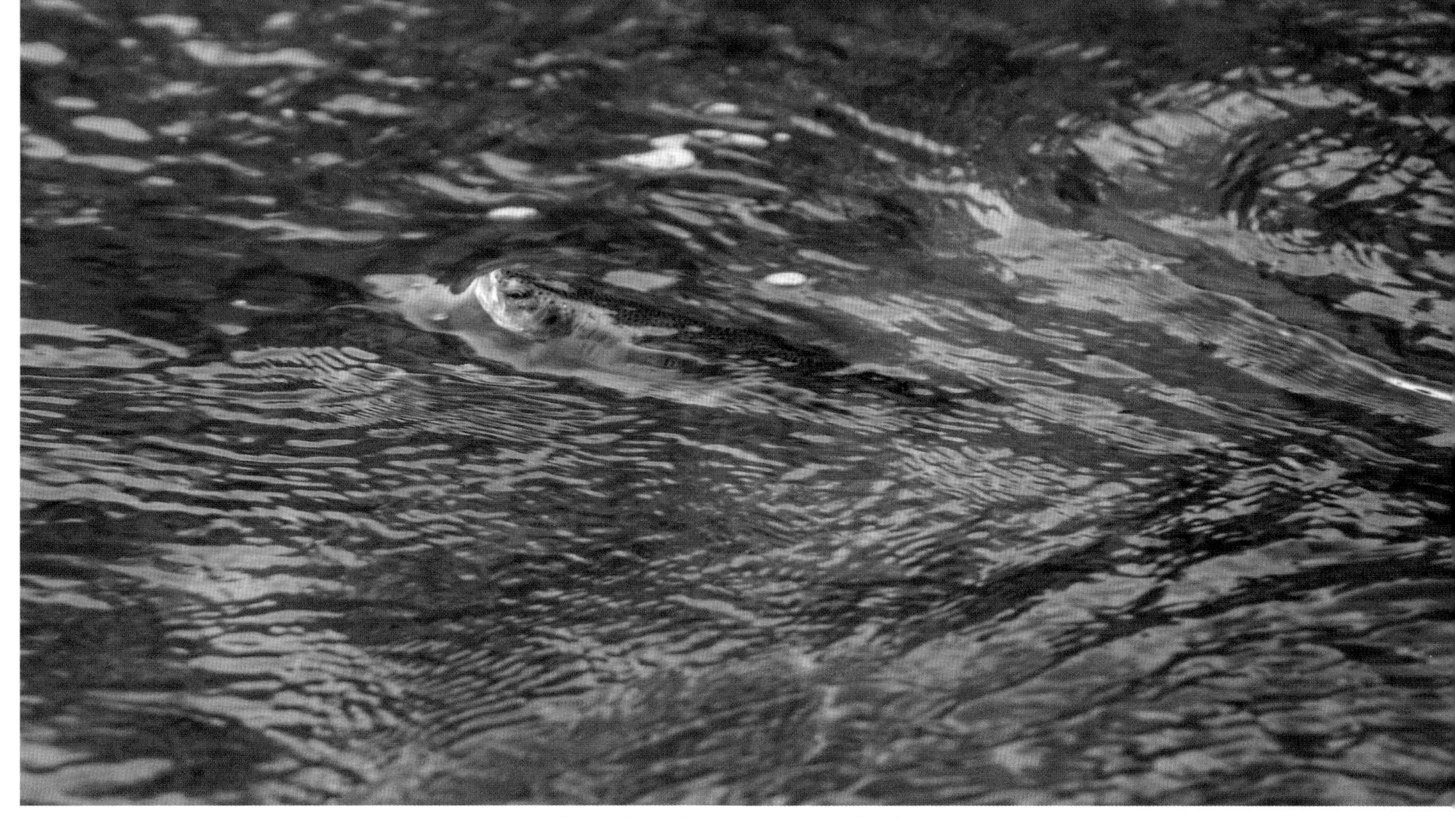

This rainbow rising in faster water has to work harder and is also a lot more difficult to spot.

ber of drifting insects produced by the river, plus the rate at which those insects pass by the trout's position. Because a trout has no control over the rate at which insects hatch or drift, it must choose a spot to maximize the rate of drift near its position.

But that is not the entire story. A trout can't hold in very fast current and survive for very long. This analogy is an anthropomorphic stretch, but bear with me. Imagine that you are constantly running a marathon, and the only food available to you is peanuts thrown by the crowd along the course. In pretty short order you'd collapse from hunger—and you would certainly not put on any weight. Now imagine you only had to run between three of four feeding spots, where you could sit for hours without having to run, and you had a constant supply of peanuts at each resting spot. You'd get chubby in a hurry, but to a trout the equivalent of being chubby is getting bigger and stronger, better able to outrun enemies, and growing into a size class that makes you too big for many predators to eat. Trout exhibit what is called indeterminate growth, which means that as long as they are alive and get enough food, they continue to grow in both length and girth, so they never have to worry about being in front of a DVD screen watching some hard body from California do yoga.

And the biggest reward, if we're to believe Mr. Darwin, is that you'd develop healthy eggs or sperm at an earlier age, and over your lifetime lots of them, so that when it is time to pass on your genes, you have a better chance of continuing your bloodline.

If you watch a trout in one of its feeding positions, you'll see that the fish rests its head or belly on an object, most likely a rock or the bottom, and that somewhere in the vicinity will be a dip in the streambed, a rock shelf, or a large group of boulders that slows the current. A trout is perfectly streamlined so that, in a gentle current, it uses almost no energy but is still able to hold its position, facing upstream where its food comes from. In fast current, this is invariably close to the bottom because the current's force is always at its minimum at the bottom, since the tremendous friction between the water and the stream bottom slows the velocity of the water.

In periods of low flow, or in the middle of large pools where the force of the current spreads out over a wider area, current in mid-water or even at the surface may approach that 1-foot-per-second optimum flow, so that a feeding trout can suspend off the bottom or hover just below the surface and still feed efficiently. Finally, if the current slows to an almost stagnant state, a trout will do one of two things: It will either begin to cruise around the pool as it would in a lake or pond, looking for food, or it might move to the head or tail of the pool where the stream narrows and the current quickens, so that it will continue to get a steady supply of food.

You won't always have the pleasure of observing trout because they are well camouflaged and often feed in places where they are not visible from above. But in low, clear water you may be able to spot fish feeding from a bridge or high bank, and if you don't frighten the fish, you will learn so much about their behavior by observing them. And if the sun is right

SCAN TO WATCH VIDEO 001.

This animation of how a trout feeds, both to subsurface food and to an insect on the surface, is something that is nearly impossible to show properly in a photograph.

SCAN TO WATCH VIDEO 002.
How to get an idea of what trout are taking by observing rises.

and the water is shallow and clear enough, you may even be able to see trout as you fish for them, observing what kind of presentation and what fly interests them the most.

In a case like this, it's extremely important to recognize when a trout is feeding and when it is not. A feeding fish will sway gently in the current and make occasional darts to one side, or it may rise to the surface. A fish that is not feeding—because you've frightened it or the water is so cold that its metabolism is low, or because it is sleeping (fish sleep with their eyes open)—will appear stiff and may sway a bit, but it will not make occasional darts from side to side. A fish like this is generally a waste of time, and your time is better spent finding one that is actively eating.

Notice that we haven't even discussed cover or protection yet. Some anglers think that cover is the most important factor in catching trout and in some rivers you can catch more trout by fishing around logjams and big rocks. But cover without food won't keep a trout alive for very long. Cover with minimal drifting food, like a big rock at the bottom of a 12-foot-deep pool or a logjam off in a slow backwater, might provide protection but not enough food. That does not mean fish won't use these places as a refuge, when danger threatens, but trout can put on amazing bursts of speed for short periods, and they often feed out in the open but with a place of refuge a few tail flips away. The reason we often see trout in these deep or tangled refuges is that fish feel safe there, and there is a good chance that if you spot a trout at the bottom of a deep pool, you've already spooked that fish from somewhere else and now it think it's invisible to you.

But anglers are not the only people who have these misconceptions about trout and cover. Biologists who monitor trout populations are not exactly stealthy. They bull around in a pool with a crew of a half-dozen people running electroshocking equipment, and of course by the time they shock some trout, fish appear from under a big logjam or from the deepest part of a pool. Those fish were probably scattered all over the pool but bolted for their sanctuary as soon as the first biologist stepped into the water.

Underwater video and still shots often show trout tucked alongside logs or jumbles of rocks, and photographers often tell us that they can approach trout very closely and that the fish are not spooked by a diver. That may be the case in a few instances where the fish were feeding so heavily that they lost their caution, or where a diver approaches a fish in a very stealthy manner, but most underwater trout shots I have seen show the fish huddled together, quivering with fright and not feeding.

I remember editing a TV show and the producer kept trying to get me to use some underwater footage of trout, and I was constantly arguing that the shots were just not natural and were misleading for someone trying to learn about trout fishing. The fish were grouped together on the bottom, so close their bodies were touching. Trout are not strongly territorial, but a trout will also not tolerate another fish so close that their bodies touch, other than during an extremely heavy insect hatch when they are all getting plenty to eat and couldn't care less about personal space. But when fish are bunched together in the bottom of a pool, you can be sure they are scared out of their wits. Like people in a tornado shelter, personal space requirements also break down in times of danger.

You may be getting bored with this science lesson; many fly fishers couldn't care less about trout biology, and I'll admit, a lot of the anatomy and reproductive behavior stuff bores me as well. But trout feeding behavior, and understanding how it works, is essential to becoming a crafty fly fisher, who can predict when and where fish will feed and how to pitch a fly to them. So let's look at what we've learned so far

That jumble of natural and man-made cover against the far bank is a great place for an ambush feeder to hide, but feeding trout might also be on the seams at the near side of the fast current or even along the change in depth right in front of the angler.

and how we can apply this knowledge to catch more and bigger trout on a nice day in June when you have the whole day unfolding ahead of you, with nothing to worry about except falling in the water and how you'll find your way back to the car after dark.

Feeding fish will be found in slower water, usually on the edge of faster water. Knowing this will help you avoid raging torrents without any breaks in the current that make it impossible for trout to feed. At the other end of the scale, stagnant backwaters are usually devoid of trout, unless an extremely heavy insect hatch blankets the water with food and trout can afford to cruise in very slow water, picking up helpless insects.

You can avoid fishing in unproductive water by looking for seams, or edges where trout can relax in slower water but have quick access to a constant supply of food in faster water. And these seams aren't always vertical seams, such as the seams on the edge of water as it tumbles into a pool. Seams are also horizontal, where a shallow riffle plunges into a deep pool, or a slightly deeper pocket in a fast riffle where fish can stay out of the fastest current.

By being stealthier and looking for places where it's easy for a trout to feed, you'll find more trout in an agreeable, feeding mood instead of fish quivering in fright. You may not want to waste your time on a trout you see at the bottom of a pool below a bridge, especially if the fish shows no sign of feeding. By looking for seams and shallow water on the edge of deep water, you may be able to catch fish that less careful anglers stumbled through on their way to find the next big logjam.

If you see a fish rising, you'll now realize the trout's observation position is upstream of where you saw the rise, so you will need to cast slightly above the place where you observed a rise. Because fish get pushed backward by the current more in faster and deeper water, you'll learn to lead a fish in a deep run by 3 or 4 feet, but may only need to cast 6 inches above a trout in a shallow riffle.

Perhaps the most valuable lesson is that if you see a nice trout rising but fail to hook it, you know that the same fish will be there later in the day, next week, or even next year if the water level has not changed drastically. And even if that same fish is not there, another one will probably move in. Trout find these good feeding spots quickly, so a good spot today will be a good spot in 10 years, unless severe flooding has moved rocks around or deposited a gravel bar where there once was a nice, deep slot. This knowledge, more than anything else, is why guides and local anglers do better on their home water than visiting anglers. They know right where to go, and they don't waste time fishing unproductive water. They have learned by past observation that no matter how fishy a piece of water looks, there is something about that spot that the trout don't like, and it's probably something about the subsurface hydraulics that makes it a poor feeding spot.

Later we'll go into more detail about hydraulics and reading the water, but now you've got the basics of drift-feeding behavior and how you can use this to find and catch more trout.

Chances are a large brown trout like this is an ambush feeder at least part of the time.

HOW DO AMBUSH FEEDERS BEHAVE?

If a trout lives long enough to reach about 14 inches in length, it may switch from drift feeding to ambush feeding. Something in a trout's nature knows it can get the same number of calories by chasing down a 4-inch sucker, sculpin, or even a juvenile trout as it can by eating 400 midges. But these fish are not just piscivorous, because a crayfish, frog, or hapless mouse swimming across a pool in the middle of the night can give the same benefit. It's a simple matter of calories ingested versus the amount of energy needed to capture those calories. This kind of dietary modification happens more often with brown trout than any other species of trout, but any large trout can become ambush feeders.

Whether or not this occurs depends on habitat. In an infertile stream with few minnows or sculpins or crayfish, trout may never switch to ambush feeding. I remember sitting on the banks of the Bighorn River with Alan Kelly, who was a US Fish & Wildlife Service biologist assigned to the Bighorn in the 1970s. The superb trout fishing in that river was formed when Yellowtail Dam was completed in 1967, transforming a warm, silty, flood-prone lowland river into a cold, clear, stable trout stream due to coldwater releases from the base of the dam. He told me that in the early days, even though the trout had an abundance of invertebrate food, they were smaller than they are today. Gradually, as populations of baitfish moved up from the Yellowstone River, into which the Bighorn flows, trout, especially brown trout, began growing to lengths of over 18 inches because they now had a steady supply of smaller fish for prey.

Sometimes trout grow very large without becoming ambush feeders, again by virtue of habitat. Trout in many tailwater rivers below dams feed on a near-constant supply of aquatic worms, midge larvae, and caddis larvae nourished by the nutrient-rich water coming from the reservoir above. In some tailwaters, small freshwater shrimp of the genus *Mysis* and baitfish also get crippled or killed after passing through the turbines at the base of the dam, and trout wait below with open mouths to catch this high-energy food that is easy to capture.

So not all trout are ambush feeders, and not all ambush feeders ignore drift feeding. It's not a mutually exclusive deal. Eight-inch trout will attack and eat baitfish if the baitfish are crippled or trapped in shallow water. Five-pound brown trout that normally feed after dark on mice or frogs may rise to eat insects off the surface of the water, usually during hatches of larger insects like the Green Drake mayfly that hatches in June on Eastern rivers or the giant Salmonfly stonefly that hatches on Western rivers in early summer. These fish may only feed on drifting insects a few days a year, but for the lucky fly fisher who happens to be on the river during one of these hatches, it's possible to catch the trout of a lifetime.

Trout are just so good at determining the relative benefits of food capture versus the energy expended that we're tempted to give them credit for thinking and analyzing the situation. But don't forget that's pretty much all they do, in addition to spawning a few weeks a year and avoiding predators, so they have to be wired somehow to make these choices without an internal debate. They make the right snap decision or they die and don't pass on their genes.

At this point you might be thinking, "Hey, why should I bother with nymph and dry-fly fishing and have to worry about reading the water and matching the hatch and all that other stuff when I can just fish a streamer fly, imitating a minnow or crayfish? Didn't he just say that even small trout will eat a minnow? So if I just fish streamers, I'll catch the biggest fish and the most fish and they will come out and attack my fly, so I won't even need to know where they are." Sorry, in practice, although you probably will catch more big fish if you just fish a streamer, on most days you'll go through long boring periods of casting practice and no fish.

Here's why: Although you may feel like you're imitating a crippled baitfish with your streamer fly, and you might try all kinds of clever retrieves and fly patterns, we just don't know how to imitate a crippled baitfish with a fly. It's probably a question of smell and the vibrations sent through the water by a crippled baitfish as opposed to how it looks that gets trout excited. I proved this by accident once on the Madison River. I had spent about two hours fishing a streamer in some great-looking water without even a touch. I was fishing close to the bottom with a heavily weighted streamer, and on one retrieve I felt a slight resistance and was surprised to see that my streamer had impaled a large sculpin. Now, bait fishing is illegal on that stretch of the Madison, but I looked around and there was no one in sight, so I left the sculpin on my hook and heaved it out into the current. The sculpin had not been in the water more than three seconds when I felt a heavy strike and my line began moving upstream. I never did hook the fish (and by the way, I'm sure the statute of limitations has expired on my attempted transgression), but it sure brought home the frustration of trying to imitate a crippled baitfish.

It's considered not sporting to soak flies in Essence of Sculpin, but consider that trout can detect a single molecule of amino acid in 10 billion molecules of water. I'm personally not convinced that adding scent to flies is all that unsporting because we get our own amino acids on our flies (which must be repulsive to trout) and we also coat many of them with pungent head cement, superglues, and epoxy. So wouldn't adding scent to flies just be a way of masking unnatural scents, applying the same philosophy as we do when using light tippets to convince trout our flies are not attached to anything? I have not experimented with scents on trout flies, but I wouldn't berate you if you decided to try it.

The other factor is the vibrations that a crippled minnow sets off in the water. Trout possess inner ears that detect vibrations in the water, and the inner ear also works in conjunction with the outside surface of the air bladder to detect changes in pressure waves in the water. Trout also have vibration sensors called neuromasts on the outside surface of their bodies. The ones scattered over the surface of the skin help a fish orient itself in the current, even in darkness, but there is a concentration of these cells along the side of the fish in canals that constitute a trout's lateral line system, which is extremely sensitive to faint changes of pressure caused by vortices in the current. The lateral line system allows trout to hunt for prey

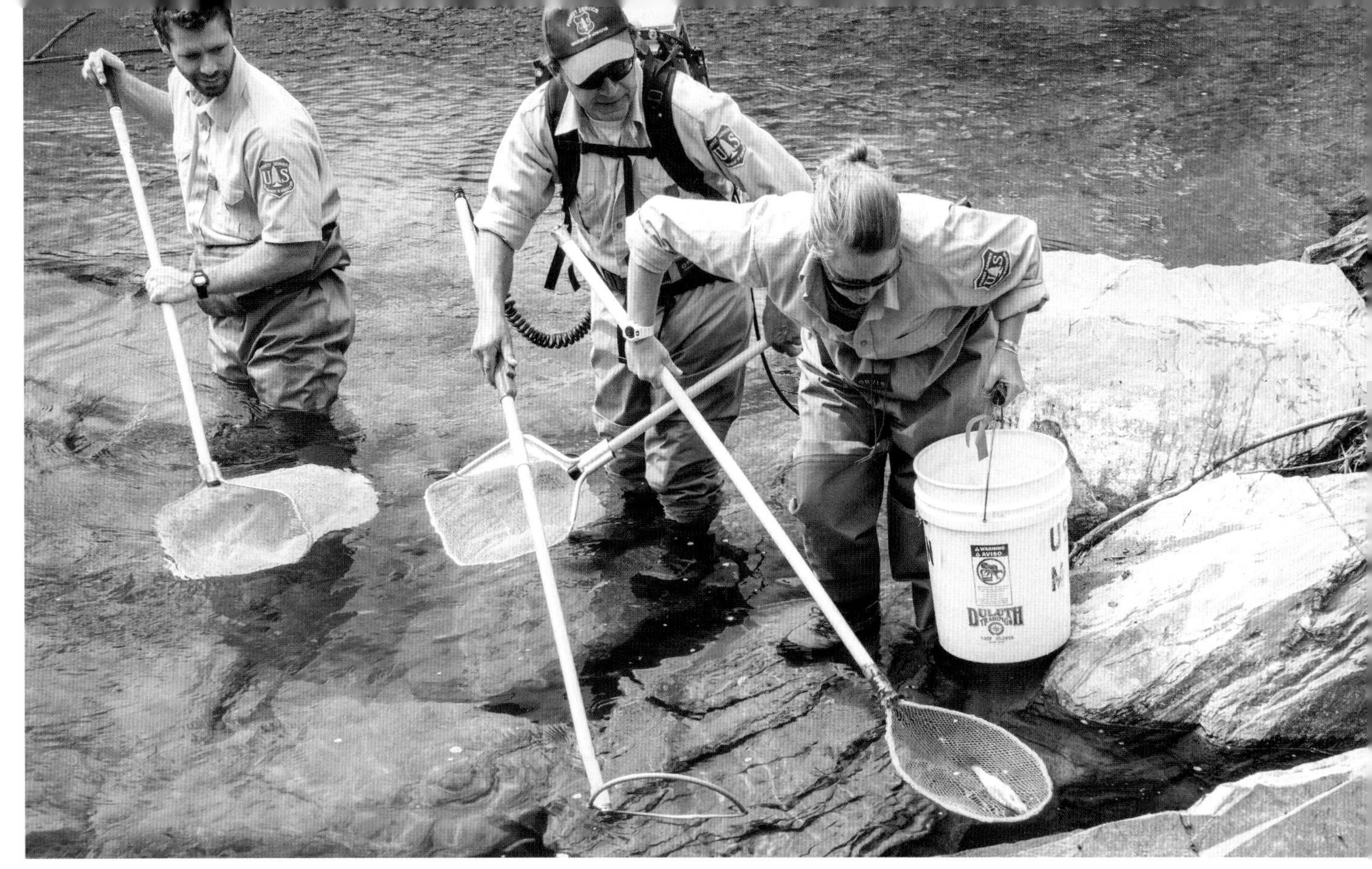

It's no wonder many biologists tell us trout are found near cover. When three people with nets and a generator go plowing through a stream, of course they will find the trout under cover. But the same trout may feed quite a distance from their refuge.

under almost complete darkness, but it is also used during the day to warn trout of the approach of predators and the sounds produced by larger prey.

It's likely that the vortices produced by a healthy dace swimming in the water are far different from the tiny currents produced by a dace struggling to maintain its equilibrium. Fly tiers have experimented with rattles and cup-shaped devices to produce vibrations in a swimming fly, and we're quite certain that bulky heads on flies like the Muddler Minnow produce vibrations that are at least somewhat interesting to trout under certain conditions. And many spinning lures have appealing vibrations that attract fish and fool them into thinking whatever they are eating is at least close to a minnow or crayfish. But we have a long way to go, because a crippled natural baitfish will be attacked almost every time if a fish is hungry, whereas our flies and spinning lures produce a far less predictable result.

But this is not even the toughest of your problems if you plan to become a streamer purist. The chances of finding a fish in the mood to eat a baitfish are not high. One meal of a large minnow or crayfish might hold a trout for several days because trout do get satiated, and they have to digest what is in their system before they are hungry again. The warmer the water, the higher their metabolism, and in water below 50 degrees F, a juvenile sucker could last a trout nearly a week before it feels the need to hunt again. So to expect to have your streamer landing in front of that 22-inch brown trout at a time when it's ready to feed is not a high-percentage gamble.

There are ways to even the odds in your favor a bit. One is to fish your streamer during periods when predators have an advantage over prey, which is typically in low-light conditions. Just after dark, all night long, and early in the morning are times when a trout hunting with its lateral line system has an advantage over baitfish, which apparently are not as good at evading predators when it's dark as they are under bright sunlight. When the light is good, small fish are able to spot a predator coming, and they are far more maneuverable than a big trout, so they can switch directions quickly. Trout are good at turning on the afterburner for speed, but their brakes are not as reliable, so they can't spin around and chase a fish that switches direction quickly because of its small body size. Trout have an innate sense of their limitations, and I've seen days when just a dark cloud will make them respond well to streamers, only to turn off completely as soon as the sun comes out.

A sudden thunderstorm that raises the water level and decreases the clarity of the water also puts these big trout on the hunt. Vermont worm fishermen know this, and a half hour after a strong thunderstorm I can count on two old guys from the next town over plying the river in my backyard with their night crawlers. They know they can't interest the big browns in the middle of a bright afternoon, but in dirty water these fish will be on the prowl, ready to play.

Even fishing after dark, when science has proven that trout, especially large brown trout, spend most of their time feeding, is not as reliable as you might think it is. Remember that these trout may only feed every few days, and combine this with another fact scientists have discovered: Large trout can and will roam for a mile or more at night searching for prey, returning to their undercut bank or logjam before the sun comes up. So even if you know a pool holds a giant trout, that fish may not be hungry the night you decide to try for it, and he might not even be home when you come calling. He could be a mile upstream or downstream, dining in shallow water that you would never think of fishing during the day.

Streamer fishing is productive and can sometimes work even on a bright day, by covering a lot of water. If you fish from a drift boat on a large river, you might have a satisfying day catching a half-dozen nice trout on streamers by appealing to the ambushing tendencies of some of them. But on a day like this, you have to realize that you may have shown your fly to thousands of trout in 10 or 12 miles of water. Sooner or later, if you know where to look for these bigger fish, and you have a fly that will entice them, and you work diligently to hit every possible spot as the boat is moving, you are bound to find one that's ready for a meal. And if you happen to be on the river during a rainstorm, or you get on the water before the crack of dawn, or a low ceiling keeps bright light off the water all day, you can really rack up the numbers on big fish. But if you are wade fishing on a bright day and can't cover a lot of water, don't expect a streamer to be a magic cure.

If you happen to know where one of these non-drift-feeding trout lives and could observe it without scaring it, you'd see that it lives with sculpins and dace just a tail flip away, but for most of the day, and perhaps even most of the week, it ignores this potential prey. There was once a large logjam on the river in my backyard that constantly surprised me because I never saw a trout feeding next to it. Along the logjam was nice depth, hatching insects drifted right past its edge, and I could see schools of blacknose dace living in its shadows. Every few years the state runs an electroshocking survey in the river on my property, and the first time they ran the electrodes through this logjam, I watched as the normally taciturn biologist for my region suddenly raised his voice an octave and began barking orders as he and his crew tried to capture a large brown trout that was momentarily stunned and then barreled into the deepest part of the jam trying to escape the tingling electric current. They finally captured the fish, and it was about 2 feet long.

To some people that's not a remarkable size, but bear in mind I fished this stretch of water religiously for years and had never even spooked a fish this big, much less seen one feeding. The largest fish I had ever seen in this water before the electroshocking was about 14 inches long. And this fish was not a fluke, because two years later the crew captured another fish of the same size, but not the same individual—I had photographs of both fish and their spot patterns did not match (the spot patterns on a trout stay with it for life and are as unique as fingerprints). In between those years of electrofishing, I saw one of the big browns exactly twice. During a rainstorm I had hooked a 6-inch rainbow on a dry fly in the riffle above the logjam, and as I played the fish, it swam below me to the edge of the jam. In a flash one of the big browns burst out from beneath the logjam, took a swipe at the struggling rainbow, and then just as quickly slunk back under the log. The conditions of a crippled fish and the lower light, both of which make a normally swift and agile baitfish more vulnerable, put that big brown into feeding mode.

Of course, you probably guess that I returned to the edge of that logjam with a streamer every time it rained, and I caught that fish (or its twin) once during two years of trying. I had learned long ago that in certain rivers with many large fish and high baitfish concentrations, you can target these ambush feeders on a regular basis at certain times of year, but if you want to enjoy steady action on a trout stream, you are far better off concentrating on the drift feeders. And in very productive waters like tailwaters and spring creeks, even the largest fish in the river are drift feeders a majority of the time, so targeting drift-feeding trout does not always limit you to smaller fish. I know of a tailwater river in Colorado on which it is possible (but nowhere near easy) to catch 10-pound drift-feeding rainbows on a size 22 nymph—but you could throw streamers at these fish from dawn until dusk and the only reaction you'd get from them is they would slide off to the side when your streamer got too close.

ARE TROUT ALWAYS FEEDING?

You'll run into times—sometimes it feels like most days—when trout don't appear to be feeding. Trout are extremely

If you don't kill fish yourself, it does not hurt to befriend a bait fisherman because opening a trout's stomach is the best way to find out what they're feeding on. This trout from my backyard was feeding on land snails, but no amount of observation or catch-and-release fishing would have tuned me into that.

adept at hiding in plain sight, and if they are not visibly feeding on the surface, they could be just a few feet deep in clear water. Unless the sun is just right and you are in the perfect position, you won't see them. So if fish are not rising, the only scheme you can follow is to fish water that should hold trout and keep changing strategies and flies until you get some interest. But when you fish for three hours in a spot you know holds trout, with a fly you know should work and you don't even get a bump, you should learn some excuses to keep your frustration level down. There are truly times when trout do not feed at all—or if they do feed, they are pretty half-hearted about it.

Your first excuse could be that trout are just not where you think they are. During the summer, the fish in the small river in my backyard are abundant. Every deep riffle and pool holds at least one fish and sometimes dozens in July. But in April, when the trout season opens and I get the itch to catch some trout on a sunny afternoon, I've learned that my backyard stretch holds few fish, because the water there stays cold during the summer. I'm within 7 miles of the headwaters of the river, and when water temperatures downstream of me reach 70 degrees and the flatter, wider water 5 miles downstream gets too shallow to protect trout from marauding ospreys, mink, and mergansers, the fish migrate upstream to find better habitat and stack up in my backyard. It took me years to realize this. I thought I was just not using the right fly in April, or the water was too high and I was not getting down to the fish.

Luckily, I have a special process for finding out if there are many trout in my river. I wait for Greg and Gib to show up. These two are the local worm fishermen who park in my driveway and always let me know when they've caught fish (they usually only keep one fish each). They're good at their game, so when these two veteran bait fishers (Gib is about 90 years old) can't move a fish with night crawlers rolled along the bottom, I know that the trout population is pretty sparse.

Next on your checklist for getting skunked could be water temperature. Trout are cold-blooded and their metabolism is low below 45 degrees, so at these temperatures they find a place out of the current and feed little, or if they do feed, they only grab something that passes right by their snouts because they don't have the energy to chase their prey. You typically experience this problem early in the season, but in some rivers it can happen all summer long.

For instance, the West Branch of the Delaware River is a bottom-release tailwater river, which means its flow comes from the bottom of a reservoir. The water at the bottom of Pepacton Reservoir remains at about 45 degrees year-round. On one August fishing trip, I arrived at the river to find that for some reason the water regulators decided to open the floodgates, dropping the temperature from a perfect 60 degrees to about 50 degrees where I was fishing 5 miles downstream of the dam in a matter of hours. Where fishing was red-hot just a day before, the trout all but shut down with a sudden decrease in metabolism, and you would have sworn there was not a trout left in the river.

Even if the water temperature is perfect, trout will stop feeding if they are frightened. A flotilla of inner tubes or canoes wallowing in a pool will spook all but the smallest trout, and fish that are frightened bolt for cover and stay huddled in deep

Boats, other anglers, big dogs—they all spook fish. How long they stay spooked and don't feed depends on lots of variables, most of which we don't understand.

water or in tangles of submerged brush for a lot longer than you may think. I am not aware of any scientific data on how long a trout will stay spooked and off the feed after being disturbed, and it probably depends on how badly they have been alarmed and how conditioned they are to that particular disturbance. In heavily trafficked rivers, I have seen an angler wade through a run with trout just moving aside and then gliding back into position in just a few minutes, back on the feed. In rivers where trout are not conditioned to boat or angler traffic, I have spooked a pod of nice trout that were rising, moved to another pool for a few hours, and returned to find the fish still nowhere in sight.

But even with no disturbances and perfect water temperatures, trout may not be feeding. With ambushers, it's easy to understand: It's unlikely a trout will try to chase a baitfish in bright sunlight because it instinctively knows the baitfish has the advantage of speed and maneuverability in the middle of the day, and a trout won't waste its energy unless the baitfish appears to be crippled. Plus we know that ambush feeders don't need to eat that often. Unless the light is low, these fish stay in their sanctuaries.

It's harder to understand why drift-feeding trout go through periods of inactivity during the day, but they do. Trout are not Labrador retrievers. They won't chase every little tidbit. Trout are stimulated to feed by an abundance of prey, because by feeding when prey is abundant and resting when prey is sparse, they conserve energy. For most of the season, drift-feeding trout eat most heavily at dawn and dusk, not because bright sunlight bothers them terribly, but because insects and other drifting foods like tiny aquatic crustaceans are most active at those times. The biggest problem facing aquatic insects is desiccation because they don't have hard exoskeletons like beetles and ants and grasshoppers, and their soft bodies shrivel and the insects die when exposed to hot sunlight.

I've seen empirical evidence that trout aren't greatly bothered by bright sunlight, as long as food is abundant. Many early-season mayfly hatches occur in the middle of the day when water temperatures are warmest, and I've seen trout feeding with abandon on bright, sunny days countless times during the Hendrickson mayfly hatch in late April and early June. Another time you will see trout feeding in bright sunlight is in midsummer, when aquatic insect hatches are not as common and trout see more terrestrial insects like ants, beetles, grasshoppers, and house flies drifting in the surface film. These insects are most active and likely to fall or fly into the water in the middle of the day when air temperatures are warmest, and at these times you will see trout out in the open and feeding even on the brightest days.

Baitfish like this sculpin are the favorites of trout that become ambush feeders.

Trout seem to prefer shade to sunlight if they can find a good feeding spot in the shade, but I think this is more because they are slightly less visible to predators in the shade—not because they don't like sunlight. Drift-feeding trout are sight feeders, and the brighter the light, the better they can see their prey as long as they do not have to look directly into the sun.

So what kind of behavior do trout exhibit when they are not actively feeding? During periods of cold water, from fall through early spring, the fish are in a state of nearly suspended animation. They find a deep pool where they are protected from predators by deep water, typically under a bank or in a tangle of submerged brush or piles of logs and rocks. At this point the fish will hug the bottom, practically motionless, and appear asleep. Food items right in front of them will be ignored. Once the water warms a few degrees, like on a bright winter day, the fish may begin to hover in the current, moving their bodies slightly, and if food drifts within a few inches, they'll move to inhale a stonefly nymph or midge larva. During warm spells, when evening temperatures stay above freezing and days are warm and sunny, trout might actively chase prey, even rising for hatching insects.

In spring, summer, and early fall, trout may still have periods of inactivity if food is sparse. They typically retreat to deeper, slower water, but because water temperatures are in their zone of primary activity, from 50 to 70 degrees, their metabolism is active and they can be induced to feed in a couple circumstances. One is when an aquatic insect larva drifts within about 10 inches of their position. If they recognize it as food and they don't have to work too hard to inhale it, they'll feed. This is why, during periods of inactivity, nymph fishing can be productive, but your fly has to drift close to the bottom and you have to know exactly where the trout are lying, because they won't be inclined to move very far for your fly.

Another circumstance where trout can be induced to eat when they aren't actively feeding is when a high-value, high-calorie bit of food is suddenly visible. It could be a crayfish dislodged from its burrow along the bank, a baitfish that is crippled, or a large insect like a grasshopper or cicada falling into the water. This is the reason smart anglers fish streamers or large dry flies when trout are not actively feeding: A nymph or small dry fly may not rouse them from their siesta, but a baitfish-imitating streamer or a big, meaty dry fly could make the switch from inactivity to attack feasible, since the effort is worth the calories the fish will obtain.

It doesn't always work, though. By fishing a big fly, you risk scaring a trout with something garish that they don't recognize as food. Trout have relatively short memories, and if you fish a 2-inch grasshopper fly in June, before trout have seen any big grasshoppers, you might send the fish bolting for cover instead of rising for your fly. And if fish are conditioned to eating inch-long sculpins and you throw a 5-inch fly at them, it's possible the fish will attack your streamer out of aggression, thinking another fish has invaded their space, but your streamer could also look like a threatening alien creature.

Trout can feed from dawn to dusk and beyond when food and water conditions are perfect and prey is abundant. Those are the days we remember fondly in our fishing logs. But when a river looks barren of fish and insects, you'll have to be at the top of your game and use every arrow in your quiver. I hope this book gives you a bit more ammunition to carry with you through the season.

CHAPTER 2

Water, Weather, the Moon, and the Seasons

HOW DO WATER TEMPERATURE AND DISSOLVED OXYGEN AFFECT TROUT?

Unless you live on a trout stream and are retired or you have unlimited time and resources, the times you fish for trout will be dictated by your job, your family, and by how far you're willing to travel to catch trout. For most of us with busy lives, factors like moon phases and barometric pressure are mere curiosities, because we'll fish when we can get away. But one environmental component, water temperature, is of paramount importance and overrides the effects of wind, cloud cover, changes in atmospheric pressure, and the position of celestial objects in its determination of how the fish will act. And because water temperature is also the key player in determining insect hatches, it sets the playing field both for the fish we chase and the prey we try to imitate.

Because temperature regimes follow a predictable seasonal fluctuation, with some random outliers due to unusual weather patterns, we can determine, with relative accuracy, what water temperatures will be like in a given river at a given week, years in advance. And once you get to the river, water temperatures can predict when fish will feed most actively or when it's dangerous to fish for them.

Let's look at water temperatures as background to a trout's survival. Water temperatures below 32 degrees are lethal for trout because fish don't do well encased in ice. At temperatures just above freezing, trout feed little, although if food is abundant and the fish have been acclimated to cold temperatures, they will feed. This is especially if the water temperature is increasing, as it would on a sunny day on a small stream in Colorado in January.

I remember fishing the upper Roaring Fork one winter day with Pat McCord, a very savvy Colorado guide, and when we started out in the morning, the water temperature was 40 degrees. I didn't have much faith in catching anything at that temperature, but we fished anyway. As we worked upstream, the sun came out and Pat said, "You just wait—when the water hits 42, the fish will go on the feed." Sure enough, as we dipped our thermometers in the water what seemed like every five minutes (and were reminded of the old saying about a watched kettle), once the water hit that magic number, fish began to take our nymphs fished close to the bottom, and when the temperature hit a very balmy 45, we even saw a few fish rising to midges.

As water temperatures rise, a trout's metabolism increases, they get hungrier and more aggressive, and coincidentally

Water temperature can tell you a lot about trout feeding behavior. A thermometer is a small tool that can pay big dividends.

insect hatches become more abundant. The correlation of insect hatches and trout feeding is not happenstance: Trout and aquatic insects have evolved together for hundreds of thousands of years, and it doesn't do you any good to have your metabolism running in high gear if there's nothing around to eat. Between 59 and 64 degrees, a trout exhibits maximum growth. Its metabolism just keeps increasing as water temperatures rise. But in the upper 60s trout run into a roadblock, actually a double whammy, because as water temperatures rise, the amount of dissolved oxygen the water can hold decreases.

Trout can survive, barely, at oxygen levels of about 3 parts per million, but that is with no activity that might increase their metabolic rate and their need for oxygen. And they need it at about 9 parts per million for high activity and growth. At 35 degrees, water holds about 13 parts per million of oxygen and a trout's metabolism is slow, so oxygen is never an issue. But as water temperatures rise, dissolved oxygen disappears in a straight-line relationship. At about 70 degrees trout can survive because the dissolved oxygen level is still at about 7 parts per million, but any feeding does not contribute to growth, and any stresses that make them expend energy can kill them because they can't get enough oxygen to support metabolic activity and literally suffocate.

You can put all the science to work when you go fishing. Let's look at coldwater temperatures, below 45 degrees. In this range a trout will seek slower water, where it can hold its position while burning few calories, so right away you know you should probably avoid the faster runs and riffles. If you do fish faster water, you should look for deeper pockets or slots behind large objects where a trout can stay out of the current. Places that held actively feeding trout last summer, when insects were abundant and a trout's metabolism was in high gear, may be devoid of fish until things warm up. So the logical places to look are slow pools or long stretches of flat water.

Also bear in mind that a trout won't move very far for a meal, and no matter how tasty your streamer looks, the fish won't chase it across the current. Trout won't be hovering in mid-water looking for food either. They will stay in their comfortable spots in deeper water, close to objects that break the current. And their feeding is very passive—I like to think of fishing for trout at these times as spoon-feeding the fish, as you almost have to lead it into their mouths. This means you have to pull everything out of your bag of tricks to get a slow, deep presentation in most spots. Long leaders, strike indicators, weight on the leader and/or weighted flies, and, most importantly, proper presentation and line manipulation to achieve a perfectly dead drift, or at least as little fly movement as possible, is critical.

When I think of this type of fishing, I'm always reminded of a run I fished one April. By "run" I mean a piece of water that is deeper than a riffle, with moderate current, but not so slow and defined that you would call it a pool. Many anglers pass up this kind of water. This particular run is the deepest in the river for a half mile either way, and the bottom is a field of grapefruit- to basketball-size rocks, so I always knew some of the resident rainbows would be tucked into the bottom between the rocks. The water was cold, probably 45 degrees, but it was clear and not too high, so I knew I could probably catch a fish or two if I worked hard enough.

I began by fishing to the deep pocket from about 30 feet away, using a strike indicator and a pair of weighted nymphs. I could see by the action of the strike indicator that the flies were not getting a dead drift because the indicator was whisked out of the current and pulled downstream, which I could tell by noticing it was moving much faster than the bubbles on the surface. I got closer to the run by wading out into the current, so I could keep my rod higher and thus keep most of the fly line off the faster current. Now I was at least getting a dead drift, as the indicator was moving at the same speed as the bubbles on the surface. But I was not snagging bottom occasionally, so I knew I was not getting anywhere near the bottom, and I figured the fish were not inclined to dart up into the current above them in cold water.

The fish might have been able to see my flies, but they were having no part of them. To get my flies down deeper, I added some sink putty to the leader about 6 inches above the flies. Now I could see the indicator hesitate occasionally, so I knew I was getting close to the bottom with my flies. Still, no fish. (I was not worried about the flies I was using, as early-season fish are not terribly picky about fly pattern, plus I knew what kind of nymphs these rainbows like from previous experience.) It was not until I got into a zone where I could visualize my flies drifting right into the trout's mouths that I began to catch a few little rainbows. I had to concentrate on steering my flies right into the deeper, slower pockets in the run, keeping all of my fly line off the water, so that there was a straight line between my rod tip and the indicator, and the front end of the fly line and the entire leader above the surface followed that straight, imaginary line.

So that's fishing in cold water. It requires tight concentration, knowledge of where the fish might be, and getting your flies down to those fish using a combination of presentation, line manipulation, and adjustment of weights and strike indicator depth. Later in the season you can get sloppier because the fish will chase your flies. When the water is cold, you have to bring your flies to them. That does not mean trout won't chase a streamer or nymph in cold water, or that they won't rise to a dry fly. I've seen it happen. But if you play the odds, your best chance of connecting with a trout will be to fish slow and deep, and you'll have to concentrate harder than you do with any other kind of fishing.

MOON PHASES AND BAROMETRIC PRESSURE

When you've taught a skill for as long as I have, you get a sense for questions no one else has answered satisfactorily by the number of times people ask you the same thing. Hope springs from questions about moon phases and barometric pressure often, but I have to confess that not only don't I have any strong empirical evidence for the effect of these two variables, I have never found any trustworthy science that gives me any answers.

Fishing in cold water requires lots of fuel for the angler!

Moon Phases

Moon phase has the potential for two effects on trout: the astrological pull on the earth, and the other more mundane effect of influencing the amount of light in the sky after dark. The pull of the moon's gravity is the basis for tides, which do affect saltwater species greatly, as it influences inshore depths, currents, and the flushing rate of estuaries. Moon phases definitely push anadromous rainbow trout and Atlantic salmon from estuaries into flowing waters, and a high tide often signals movement of these fish upriver. However, high water caused by storms or hydroelectric releases below dams serve the same purpose, so rather than the moon phase itself acting in some mysterious way, the moon's effect on water levels is the main stimulus. Far inland, stream trout are not affected by tides, and although you can argue that all trout have anadromous ancestors, there is no evidence stream trout are influenced in the slightest by the gravitational pull of the moon.

However, on clear nights when the moon is not blocked by clouds, it does have strong effects on trout feeding behavior after dark. For trout feeding on insects in the drift, where they need some light above the surface to zero in on their targets, moonlight allows them to feed well into the night. Happily, with any luck, it also gives us the ability to see rises and maybe even track our dry flies well past sunset. But don't think it will be easy. Whether because I can't see my fly and thus don't always know where it is or the fly is dragging, I've always found trout feeding well into the darkness to be very tricky to catch. I don't mean those easy fish a half hour after the sun goes behind the hills—I mean those fish that are still sipping about the time late-night talk shows begin. Let cloud cover move in, though, and you'll stop hearing rises because the fish are no longer able to spot their prey against the skylight.

Ambush predators, mostly large trout (and especially brown trout), feed by sensing vibrations on their lateral line and are affected in an opposite way by moonlight. Fishing large wet flies or streamers after dark, fishing on the swing and going entirely on feel, you'll do much better on nights without moonlight. But it isn't the moon phase. I remember one night many years ago on a favorite night-fishing stream when I switched to a big unweighted Muddler Minnow just after dark. The night was so dark, I felt like I was trapped inside a muggy closet, and it seemed like big brown trout inhaled the fly on every cast, or at least bumped it every time I slid the fly through the tail of a big pool. It was too good to last. The clouds above me parted, revealing a full moon glaring down at me, and immediately the fish stopped taking—I mean like someone flicked the off switch. That night was not an isolated event either. Night fishing that is terrific ends when the moon comes up over the hills, and any kind of moonlight at all, in any phase, detracts from the effectiveness of fishing at night, while cloudy nights and new moon nights can be spectacular.

You may have heard of "lunar tables," or "Solunar tables." These show up in the strangest places, from magazines to websites to phone apps and watches. They are all based on a theory developed by John Alden Knight (also famous for inventing a famous bucktail called the Mickey Finn) in the 1930s based on the position of the sun and moon, plus the tide phase. According to the theory, there are two major feeding periods a day when the moon is directly overhead or directly underfoot, flanked by two minor feeding periods when the moon rises or sets. Fishermen and hunters hold great stock in these table; in fact, the tables are supposed to predict the feeding times of any animal, from red squirrels to bluebirds to catfish. Many people also hold great stock in getting rich on a weekend trip to Las Vegas, which in my observation is slightly more reliable than the Solunar tables. Knight should have quit while he was ahead with the Mickey Finn.

I'm only giving you my observation of the effectiveness—or better, ineffectiveness—of these tables. Many experienced anglers, particularly tournament bass anglers, swear they see better fishing during major feeding periods. The *Farmer's Almanac* has survived even longer with less of a scientific pedigree. So if you still believe that a furry creature brings you chocolate in a basket once a year, get a copy of the Solunar tables and only fish when it's a major or minor feeding period. I'll stick with advice from a charter boat captain buddy, "Go early and stay late," and keep my eye on wind, water temperatures, precipitation, cloud cover, and the height of the sun.

Barometric Pressure

There is no doubt that a change in barometric pressure can influence the activity of both stream trout and their prey. But it is not the change in pressure that does the deed—it's the accompanying weather change. The idea that fish can foretell a change in barometer before it happens, or are affected by a change in atmospheric pressure without a corresponding change in weather, remains a theory with no empirical evidence. Once you examine the science, it's easy to see why.

A high-pressure system reads about 30 inches of mercury. A hurricane pushes the mercury down to about 28 inches. If you convert the 2-inch difference in mercury to atmospheres (atm), this is a difference of about .10 atm. The difference between a high-pressure system and a passing cold front is about half of that, or .05 atm. Now let's take a trout feeding in a typical pool, where the fish lies in about 3 feet of water. When this fish spies a passing mayfly on the surface and rises up to eat it, and then returns in a matter of seconds to its lie on the river bottom, it has just gone through about .10 atm of hydrostatic pressure change—roughly the same amount of pressure change if a sunny day had flashed into a hurricane in seconds!

I've heard anglers say, "Oh, it's the background pressure change they notice," but it makes absolutely no sense at all for a fish that constantly changes depth when feeding to be influenced by pressure changes happening above the water column. It's the weather, pure and simple.

WEATHER

Now we're getting to the good stuff. Weather has the biggest impact on when and how much trout feed not only because it affects their metabolism directly, but also because of its effect on aquatic insects. Trout don't need to check Weather Underground every few hours, but if insects had smartphones, you can bet they'd have their eyes glued to the weather.

Sunlight

Insects are most vulnerable once they've risen from the protection of the streambed and have to navigate an extreme

It is most likely the change in light levels, wind speed, and precipitation that accompanies a change in atmospheric pressure that affects fish behavior, not the change in pressure by itself.

environment full of predators ready to suck them in or sweep them from the air. But their biggest threat is an environmental one: desiccation. Thus insects have evolved to hatch at precise times, when the water is warm enough to get their metabolism going, but when the sun does not beat down on them. And I would think that a creature so dependent on terrestrial weather conditions, unlike trout, would have an innate behavioral response to weather.

This is why insects hatch and return to the water for mating flights in the evening or morning on sunny days. The only exception to this is early in the season, when water temperatures are too low for insects to expend energy hatching except in the warmest part of the day. (What these early insects lose in desiccation for their midday habits they benefit in a lack of predators like swallows and bats and cedar waxwings so early in the season.) At no time is this behavior more apparent than on a partly cloudy day in midseason, when the air temperature is warm and water temperatures optimum for insects and trout. You'll be standing in a pool with no feeding activity when the sun goes behind a big cloud, and instantly caddisflies or mayflies appear on the surface and struggle to hatch. Trout spot this and begin to feed heavily. Then the sun comes out, and the surface of the water is soon as clean as a polished mirror with no bugs marring its surface, and the trout sink away out of sight.

There is also an apparent reaction of trout themselves to dark clouds in the middle of the day beyond the stimulation of insect hatches. I was floating the lower Eagle River in Colorado with a guide buddy, John Packer, and after catching a few fish on nymphs, I asked him if streamers would work. He cocked his head up to the sun and said, "Yeah, in about five minutes." I looked up and saw a dark cloud sliding toward the sun. "Will it really make that much difference?" I asked him. "Put your streamer on right now and try it," he replied.

While the sun was beating down, nothing touched the streamer. As soon as the sky darkened, fish began chasing the streamer and a few hit it. But once the sun came back out, I stopped even getting hits. Because streamers are notoriously hit-or-miss depending on where you are in a river and we were floating downstream, hitting different water every few minutes, I was still not convinced the streamer love was not a coincidence. But after two hours of fishing the same streamer and observing the number of strikes I got when it was sunny compared to when the sky darkened, I was convinced.

Despite the fact that we usually observe increased action on trout streams in periods of low light, especially during hatches in the warmer parts of the year, sun is not always a negative factor in fishing success. You hear platitudes like "Trout have no eyelids and can't squint, so they stay out of the light" and "Big brown trout always feed in the shade." It's true that not only do trout have no eyelids, but their pupils can't contract to restrict bright sunlight from hitting their retinas. However, they can adjust the depth of the light-sensitive cells in their retinas, and this seems to be sufficient to allow them to feed comfortably even with the sun directly overhead.

If you spend enough time on trout streams, you'll notice conflicting evidence of their reaction to sunlight. In some rivers, on some days, you see trout right out in the open, as often in bright sunlight as in shade. But other times and in other places, they will show a definite preference for shady areas.

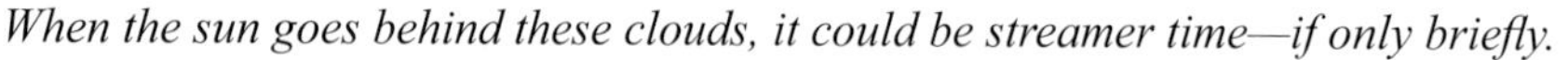

When the sun goes behind these clouds, it could be streamer time—if only briefly.

Trout have no problem feeding in bright sunlight and will regularly do so if insect food is available.

My thought on this is that their apparent preference for shade is more closely related to protection from overhead predators, as a trout is far less visible in the shade than it is in bright sunlight. This is partly because, despite being well camouflaged against the stream bottom, they etch sharp shadows on the bottom in bright sunlight—an advantage we anglers use as well as avian predators.

Trout are not negatively phototropic by any means. They are sight feeders, and the better they can see, the more they can eat. But how much time they spend in the sun is determined by the amount of insect food available and the density of birds of prey on a particular river. And even with lots of eagles, ospreys, and mergansers around, the density of the food supply can temper the caution of trout. During a heavy hatch on the West Branch of the Delaware, I've watched wild brown trout continue to feed, even with mergansers blowing up in the shallows just a few feet away (apparently chasing baitfish or trout fry) and ospreys and eagles casting their shadows as they glide by. In contrast, a merganser blowout on the river in my backyard in Vermont spooks the fish for as long as six hours—but it has nowhere near the food supply of the Delaware.

There are also positive influences of sunlight on insect activity. A species of caddisfly hatches in early June in many of the rivers I fish, a size 16 cream job with a pale tan body that seems to hatch only in bright sunlight. You'll have trout rising all around, and when the sun goes behind a cloud, the trout stop feeding (on the surface at least) and the caddisflies stop hatching. As with many insects, the reaction to sunlight seems to be nearly instantaneous (this time in a positive direction) and can switch on and off as quickly as you can turn the key in your car.

I've also seen an interesting phenomenon, in both Eastern and Western rivers, where some kind of small sulphur-colored mayfly hatches when the sun is out and a Blue-Winged Olive mayfly hatches during periods of cloud cover in the same riffle. This can drive you absolutely nuts on one of those days where big dark clouds move quickly across a blue sky until you figure out what is going on. Rather than switching flies every time cloud cover changes, it's a good idea to fish two dry flies at the same time—typically a size 16 PMD (Pale Morning Dun) and a size 20 BWO (Blue-Winged Olive) hanging behind it.

You can't use sunlight to predict trout fishing in a vacuum, though. Sunlight is the primary determinant of water temperature, so the amount of sunlight, and when in a daily cycle the sunlight occurs, determines both the absolute temperature of the water and the rate at which it changes during the day. Understanding the effects of temperature on trout populations is a critical key to taking your fishing game to the next level.

Temperature and Dissolved Oxygen

Temperature affects both the metabolism of trout and the amount of dissolved oxygen in running water. At cool water temperatures, oxygen is not a problem and water holds much more dissolved oxygen than a trout needs. For instance, at 59 degrees, water holds about 10 parts per million (ppm) of oxygen, and a trout needs about 3 ppm for a basal activity (breathing, holding its position in the current) and 8 ppm for increased activity like fast swimming. However, in an unfortunate congruence of biological processes and the physical properties of water, as water temperature increases, the amount of dissolved oxygen it can hold decreases but the metabolism of a trout increases—and thus its demand on the oxygen supply for respiration hits a peak as less and less dissolved oxygen is available. At some point, there is not enough oxygen available even for basal metabolism, and even a trout lying quietly on the bottom of a pool will suffocate because it cannot get enough oxygen. The lethal temperature is somewhere around 78 degrees, but this lethal point can be mitigated either up or down depending on conditions.

For instance, brook trout living in unusually cold waters, as in the subarctic regions, where daytime water temperatures may not get above 40 degrees, will die when water temperatures hit 70 degrees. However, brook trout acclimated to water temperatures in the mid-60s can survive up to 78 degrees. Redband trout in Nevada, where summer water temperatures are much higher than for most trout populations, continue to thrive in temperatures as high as 83 degrees. Other mitigating factors include how long trout are exposed to these temperatures. If the water temperature spikes to 75 degrees for an hour but drops back down to 60 degrees at night, wild trout suffer little mortality.

Much of this high-temperature discussion is academic until you bring the activities of other species into play—especially humans. It's been observed that trout lose their competitive edge against warmwater fish in temperatures above 70 degrees, which might tell you to stay away from rivers that have daily summer temperatures this high unless you prefer catching smallmouth bass. But even more critical, and subjective, is at what point is it ethical to stop fishing for trout if you want to release them unharmed.

Trout are quite happy at 70 degrees until they have to exert a lot of energy, the most demanding of which is swimming fast. At high activity levels, a trout's oxygen consumption can increase to four or five times that of its resting rate. Thus you risk suffocating a trout if you play it for long periods above 70 degrees. In the best scenario, you will need to revive the fish for a long time. But at times the trout is dead by the time you get it to hand, especially if you're not skilled at playing trout quickly.

The practice of floating down trout streams in inner tubes on hot summer days is especially worrisome. Trout in 74-degree water are in little danger if they aren't pestered. But introduce dangling arms and legs below the surface and splashes above, and the trout are constantly harassed and pushed into physical activity in trying to escape these perceived threats. They may be pushed beyond their needs for respiration. I'm not aware of any scientific studies on this issue, but the potential is there and it bothers me.

At the low end of the temperature scale, oxygen is not a problem, and unless water freezes solid, trout don't experience any physical problems. However, their metabolism is slowed down, and although trout feed in water as low as 33 degrees, it takes little food to satisfy them, so they just don't feed as much. Nor will they move far for their food. Trout in places like glacial runoff rivers or in the far north *do* get acclimated to water temperatures that never get much above the high 40s, but these fish seldom grow very large or very fast because trout that live in these extreme conditions never hit optimum conditions for growth. In fact, biologists have shown that trout in environments where temperature fluctuates 15 to 20 degrees daily grow faster—and eat almost twice as much—than trout raised in a near optimum but constant temperature of 56 degrees.

Again this might be academic, but it is valuable information for the fly fisher, because I've seen empirical evidence of this on the river. Trout feed more heavily on days where

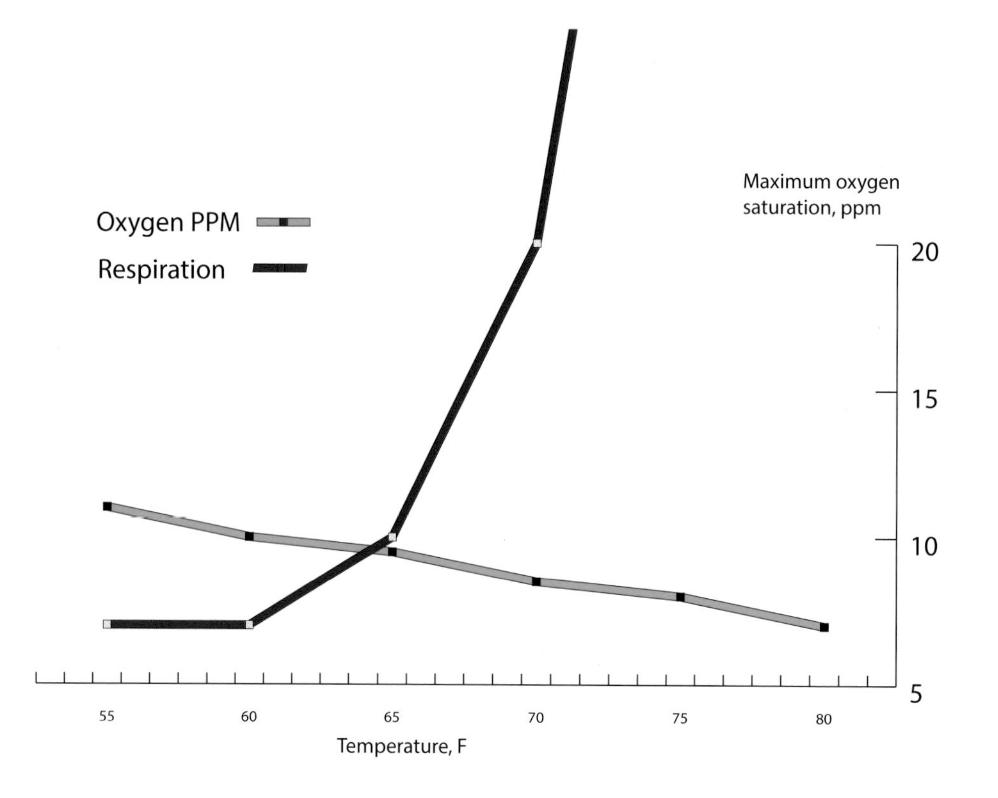

This chart makes it clear that as the temperature rises and trout respiration increases, the amount of oxygen the water can hold decreases, putting a big stress on trout survival.

the water temperature rises 10 degrees during that day than on days when the water temperature is steady—even if it is at an optimum temperature. Even in the summer, when water temperatures are what we would consider relatively high, I have almost always found that the time between 8 a.m. and noon is the period of highest feeding activity and the fish are far more active than they are in the evening, which is often seen as the best time to go trout fishing in the summer. It is not in my experience.

I remember the late Leonard Wright, author of *Fishing the Dry Fly as a Living Insect* and *Fly Fishing Heresies*, telling me about his observations on the Neversink, where he lived and carefully studied a trout population for many years. He was convinced that it was the rate of temperature change, rather than the absolute temperature, that was important for trout feeding. His observations showed that a slow, steady rise in water temperature was the best indicator of good fishing (as long as the water temperature was not close to the lethal range for trout, of course). Not only do my observations back this up, I've seen many instances where sudden changes in water temperature slow down trout feeding.

One year the Hendrickson hatch on the Battenkill was spectacular, with water temperatures in the morning starting around 42 degrees and peaking at 52 degrees in the afternoon. Both insects and fish were very active, and the catching was better than in most years. Then a period of balmy weather set in, with daytime air temperatures of 85 degrees and warm nights, and water temperatures that reached 63 degrees in the afternoon. The fishing went quickly downhill. You would have thought the opposite, because that water temperature range was smack dab in the middle of what is considered optimum for trout. But I think that the fish, used to temperatures in the 40s and low 50s for a few weeks, were not prepared biologically for the warmer water temperatures and it slowed them down. This was not an isolated case, as since then I have seen many days where unseasonal increases in water temperature made for slow trout fishing.

Even more detrimental to fishing is when water temperatures decrease suddenly. One August I went with some buddies to fish the West Branch of the Delaware. This river, although very difficult, is still productive in high summer because stable flows and water temperatures keep both trout and insects active. We were on the lower river, where water temperatures had been in the 70s, but a sudden release of 45-degree water from Pepacton Reservoir 10 miles upstream brought water temperatures down quickly to the mid-50s. We tried nymphs, streamers, wets, and dries, but in places where we normally caught lots of fish in August, the water seemed barren—even though we knew we were fishing over hundreds of trout. Water temperatures were in the optimum range, but the sudden drop in temperature probably brought the metabolism of the trout to a screeching halt.

Rain—and Snow

The old cliché about fishing being better in the rain is one platitude you can hold stock in. It's rare, in my experience, to find an instance where rain does not make fishing better. Undoubtedly it's not the rain itself, but what rain does to the physical environment that makes the difference. One reason you'll read about is that rain increases the dissolved oxygen

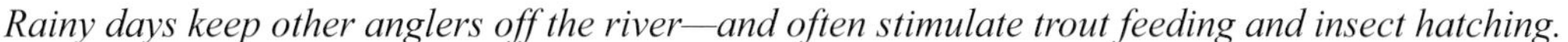

Rainy days keep other anglers off the river—and often stimulate trout feeding and insect hatching.

in the water. This may be the case in calm lakes, which have less exchange with the atmosphere, but in stream trout fishing, rain is probably inconsequential in adding more oxygen to the water because a stream's natural turbulence overshadows the additional gas exchange rain provides.

Unless blown ahead of the thunderstorm, rain is accompanied by darker skies, so the decreased light makes trout lose some of their caution because they are not as visible to predators. And rain's drumming on the surface of the water offers even more protection because the surface, even in still pools, is more disturbed. The noise of the rain does not seem to bother adult trout in the slightest, but the darkness combined with surface disturbance does seem to disorient small baitfish. Larger trout that feed on baitfish almost exclusively sense that they have a predatory advantage over the baitfish, which are normally too fast and maneuverable for adult trout to catch in bright sunlight. It's like the difference between turning a corner in a hot sports car as opposed to a dump truck.

Don't let a little snow stop you. Snowy days, especially during early fall storms, can be some of the finest fishing days you will ever see.

The darkness that accompanies rain also stimulates insects to hatch. In fact, some insects seem to hatch in large quantities only during rainy weather, like the Blue-Winged Olive, or *Baetis*. On sunny days, you see them dribble off the river all afternoon, but during rainy weather they hatch in large concentrations, which bring them to the attention of trout in short order. I would have to say that fully half of my memorable fly-fishing experiences have centered around *Baetis* hatches on "lousy" days, and because *Baetis* are the most abundant mayfly in the world, these wonderful experiences have occurred from England to Maine to California. I understand from more well-traveled anglers that these hatches are just as much of an event in Argentina and New Zealand. Other insects that normally hatch only in the evening will also hatch during rainstorms, most notably the big Green Drake and March Brown mayflies of the eastern United States.

Rain also stimulates feeding by trout because it makes it more difficult for aquatic insects to leave the water. Some actually get pounded by raindrops and fall back to the surface, and even those that manage to dodge globules of water emerge more slowly because of the high humidity. Insects can't leave the surface until their wings partially dry, and this process is slower in humid weather. Trout know insects that leave the water slowly are easier prey and are more likely to respond to the easy source of food that is not about to fly away an instant after it reaches the surface of the water. Combine this with terrestrial insects knocked off leaves, twigs, and grasses, and you have the makings of a trout banquet.

There are good rains and better rains. The better rains are the ones without much wind—those dank, low-ceiling days with all-day drizzle and fog. Not only are these days typically darker, but they are not as often accompanied by wind, which does not bother trout feeding under the surface but often seems to inhibit surface feeding. Days like this can be banner fishing days, and if you have the flexibility to fish on short notice (because who trusts long-term weather forecasts?), you will seldom be disappointed on calm drizzly days, regardless if you like to fish dries, nymphs, or streamers.

The one caution I will advise is that you don't give up on fishing the minute rain starts to fall, because at first what I have seen is a reduction in trout feeding, but only briefly. It's as if the trout are frightened at first by the sudden noise and surface disturbance of raindrops hitting the water, but they soon adjust to it. Maybe you've left your rain jacket in the car and don't want to get drenched to the skin, and so the onset of rain is an excuse to quit fishing. I'd advise you to either tough it out and get wet, or if your car is not too far away to fetch it. Because if I'm not mistaken, you'll soon be into better fishing than you had previously in the day.

Everything I've said about rain also applies to snow, but of course snow in the middle of a long cold spell won't do much to increase feeding. Water temperatures are already low, probably too low for many insects to hatch or for trout to do any but minimal feeding, not moving much to feed because of their low metabolism. However, sudden early-season snow often stimulates a trout feeding orgy beyond anything you've seen in months.

One year I was in Denver with some colleagues, fishing the South Platte prior to a trade show. We were staying in a cabin up in the Front Range and were to meet up with a couple of guide friends, Monroe Coleman and the late Kevin Gregory. When we flew into Denver, it was a typical hot, painfully bright September day with temperatures in the 80s. The next morning when we woke up, one of the guys went out to grab a smoke and came back inside covered with snow. When Kevin and Monroe arrived at the cabin, their eyes were wide as half-dollars and they were breathing like they had just run a marathon. "We gotta get to the river right now. It is going to be an epic day. We haven't even seen a cloud in weeks, and this dark weather is really going to turn the fish on."

Kevin and Monroe knew the moods of the South Platte like their own. As we descended the steep, rocky trail into Cheesman Canyon, even from hundreds of feet above the river we could see fish rising everywhere. Blue-Winged Olive mayflies, tan caddisflies, Pale Morning Dun mayflies, and midges covered the water. The dark day stimulated hatching, but the sudden drop in air temperature and snow didn't let them dry their wings, and they floated until they drowned or got eaten by a trout. We were all dressed for late summer, with only raincoats for protection, but it took a few hours for anyone to notice we were shivering. We built a small makeshift fire along the bank, in the shelter of a huge rock overhang, and would warm up enough to get back to the river and then fish until we couldn't stand it anymore. Late in the day someone suggested we get out of the canyon and get truly warm and dry, but as we walked out we spotted more big fish rising. Gritting our teeth, we walked back down to fish for a few more minutes.

We finally got out of the canyon at dark, and two of our party still suffers from the frostbite they got that day. We all still feel it was worth it, for a day of fishing that we may not repeat for the rest of our lives. Weather is more likely to put a damper on your fishing than make it spectacular, but we live for those exceptional days.

Wind

For the most part, wind is the bane of fly fishing. True, it can help on flat water with spooky fish, like permit in subtropical waters or trout in very clear lakes, but I can think of few times that wind made better fishing on a trout stream. Of course, it makes casting harder, and if you can, try to get the wind behind you. But so much about trout fishing is approach, and often you just can't change positions because it will put your backcast into the trees, or it will force you to fish directly downstream, or otherwise make a mess of your presentation. One thing that will help is to shorten your tippet, or if the wind is really bad, shorten your leader by going to a different length. If you're having trouble putting your fly on target with a 9-foot leader, put that one away and replace it with a 7½-footer. Because the surface of the water is riffled, the fish may not be spooked by the shorter leader.

Wind will sweep terrestrial insects and resting adult mayflies, stoneflies, and caddisflies into rivers. After hatching, adult mayflies and caddisflies leave the surface of the water

When the water's surface is calm, this trout is happily rising.

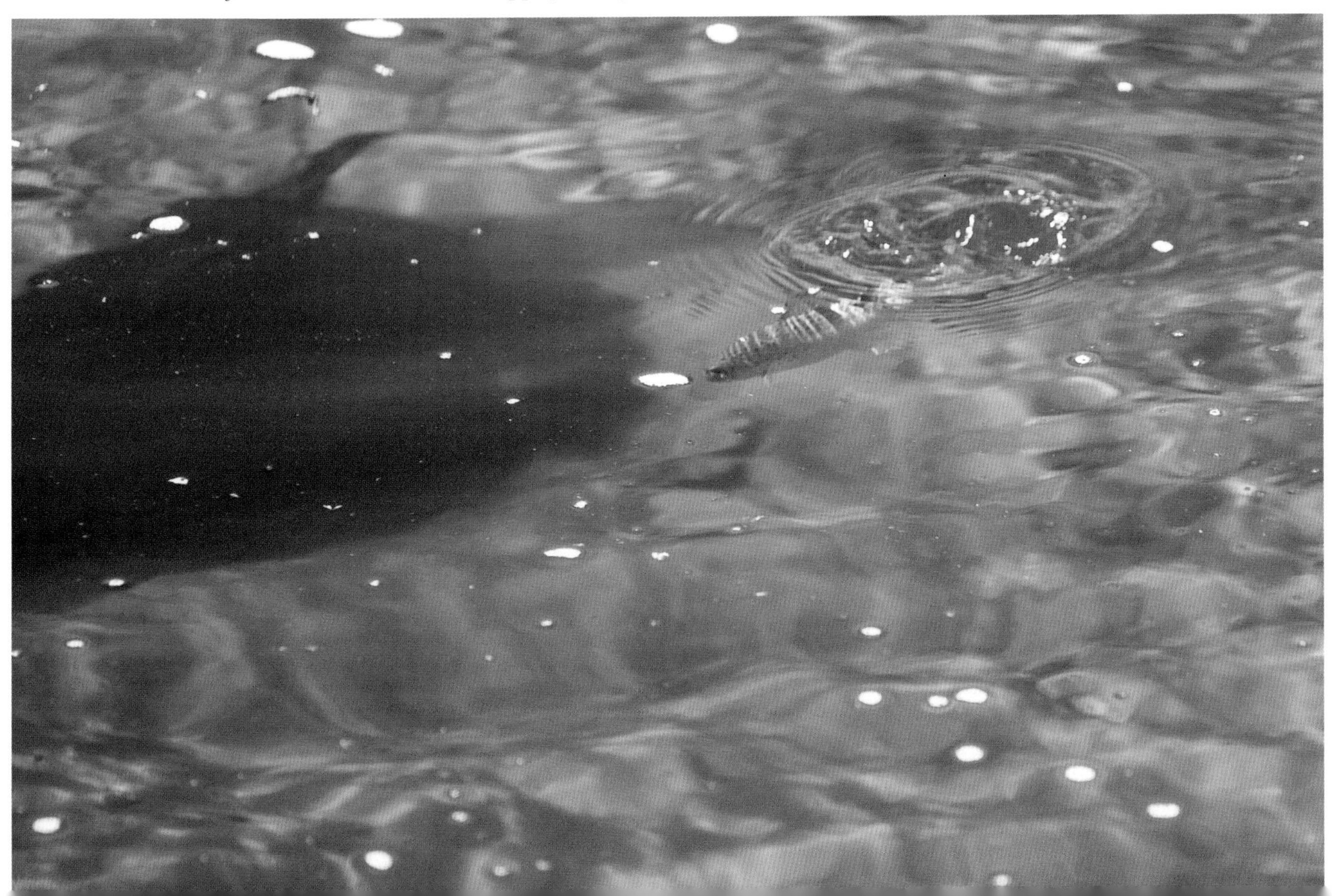

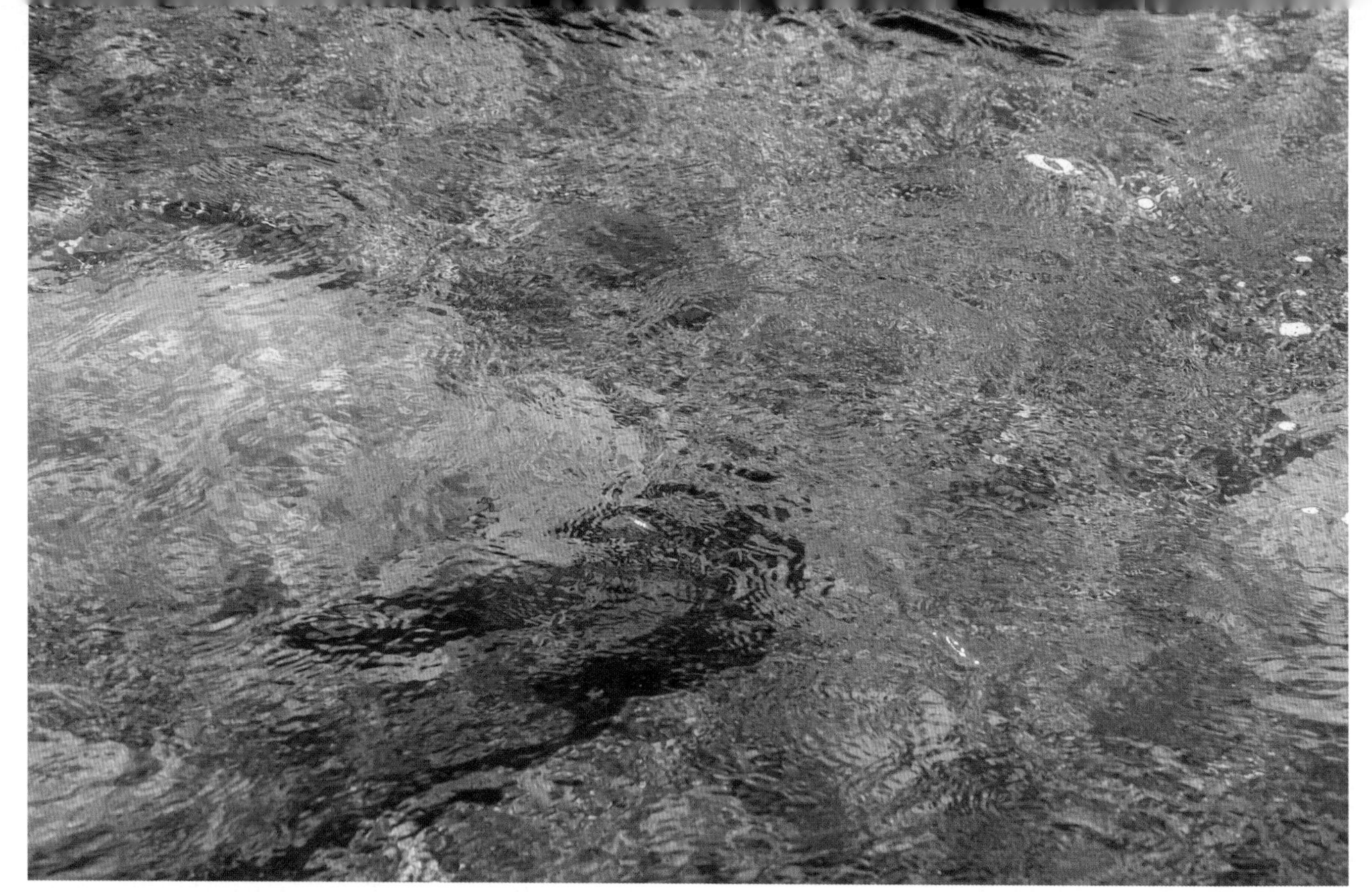

But when the wind riffles the surface, the trout stops feeding. It is not just that you can't see it feeding—it really does stop until the wind drops.

and rest in streamside brush while they molt and wait for the right conditions for mating flights. Stoneflies hatch by climbing out of the water onto rocks and logs along the edge of a river, so until they return to the water on mating flights, it's tough for trout to get at them. All of these insects lie just out of reach of trout, and most are pretty clumsy, especially big stoneflies, so a brisk wind can shove them into the water, where the trout soon notice them. Other big meaty insects, like grasshoppers, beetles, and damselflies, will also find themselves marooned by the wind.

All of this is tempered, though, by the effects of the wind on the mood of the trout. It's less of a factor in riffled water, where the surface is already disturbed and the trout that live there are used to feeding through a distorted surface. On smoother water, I have seen days where wind does not bother surface-feeding trout at all, and other days when they would only rise in breaks between gusts. The very best days with wind in slow pools are those where strong gusts alternate with periods of calm, like summer weather with thunderstorms in the vicinity. Winds push bugs into the water, and trout take advantage of the insect soup during periods of calm when it's easier to see their prey. In slower water, you can also look for little pockets in the lee of the wind. If these places are otherwise suitable for trout, meaning sufficient depth, some current, and protection from predators close by, the trout there may be feeding heavily on windblown insects.

Wind does not seem to affect trout feeding below the surface much at all, but it does limit the way you can present your fly. When fishing a streamer, your rod should be low to the water, and since you are probably moving the fly most of the time, the wind is only a problem when you try to cast. And if you're using a sinking line, which is denser than a floating line and less likely to be grabbed by the wind, you might not even notice a stiff breeze.

Nymph fishing gets tougher in the wind, even if the ruffled surface doesn't bother the trout feeding a few feet down. With nymphs, you often keep your rod tip high to lift most of the line off the water so you can get a dead drift, but a strong wind pushes your line around so much that it will often move the line in ways you don't want it to move. The best course of action here is to leave less line in the air, which forces you to keep your rod tip closer to the water and out of the wind. It's tough to get a good drift with just a few feet of line out unless you fish about a rod length away, but by keeping your rod tip just above the water and following the leader as it drifts downstream, you may get a decent presentation. Most likely you won't even have any fly line out of your guides, just the leader, but it's about the only game in town if you want to high-stick nymphs.

Strike indicators get pushed around by strong winds, blowing your drift off course and introducing unwanted drag. You can lessen the effect of the wind by using a small round indicator if you've been using yarn, because a small round one catches less wind. As with high-sticking, keeping the rod tip close to the indicator will help, but again you'll be forced to make very short casts.

One of the best ways to fish nymphs in a strong wind is to fish directly upstream with a floating line, without a strike indicator. You can keep your rod tip relatively low when fishing straight upstream because you don't have to worry about your line going across conflicting currents, and all you have to do is watch for a pause at the end of your floating line. It's not as easy as high-sticking or using a strike indicator, but if you want a dead drift when fishing nymphs in the wind, it's an efficient way to do it. You may get so good at this kind of nymphing that you declare your independence from the strike indicator crutch more often. Another way to deal with wind when fishing with subsurface flies is to swing a soft-hackle or winged wet fly across the current. These flies work best when swung in the current, and because most of your line is anchored on the water when swinging a fly, you'll stay out of the wind.

TIME OF DAY AND THE SEASONS

Most of us fish when we can and don't have the luxury of picking optimum weather for fishing trips. But often when family, work, or vacation keeps us from fishing all day, we can at least choose the few hours we can sneak away.

The time of day that should be best varies with the season. Notice I said *should*, because no sooner do you make predictions about trout than they prove you a raving idiot. All we can do is make educated guesses and hope for the best. But since you are interested in upping your game in trout fishing, it makes sense to experiment with different seasons and different times of day. You may be delighted to find great fishing at a time of day when it isn't supposed to be great, or you may struggle through a difficult day catching only a single fish. But that single fish is one you'll remember more than others, and the iterations you went through to catch it may open your eyes to a whole new technique.

The time of day you fish affects both the amount of light and the water temperature, and not only does it affect the trout you're after, it also affects their prey. We've already looked at how light, weather, and water temperature come into play, so let's examine those factors in relation to the time of day at various times of year. Also, let's look at the kind of fishing you can expect during each season, and what you can expect from the fish during a year's progression.

Winter

You might suspect that winter is the easiest season to predict good fishing times, because water temperatures may only get into the range where trout even begin to feed for a brief period in the middle of the day, and in most cases that's correct. Depending on local weather conditions, in a stream that is fed mostly by runoff and surface water, temperatures will be in the mid-30s at dawn. On a sunny day, waters might rise to temperatures in the 40s by late afternoon, and I stress *late afternoon* because water has a high heat capacity. In fact, it takes more energy to increase the temperature of water than any other liquid. For instance, water has a heat capacity five times that of rock, which is why you can sit on a streamside boulder feeling pretty toasty in the middle of the day, but the water can still be piercingly cold. This is actually beneficial to aquatic organisms, because it prevents cold-blooded creatures from being exposed to extreme temperature changes in a short amount of time—something that would shock their systems with often fatal results.

Thus even though a winter day might be balmy at 11 a.m., the water could still be too cold for much feeding activity. If you have a limited number of hours to fish during the winter, or if you don't want to freeze your toes and fingers before the fishing gets good, it's probably a safe bet to sleep in and have a late breakfast. One day in the middle of January on the South Platte in Colorado, I plugged away with nymphs all morning without a strike while the water hovered in the low 40s. By about 3 p.m. the water had risen into the mid-40s, and I was able to hook nice rainbows on a regular basis for an hour or so, until the sun got so low it was hard to see my indicator. Those fish may have continued to feed for another hour or so, but since I couldn't see what I was doing, I quit.

I was also lucky enough to find pockets that held trout, because you don't find them everywhere during the winter. One pool held what appeared to be a whole school of rainbows in a spot that was no more than 20 feet long. It was in the lower third of a pool, dead center in the river. So once I had pestered those fish enough, I went immediately to similar pockets in other pools and found more concentrations of fish. Fish typically seek out the deeper portions of pools where there is slower water but still some current. The deeper pools are not any warmer, but in places that suffer long bouts of air temperatures below freezing, the bottom of the river can form what is called anchor ice, where ice covers the bottom of the stream, making the area inhospitable for trout.

Anchor ice is more likely to form where the water is in contact with more air, as in shallow riffles and faster water. Trout get gradually pushed into these places, called "winter refuges" by biologists. I'm not saying you won't find trout in riffles and runs during the winter. On warm days, they might move from these refuges into the shelf below a riffle at the head of a pool, because they are more likely to find food in riffles than in deep pools. But even on these warmer days, they will shy away from anchor ice.

In streams that are closer to a source of groundwater, or are fed more by subterranean springs than surface water, all bets are off. Even in the dead of winter, groundwater reflects the average yearly temperature of a region, and during the winter it will be warmer than surface water, between 40 and 50 degrees, in most places in the world that support trout. In these streams you can find trout feeding anytime during the day, even at dawn if food is available.

I used to fish Letort Spring Run in Pennsylvania every March with the late Tony Skilton, who grew up in that area. Neither of us could get away at the height of the season because we taught at a fishing school, so we had to visit when we could, and March was a good time. Although morning air temperatures were often in the 30s, we could count on sight-fishing to large brown trout at dawn, when the fish would slide out of their nighttime haunts to forage in shallow water for scuds and sow bugs, small freshwater crustaceans that are often the most abundant trout food in spring-fed waters. In most trout streams I would never think of fishing at dawn in March, but apparently neither did anyone else because we never saw another angler on this popular stream.

In winter, seek out the deeper, slower water that provides trout with a cold-weather refuge.

How do you find these spring-fed waters? Winter is actually the easiest time, because they stay ice-free or only have ice in stagnant backwaters, even on the coldest days, and you will never see anchor ice on them. An abundance of weed growth is also typical on these streams, and although aquatic weeds die back somewhat in the winter, you'll still see some remnants of weeds on the bottom and along the edges. One final way I find spring-fed areas is to drive along rivers on very cold mornings, when the air is still. Spring-fed places will steam on very cold mornings, as the warmer water forms an ice fog when it comes in contact with much colder air.

You'll find similar conditions in bottom-release tailwater rivers, where the water released from the bottom of a deep reservoir reflects the average mean temperature of a particular region. For instance, water at the base of Cheesman Reservoir on the South Platte River in Colorado, at the beginning of the Cheesman Canyon trout-fishing stretch, averages about 42 degrees year-round. It's common knowledge that this trout fishery is great even in the heat of a Colorado Front Range summer, but equally important is that the release water is often warmer than the air temperature in the depths of a Colorado winter. A temperature of 42 degrees is not exactly optimum for ravenous feeding by trout, but it's a heck of a lot better than temperatures in nearby streams that are not influenced by a dam release, where water temperatures are typically in the mid-30s during the winter. That extra 10 degrees can mean the difference between no feeding and at least sparse feeding by trout, especially when a warm day with abundant solar heat raises that base temperature a few degrees.

Early Spring

Lengthening days and warmer daytime temperatures have a positive influence on trout feeding as water temperatures rise, but as far as fishing success goes, the water temperature increases are often balanced in a negative way by increased flows. In the early spring, late March through April, you have to catch conditions just right, and it's often a time of great reshuffling in trout habitats due to a number of factors, first of which is runoff.

I have taken an annual trip to Montana in April for many years. The increased day length in early spring makes insect hatches more abundant, and mayflies like the Western March Brown and the tiny Blue-Winged Olive are joined by large stoneflies like the *Skwala* and caddisflies like the Mother's Day Caddis. Midges, which are active all winter long, get even more abundant and can form large mating flights, with thousands of individual flies falling on the water in a few square feet of river, getting the trout to feed actively. On streams with constant flow, protected from runoff fluctuations like the spring creeks of the Paradise Valley near Livingston or tailwaters like the Bighorn and Missouri, the fishing is predictable and productive, even though the weather may range from 70 degrees and sunny to 25 degrees and blinding snowstorms. The bugs don't care and neither do the fish (in fact, often the lousier the weather, the better the fishing, if you can stand it), because flows and water temperatures are stable.

However, if you have your heart set on fishing rivers that are not influenced by groundwater flows or dams, like the Gallatin or Yellowstone or Bitterroot, the fishing is much more of a crapshoot, and surprisingly your biggest enemy is balmy weather. A spell of sunny, 70-degree weather the day before you fish melts snow in the mountains, and this water quickly rushes downstream, raising the flows and picking up sediment, neither of which are good for fly fishing. The fish may still be feeding, but it's doubtful you can get many of them to see your fly in the turbid waters and even tougher to get your fly close to the bottom, where the fish will be lying to get away from high flows. You can get lucky and find a backwater where fish may be congregated and at least have a chance of showing your fly to one, but the fishing will be exponentially more difficult. The best fishing in early spring on these rivers is a gradual warming trend after a cold snap, when all the water trapped in ice and snow is still locked up in a solid form, or at least released gradually instead of in one major pulse.

To add complexity to spring fishing, you have to factor in the spawning migrations of both rainbow and cutthroat trout. Rainbows begin to migrate toward shallow gravel bars, where they find optimum spawning conditions, anytime from December through May. Not only does this timing vary with altitude and water temperatures, but there is also an indication that it varies with genetics. Because rainbow trout have been hybridized many times over the past 150 years and transplanted all over the world, you can even find distinct popula-

An early April hatch of Blue-Winged Olive or Baetis *mayflies. You will see more of them on dark days than bright days.*

tions of rainbows in a single river, some spawning in February and some spawning in April. These fish may move a matter of yards or many miles to spawn, choosing the main channel of a river or a small tributary stream, depending on how much they have migrated as adults to find suitable living conditions. They are imprinted to spawn in the same place they were hatched, and where they end up living as adults may be some distance from where they were born.

Cutthroat trout spawn later in the season than rainbow trout, usually March through as late as July in high-altitude rivers. They also hybridize with rainbows in some populations, depending on whether their chosen spawning sites overlap both in time and space with rainbow trout spawning. For instance, in the South Fork of the Snake River, cutthroat and rainbow trout spawning overlap in many side channels of the river, but in some tributary streams the cutthroats stay reproductively isolated.

Brown and brook trout, fall spawners, generally remain in deeper winter pools in early spring. Some migrate to shallower runs and riffles as insect hatches become more frequent, because insects hatch more abundantly in riffles than in deeper pools, and the fish move to places they can get food more readily. Browns may also follow rainbow trout on their spawning runs to take advantage of loose eggs that don't get trapped in the spaces between pebbles on the bottom.

Because water temperatures continue to peak toward the optimum temperature for trout in late afternoon in early spring, your best fishing opportunities will still be at that time of day. However, where you find the fish depends on whether the water you are fishing has just brown trout or brook trout, or contains rainbows and cutthroats. Deeper, slower pools will hold rainbows and cutthroats that have not begun their spawning migration or have already finished spawning. Shallow gravel runs, particularly in the tails of wide pools, and side channels will have rainbows and cutthroats that are moving to spawn or actively spawning. But because there is so much variation in these species, there are no calendar dates you can reference to find out where they will be, other than the history of the river in question based on your past fishing experiences or those of other anglers.

Late Spring

In places without heavy May and June runoff, late spring is the banner time of the year for fly fishing. Water temperatures climb into the optimum range and stay there all day, plus the late spring is the heaviest period of aquatic insect emergences. Trout are genetically programmed to feed heaviest when their prey is most abundant, so it's not a lucky accident that the heaviest period of trout growth coincides with the heaviest hatches of the year. Trout can and will feed in all water types, all day long. Many have left the security of deeper pools for faster, shallower water because they can optimize their food intake closer to the areas of a stream where insects emerge, typically shallow riffles.

The notion that trout feed more actively in the evening, the famous time known as "the evening hatch," can mean some missed opportunities for you as you learn more about trout fishing and trout behavior. This fallacy has arisen mostly from fair-weather fly fishers in the eastern United States, who just fish on pleasant, sunny days and see a great increase in trout feeding as soon as the sun drops below the trees. But this has little to do with trout themselves and a lot more to

FISHING FOR SPAWNING TROUT

This is probably a good place to discuss fishing for spawning trout. I have no dog in this fight because I believe you should fish for trout any way you want, as long as what you do is not damaging to a fish population or to the fun of other anglers. Some people believe that fishing for spawning trout is unethical, and I respect their views. There is no biological proof that fishing over spawning trout, where the fish are released unharmed, hurts a population.

In the past, many states planned their legal fishing seasons to protect spawning trout, because when spawning they are extremely vulnerable. The fish are typically in shallow water, and their nests, or redds, can be spotted easily because as the female builds a redd, she cleans off the gravel, leaving a pale spot on the bottom. Targeting these fish and taking them home for food can put a big hurt on a trout population, but catching and releasing them is pretty benign. When fish are spawning, they fight, especially the males, and tear into each other viciously. They exhaust themselves jumping waterfalls and in the act of spawning itself. Catching a fish, exercising it quickly, and releasing it will do little harm to the fish itself or the trout population in general because oxygen levels at spawning time are near optimum and the fish recover quickly and go right back to what they were doing.

If you want to fish for spawning trout but still feel funny about fishing for ones in the act of spawning, consider fishing only downstream of the redds. Often a number of males will compete to mate with a single female on a redd, and the less dominant but very aggressive males hold downstream of a spawning pair, hoping the male will vacate the nest so they can move in. Also, trout of all species plus baitfish will hold below a redd feeding on loose eggs that get dislodged from the gravel. This is an easy source of high-quality food for species that are not spawning, but even the fish in the act of spawning eat their own eggs. It's an adaptive advantage because any eggs that don't get deposited in the gravel are wasted biomass since they will never get fertilized and grow, so even the species spawning will eat their own eggs to recapture this energy source.

Rainbow and cutthroat trout spawn in the spring. Whether you fish for them over their redds or not is up to you, but many anglers frown upon it.

Late spring, when everything from leaves to many insects pop, is one of the best times to be on a trout stream—as long as heavy spring runoff doesn't get in the way.

do with their prey. Aquatic insects are programmed to hatch more frequently when light levels are too low for birds to feed on them but not dark enough for an abundance of bats. Trout naturally follow this rhythm on sunny days. Yet a single day spent during a dreary, rainy spell with a low ceiling and low light levels, the kind of day when birds like swallows and cedar waxwings stay sheltered under leaves and don't feed as actively, will show you that the evening hatch is not always the best time to fish.

I was staying at a friend's house on the Delaware River one week in May, and had been experiencing great fishing to a size 18 mayfly spinner every day just before dark. Although I don't like to miss any time on the river that time of year, I did need to replenish my fly box with Rusty Spinners, and at noon was sitting at his kitchen table tying flies on a warm but dreary day with drizzling rain, figuring I wouldn't miss much fishing in the middle of the day. As I looked away from my vise, I glanced down at the shallow flat in front of his house and noticed a rise. Then another. Then several. I packed up what flies I had completed and slapped my waders on and hurried down to the river. The same spinners that had been falling at dusk covered the water, and big fish were rising everywhere.

The fishing that afternoon was probably the best I have ever had on the Delaware, as one big fish after another inhaled my Rusty Spinners. By the time that magic evening period arrived, the fishing stayed good but got no better than it had been all day, and in an unusual move for me, I left a river full of rising fish because, for once, I just didn't want to catch another trout on a dry fly.

The evening hatch phenomenon also falls flat on most Rocky Mountain rivers, where because of lower water temperatures the heaviest late-spring hatches occur in the middle of the day. The famous Pale Morning Dun and Green Drake mayflies both hatch any time from mid-morning till dark, but on most days they are heaviest in the middle of the day, even in bright sunlight. And the trout feed just as eagerly as during an evening hatch on an Eastern stream, even at high noon.

The inclination of trout to feed all day long and feed heaviest in conjunction with an abundance of prey goes beyond just waiting for aquatic insect hatches. Subsurface food is always available to trout, but a fish's ability to prey on that food varies with its vulnerability.

For instance, if you like to fish streamers, your opportunities are not equal during the course of a day or week on the river. Trout have an innate sense of determining when they have an advantage in catching and eating smaller fish. The smaller fish are more quick and nimble during the daylight hours, when they can see a predator approaching. After all,

base of the Navajo Dam on the San Juan River in New Mexico are about 44 degrees year-round. Air temperature ranges from the 40s in January to the 90s in July, and the fishing can be as good in August as it is in May, especially if higher flows are released from the dam, as the higher volume of cool water extends farther downstream when there is more flow.

Fall

I have a love-hate relationship with fall fly fishing for trout. Next to winter, it's the most uncrowded time of year on trout streams, and the weather is more pleasant, at least in early fall. Water temperatures begin to fall back into the optimum range for trout (55 to 65 degrees) in many non-tailwater rivers, and you would think that trout would go on a feeding binge when this happens. In fact, I often read that "trout really put on the feed bag in the fall in preparation for winter" in magazines or books. This really makes steam come out of my ears, because people expect to find trout fishing as good as it is in June since water temperatures are similar. It just doesn't happen. Trout are not bears. They don't binge prior to winter.

Countless growth-rate studies have shown that trout feeding peaks from June through early July and declines steadily after. Whether it's a relative lack of aquatic insects or an adjustment in their bodies prior to spawning (especially for fall spawners like brown and brook trout), they just don't feed as much, which can make fishing difficult. You will see a few hatches and you will find trout feeding, especially in the middle of the day through early evening. Just don't count on it being a bonanza.

One common issue with trout fishing in the fall in areas with large numbers of deciduous trees is the amount of debris, especially leaves, drifting in the current. I am not sure why it puts trout off—perhaps it just annoys them to have leaves slapped in their faces all day long, or perhaps the amount of nonedible debris in the water turns them off to feeding. I do know that windy days are never as productive as calm days in the fall.

Although they don't feed as much in autumn, brown and brook trout get more aggressive as they approach their spawning time, particularly male browns. These species often begin to "stage" or move closer to their spawning areas in late August, in preparation for actual spawning from late October through December. Exactly when spawning occurs varies greatly among river systems and even among different populations of fish in the same river system, but if the stream you are fishing has brown or brook trout, you can assume that at least some of them will respond aggressively to streamers. Unlike fishing with streamers in the spring and summer, where you are trying to imitate a prey species escaping or wounded, in the fall, when fishing for aggressive fish, you want the fly in their faces as much as possible. Slower strips, or swinging the fly in front of them, is usually more productive than the fast strips you might use at other times of the year.

Fall can be a glorious time to fish, and you won't see many people on the river. But trout don't feed as actively in the fall, so the action is sometimes inconsistent.

Tailwater rivers, stable most times of year, have their period of lowest stability in the fall, when the deeper ones experience turnover. This happens because water is most dense at 39 degrees, so when the surface water hits this temperature, the heavier water on top drops to the depths below and the whole lake experiences mixing. This has a mixed bag of effects depending on the exact conditions of the reservoir. In many systems, turnover lowers the water clarity because the mixing of the water column stirs up debris from the bottom, making the water released from the bottom of the dam more turbid than it is at any other time of the year. Mild turbidity may help the fishing because it makes the fish a little less suspicious, but heavy turbidity can turn off both the fish and the fishing.

However, some reservoirs get depleted of oxygen during the summer because they are too deep for much photosynthesis to occur, and the lack of mixing with surface water combined with decaying organic matter from dead algae drifting down from above depletes the oxygen. Turnover restores oxygen to the bottom layers, so when the turbidity effects of the initial mixing lessen, the resulting water releases, with their higher oxygen content, have a stimulating effect on the fish.

CHAPTER 3

Reading the Water

People are always asking me: "Teach me to read the water." I only wish it were that easy. There is no doubt that walking up to a river you have never fished before and going right to the spot where feeding trout will be found would be a skill that would really propel you to the next level in fly fishing. It would be great if there were a set of rules that you could follow, a way to progress down a series of filters like narrowing down data in a spreadsheet to find exactly what you want.

Unfortunately, it doesn't work that way. We're trying to find a living organism, a creature that is not exactly like every other trout in a river, and where it lives in a river can depend on what experience it has had with predators in the past, how it has learned to maximize the food it gets while wasting as little energy as possible, and perhaps even some aspect it has inherited.

A trout's world is full of complex currents, and although we can predict with some accuracy where trout might be found, there are many factors that only a trout understands.

Layer on top of this a moving water environment that can change velocity or clarity or temperature in a manner of hours, that changes flow as the seasons progress, and that offers food in a nonlinear progression daily and throughout the season. And then the living food that trout eat has its own behavioral quirks. And that food can be anything from a tiny midge larva to a crayfish. And the dynamic nature of moving water affects each prey item differently. Ugh. It's a wonder we can make any kind of predictions about where to find trout.

But you really didn't want easy answers, did you? Part of the reason trout fishing appeals to us, and for some people never loses its appeal over a lifetime, is the very surprises you encounter while stalking the banks of a river or wading across a strong current. Those surprises will continue as long as you fish, but I can give you some hints on how to find these sometimes-elusive fish so that as you make your own discoveries, you don't feel completely clueless. You've already learned some factors that affect the behavior of trout—now let's look at the moving water environment to narrow down the odds of finding *feeding fish*.

Note that I said *feeding fish* and even stressed it in italics. We've all had people tell us about the big trout that live under a highway bridge in a deep pool that anybody can see by leaning over the guardrail. I always ignore these fish and never fish for them. They are invariably lying in deep water because they've been frightened by a flotilla of canoes or sloppy wading by anglers—or maybe they just lie in the comfort of deep water because they know ospreys can't grab them and herons can't poke them. Maybe they drop down into the tail of the pool at dusk or move a half-mile upstream to cruise the shallows for minnows and crayfish after dark. Anyway, I'm not interested in these fish. They're frustrating. They may not even be trout because the average bridge gawker can't tell a trout from a sucker.

This is the first maxim, perhaps the only maxim, of reading the water: Look for feeding trout. When you start thinking this way, you trace the path of drifting food through a pool, and you begin looking for places where a trout has refuge from the current but still has access to a constant supply of food. In fact, maybe I should stop right there—it's all you need to

This is classic soft water: mild turbulence, moderate depth, and not a lot of conflicting currents. It's the place you want to be when looking for trout.

know. But I know you want to look deeper; you want to move from just flailing the water with a fly somebody suggested you use to becoming a more cagey predator. So let's move on.

FLOWING WATER

Books and articles on reading the water often go into a big explanation of the differences between turbulent and laminar flow. It's an important part of the study of hydrology, and in order to read the water, you do have to dip your toe into a few pieces of this science. But most of us can only handle a few variables in our brains at any given time, and I'm going to make a brash statement and tell you that you can totally forget about laminar flow. It does not exist in any trout stream I know. Laminar flow describes the behavior of water running through a frictionless pipe, and I don't think any of us would have fun fishing in a shiny pipe. There are many degrees of turbulent water, though, from frothy maelstroms to smooth glides to near-stagnant pools. Those we will examine in detail.

We tend to think of moving water in relation to our own environment, air, but water is liquid and relatively viscous so it behaves in ways that are not always intuitive to us. Most of the literature on stream hydrology is focused on channel movement and sediment load. These are important if you are working on a stream habitat project with Trout Unlimited, but we're really concerned with what stream hydrology is doing right now, as we're standing on the bank looking for fish. What we want to learn about is the immediate response of water flow to submerged objects in a river, not the effect of these forces over years or decades.

One of the first counterintuitive aspects of hydrology that's important to us is that water behaves in a strange way when it encounters a solid—it sticks to the solid. When two rocks slide against each other, you get friction at the point of contact. When water encounters a rock, it sticks to the rock, and its velocity is reduced to zero. Of course, this layer of zero velocity is tiny, and the velocity of water moving past a rock quickly increases as it get farther from the rock, but that dead zone still exists, and it sets up helical currents and turbulence out into the main flow.

Turbulence itself is unruly and unpredictable, which is one of the reasons reading the water is not an exact science. For instance, in the textbook *Stream Hydrology* (p. 134), this is the way the authors introduce turbulence: "In turbulent flow, layers of fluid break up into 'globs' which mix with other globs in a chaotic collection of eddies and swirls." They then go on to say that "the accurate mathematical modeling of turbulence remains a frontier research topic, and the description of turbulent flow relies heavily on experimentation." I could have guessed that—any time a scientist resorts to words like

This rock garden of cobbles creates lots of moderate turbulence—a great habitat for trout.

Looking at a submerged object from underwater, you can see why trout won't be found immediately behind an object, but in other places you might not suspect. The turbulence immediately behind the rock makes it difficult for a trout to see its prey and hold position. Farther downstream, the rock still breaks the current, but the turbulence has subsided greatly, so the trout has an easier time holding position and spotting its prey. There are also areas of reduced current in front of the rock and along its sides, and trout may also be found there.

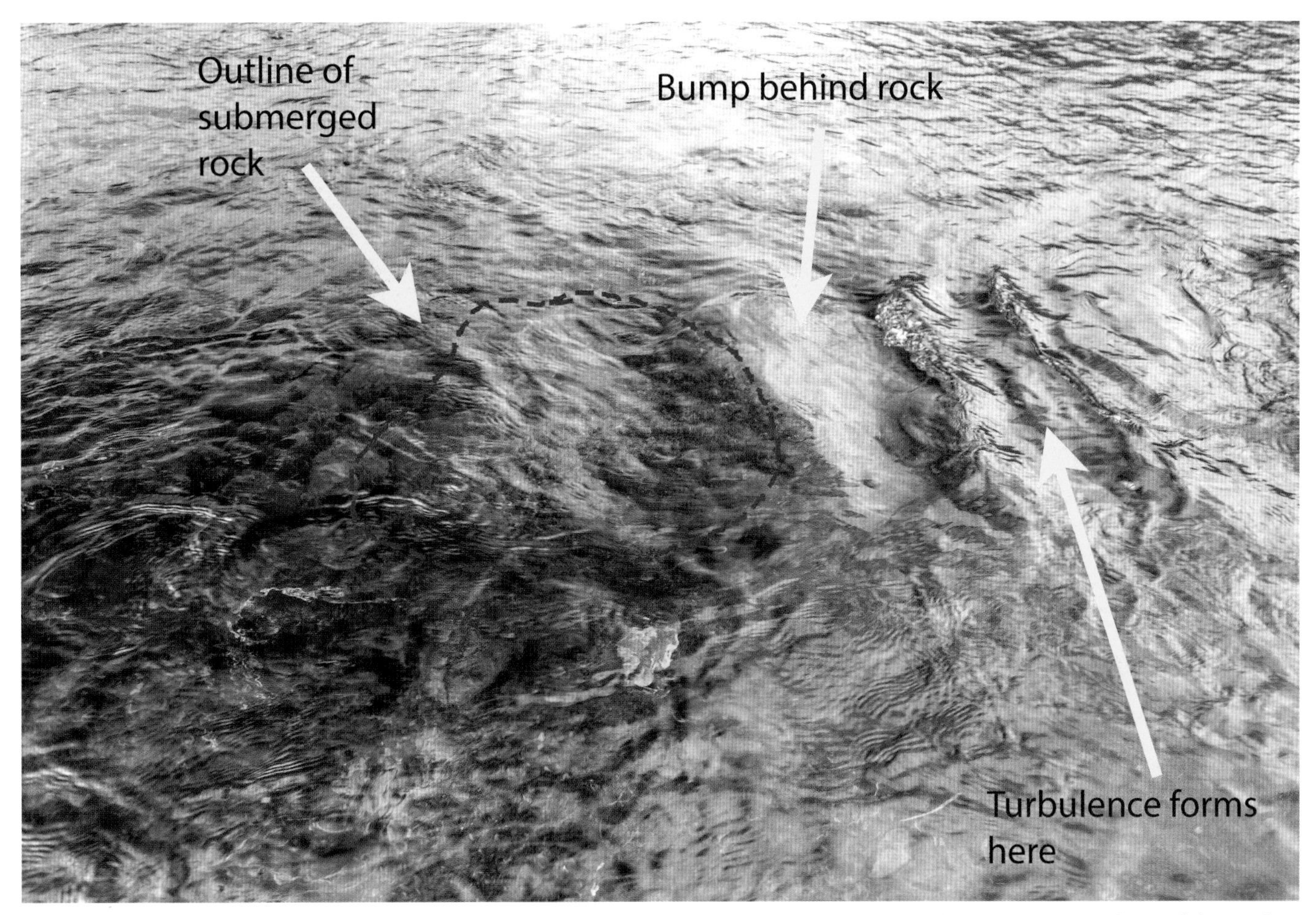

A submerged rock showing the bump and turbulence forming below the rock. If you suspect there is a trout in front of this rock, notice how far ahead of the bump you have to cast.

"globs" means they really don't have a clue how to develop a model!

What we do know in broad strokes, and in a manner that's good enough for us to predict where to find trout, is that friction between the zone of zero velocity next to an object and the main flow of the river creates turbulence. The rougher the object, or the more frequently the objects are distributed, the greater the turbulence and the greater the reduction in downstream velocity. A solid piece of slate on the bottom of a river, the slippery type where once you step on it you get pushed downstream into a deep hole, creates turbulence but a narrow lane of it. On the other hand, a rock garden of basketball-size cobbles creates a lot more turbulence, and its effect stretches closer to the surface. You can see this by the bumps in the surface of the water, and the shallower the water, the bigger the bumps (assuming the same current velocity).

Another aspect of stream hydrology involves an object like a rock or jumble of rocks on the bottom. Hydrologists in their imaginative language call these "bluff bodies" (don't forget these are the people who gave us "globs"). In front of the object is an area of low velocity due to the piling up of water molecules against the initial layer of water that sticks to the rock. This is called the stagnation point. As water slips around the side of the object, it slows down because of friction with the layer against it and streams out from the object downstream. A gap of low pressure called the cavity region is left immediately behind the object, and typically it is about half the length of the body that caused it. The water flowing past the object gets pulled back into this area, in a process called flow reversal or vortex. In this area, called the wake, there's lots of turbulence and energy dissipation.

Now bear with me, I know I'm getting a little geeky, but this stuff will help you find fish, trust me. Along with the conservation of energy and mass, fluids also must obey the law of conservation of vorticity. I'm serious. As water forms vortices along each side of the rock but in opposite directions, these vortices set up counter-vortices when they meet other currents, resulting in a rhythmic side-to-side vibration behind the object. If this vibration coincides with the natural vibration frequency of a solid, it can produce resonance, which is why your wading staff sometimes vibrates in the current. These counter-rotating vortices use up a lot of downstream current energy, and if the current is not too swift and the turbulence is not overpowering, the vortices create a nice pocket of slower water where fish can live comfortably. If the main flow of the current is very swift, the vortices will be so strong that they move a fish out of its position constantly, and at a less predictable pattern. If you see standing waves behind an object,

Don't ignore shallow water: Trout feed more often in shallow water than in deep water.

it's a good assumption that the turbulence in that area is not a comfortable place for a trout to live.

It's the nice, gentle form of counter-vortices that produces areas called seams that are so attractive to trout and so well-known to anglers. It's also part of the form that manifests itself as what some fly fishers call "soft water." Soft water is that part of a river that has everything just right, and like the temperature in your morning shower each day, you know when it's right but you can't put any numbers on it. You just know that you keep adjusting the hot and cold until you get that perfect temperature. Experienced water-readers can look at a half-mile-long pool and find that just-right area in a few minutes. After 50 years of looking at this stuff, I think I can finally verbalize just what you should look for.

There are three aspects of good water for trout, and every spot that harbors feeding fish has them. The soft water could be a sink-size bowl in front of a rock, or it can be a long glide of water that stretches down a pool as far as you can see. All water like this can be evaluated with three criteria:

- Depth
- Drift lines
- Turbulence

But like your morning shower temperature, each one has to be just right, so let's go into detail on what to look for.

Depth

Most trout are caught in depths of between 1 and 5 feet. Any shallower and they don't feel secure; any deeper and it's tough for them to get food. It's easy to understand the minimum depth figure, but the maximum one is not as obvious until you remember what a feeding trout is doing. A feeding trout lies in the current waiting for food to drift by, and because riffles produce nearly all of the invertebrate food trout prey upon, the deeper the water, the more that food is spread out in the water column. This is not as important when trout are feeding on the surface because all the food is on top of the water, but trout feed both on the surface and beneath it, so any place that funnels the food into a narrower vertical band will be a more attractive place to lie and wait for it to drift past.

Even in large rivers, you ignore shallow water at your peril. People who fish from drift boats often pass by some of the best water because it's just too shallow to get to. I can't tell you the number of times I've had to get out of a drift boat to get to the best water in big rivers like the Missouri, Bighorn, South Fork of the Snake, the Delaware, and the Madison.

One of my best places for catching trout over 20 inches long is in a large river, at the shallowest part of a wide flat that looks (and really is) pretty boring and featureless. Anglers in drift boats row down the far side of the pool, the only place deep enough to get a boat through, and my little spot is separated from the main channel by 50 feet of flat, uninteresting

If most of the water is shallow, look for places with just a bit more depth to it.

water; in fact, the place I find the fish feeding looks pretty boring as well. There is not even any cover nearby—the nearest protection is a slot of deep water about 60 feet below where the fish feed. But I know that deep water is where they go for protection, because most of the time I spook the fish and watch them whip around and make a beeline for that deep water. And, on the rare lucky occasion when I hook one, it always bolts to exactly the same place.

In large expanses of shallow water, less than a foot deep, look for the places where the water gets just a little deeper. You don't have to go probing around with a yardstick to find them. One way is to look for spots on the bottom that are darker than the rest of the streambed. It could be just a dark flat rock, but it could also be a little pocket in the shallow riffle that holds a 14-inch cutthroat.

In riffles, look for spots where the surface gets glassy and slick. In the water surrounding it, the vortices form close to the surface because the bottom is near and the turbulence does not dissipate before the water hits the surface. Where the water is deeper, the vortices will be the same size (assuming the bottom is relatively uniform gravel), but most of the turbulence will have dropped by the time the water hits the surface.

In clear, smooth water, look for places where the bottom seems to get blurred. Let's say you are looking at an expanse of smooth water in the tail of a pool. You can see every rock on the bottom in relatively sharp detail, but there is a slot about 5 feet long and 2 feet wide about three-quarters of the way across the river where it gets blurry. That deeper slot is a place that might hold trout.

Drift Lines

Drift lines, debris lines, scum lines, and bubble lines are some of the terms used to describe an indication of where the drift is concentrated as it flows through a piece of water. Drift includes twigs, bubbles, leaves, and invertebrate food—whether it falls into the water like an unlucky ant or it lives there and is in the process of hatching like a mayfly. In a stylized pool with a deep center and shallow banks, the biggest concentration of drift will be along the *thalweg*, which is a German word meaning "valley course." (Most early work in limnology, the study of fresh water, was done in Germany.) The *thalweg* is a line through a river's course that connects all the deepest points in a pool, and because of the friction effects and turbulence, we know that this is also the fastest water in a pool because it is the place least inhibited by turbulence.

Now, before you start complaining that I'm contradicting what I said about depth ("You said trout won't usually be found in the deepest water!"), notice that I said the concentration of drift will be along the *thalweg*, not in it. Especially in faster water, you will find two lines of drift, one on each side of the *thalweg*, and typically one side will hold more drift than the other side. You can observe this just by looking at the bubbles carried along. Here is where you will find the fish—in the shallower, slightly slower places to the side of the main current thread.

Sometimes the line of drift is spread out over a much broader area, covering half or more of the pool. Again, look for the bubbles or bits of leaves and other debris on windy days. When the drift line is spread out, it makes your job of

You can clearly see the drift line on the surface here—and at least three trout feeding right in it.

SCAN TO WATCH VIDEO 003.
Looking at currents to see where trout may be found.

reading the water harder—or you can be an optimist and say that fish will be all over the place. It's during the latter part of the season, or in slower pools, that the lines of drift really help you narrow down your search. The slower the water, the less food it will carry at any given spot, so in slower water the drift line really helps you narrow your possibilities.

If you see a place in a deep, slow pool that looks trouty in all other aspects but is isolated from any line of drift, chances are you won't find trout there. You'll often hear this kind of water described as "frog water" by guides and other anglers for good reason. Frogs don't like to live in or near current, and although this might be a good place to throw a streamer in case an ambush feeder happens to be prowling around there looking for a frog or baitfish, your basic drift-feeding trout will avoid these spots.

In reality, there is seldom only one line of maximum drift that follows the *thalweg*. Lines of drift often get split off into multiple threads through a given stretch of water, and in wide riffles it can be tough to see any sign of the *thalweg* because most of the water is of uniform depth. And don't always look in the middle of the river either. Often the *thalweg* winds its way from one bank to another, following the sinuous course of the river channel.

Turbulence

Turbulence is caused by vortices, as we've already seen. And all the energy that goes into that water whirling in all directions takes the downstream velocity out of the water. Trout need some protection from current; otherwise, they burn all their energy trying to hold their position. But trout do need some current to hold their position because they are so nicely streamlined that current and turbulence in the right amount actually helps them hold in position, facing up into the current where their food comes from. So some turbulence is good, and like your shower temperature, it has to be just right. Trout are very sensitive to the push of current along their entire bodies because their lateral lines and other sense organs in their skin detect minute changes in water velocity, enabling them to slide into a position where current forces from all angles help them align perfectly.

Mild turbulence is attractive to trout, and the type of turbulence to look for is the kind that just dimples the surface of the water. I've often thought it looks like goose bumps on the surface. A soft chop would be another way to describe it. Look for mild turbulence that has a steady downstream progression, because trout like their world predictable. If you look at a spot of turbulence in a stream, you will often see places where the vortices swirl from side to side and boil in one place for a moment, die out, and then boil in another spot. Trout don't like these places because they find it difficult to hold their

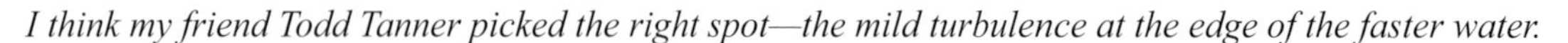

I think my friend Todd Tanner picked the right spot—the mild turbulence at the edge of the faster water.

Todd thinks there is a trout behind this rock, but to me it looks too turbulent. And he didn't catch one there.

position without working too hard and also because the swirls make the food supply coming downstream unpredictable and difficult to capture.

In the same light, extreme turbulence, like places in a stream with standing waves, won't hold many trout directly in the vicinity of the standing wave. The fish get buffeted constantly, and any trout that tries to spend much time near a standing wave burns more energy than it obtains from feeding and will either move out of the way or die of starvation. Trout don't like roller coasters. They don't do stuff for fun.

BUT WHAT ABOUT COVER?

Notice I did not say much about cover. Biologists always tell us they find trout very close to overhead cover; in fact, they often evaluate a river by how much LWD (large woody debris) is in the water. But if you have ever watched how biologists evaluate a trout population, you'll know why they find most trout in logjams and deep pools. First a bunch of people stamp up and down the bank, getting equipment ready. Then they splash around getting everything set—blocking seines, cages for holding fish, and often a canoe to hold heavy electroshocking gear. Then a half-dozen of them splash through a pool, chasing fish with their electric probes. Is it any wonder they always find fish near cover?

Trout do need that cover—they need it when cornered by a flock of mergansers, threatened by the shadow of an osprey overhead, or chased by an otter. But all they need to do is to be able to bolt to that LWD (or for that matter, a pile of submerged rocks, a deep pool, or a bed of watercress) when danger threatens. They like to be close to it—they prefer feeding areas that are close to protection—but it shouldn't be the primary focus when you are looking for feeding trout. Trout often feed 40 or 50 feet from their security blanket, but fishing just to areas of cover is like opening a hot dog stand in a tornado shelter. You'd be much better off opening your stand out on Main Street where people are happy and hungry.

Depth itself offers cover, and we often overlook the idea that riffled water itself provides cover. You can see this yourself if you spend enough time trying to spot trout in a clear stream: They are much easier to spot under a smooth surface than a riffled one, and even on a smooth surface, when the wind just gently riffles the surface, the trout seem to disappear. Overhead trout predators like kingfishers, ospreys, and eagles can see better into the water than we can, as they are

In a place otherwise barren of protection for a trout, this logjam provides both instream cover and overhead cover.

You can tell by the steep slope of the far bank (and how deep my friend Bob Gotshall is wading) that there is a deep hole here. Trout don't need any other kind of cover to feel secure here.

typically directly overhead, where the distortion caused by the difference of index of refraction between water and air is minimized or eliminated. We're nearly always looking into the water at an angle, unless we're on top of a high bluff or on a bridge looking at fish. But still, even a gentle riffle can distort the surface enough to hide a trout from predators, and fish will use riffles as cover as often as they do depth—the difference being that there is far more food in a riffle than in a deep pool. Given the choice between fishing a 2-foot riffle or a 10-foot-deep pool, I'll take the riffle every time.

The broken surface of this riffle hides a trout from predators.

OBJECTS IN THE CURRENT

When you get down to the micro level in a trout stream, objects in the water also help you pinpoint where trout feed. The most obvious items are rocks on the streambed, and usually it is not a single rock but a jumble of them, because the current in a river sorts objects by their size and resistance to current. The faster the water, the bigger the object, because smaller objects get pushed downstream in the current until it is slow enough for them to settle out. Thus, slow pools are carpeted with silt, pebbles, and sand, but as you move up to the head of a pool, you find bigger pieces of gravel, then rocks, then boulders. This is not to say you won't find a big boulder in the middle of a slow pool, but often they don't stay there because they either get covered up by the finer particles or the lack of resistance on the softer bottom moves them out of the slow water in the next high flow.

Smaller rocks or piles of rocks don't need much elaboration because you can cover them with a single cast. In other words, a bowling-ball-size rock might hold a nice trout somewhere close to it, but since you can effectively cover the pocket in front of the rock, the slow water behind it, and the mild turbulence even farther back with a single drift, it really doesn't matter exactly where a trout might be lying. As long as you can recognize the presence of a rock, either by seeing it through the lens of clear water or by the wake made on the surface, it doesn't matter.

It's when you get to bigger objects, those wider than a refrigerator, that reading the water becomes more helpful. You won't be able to cover the entire area with a single cast, and because each subsequent cast risks spooking a wary trout, you want to place your first few casts in the best spot and subsequent presentations in less-prime locations.

Most anglers make their first cast right behind a rock, in the cavity region, but in my experience that location would be my last choice, as I have both caught and seen far more trout, and bigger trout, in the stagnation point in front of rocks. At first this appears to be counterintuitive, but when you look at hydraulics and the feeding behavior of trout, it makes more sense.

Trout in front of a rock can see what's coming, and they also get more of it because food drifting down in the current gets pushed aside by the rock, straining all those drifting goodies away from the cavity region. Yes, the vortices created in the wake rotate current back in behind the rock if the current is strong enough, but that backwash drifts into the trout's position from behind, so it is not able to see the food and plan an attack to capture it. Of course, if the rock is big enough to create a whirlpool behind it, trout may be found

With a single object in the current for both protection and a reduction in current, trout are more likely to be found along the sides of the object and more toward the front. If a trout is found behind a rock, it might be a distance behind it, where the turbulence is less violent and the fish can see its prey and hold its position better.

Most times you won't find a single object but a combination of them, so look for how the combination of objects make places for trout. Trout 1 is there because of the nice submerged shelf, because it is in the tail of a little run where food is concentrated, and because it has that large rock for cover if it gets frightened. Trout 2 has the side of the large rock for protection and submerged rocks in front of and behind it to help break the current. Trout 3 is also in the tail of a little run, and it has two rocks close by for protection. Trout 4 is in the slick behind the lower rock, back far enough so that it does not suffer the turbulence immediately behind the rock.

facing downstream (but still with their heads up-current), but the vortices create an unpredictable flow and it's just not as easy to capture prey there.

Although the stagnation point in front of a rock is seldom long enough to encompass a trout's entire body, they still seem to be comfortable resting in front of a rock. I believe that because the rear half of a trout's body is in this low-velocity area, and also because the force of the water digs a small trench in front of a rock, trout are able to hold their positions here with minimal effort because of their fusiform shape: The wider front half of their body acts like an arrow and cuts the current, and the more flexible rear portion, protected from the current because of the stagnation point, does not have to work as hard.

Almost as productive as the front of a rock are both sides of a rock. Although current picks up velocity along the sides of a rock, most rocks are not perfectly smooth, so any projection from the side of the rock creates a nice cushion of slower water. A trout here has the advantage of seeing more food drifting past than it would lying directly behind the rock. The smoother the sides of the rock and the faster the current, the less likely this will be a good place—but in moderate currents the sides of rocks or rock piles are my second choice for presenting a fly.

We've seen that the spot behind a rock can be less productive than other places, because it strains a lot of the food from the current. But what happens as you progress farther downstream from the rock? A lot of it depends upon the size of the rock and the velocity of the current. In fast currents the vortices create standing waves, buffeting a trout out of position. In slower currents the vortices get more predictable and less violent, and the farther you get from the rock, the less dramatic they are because they begin to get diminished by the force of the current outside of the wake.

At some point below an obstruction, the downstream velocity of the water is still reduced but the flow is more stable and oscillations decrease in amplitude. This is another place of great interest to us as stalkers of trout, because the flow is more uniform and trout are protected from the main flow of current, and at this point prey items that flow past the rock are directed back into the wake.

I think this is the reason we catch fish when we cast behind rocks—not because fish are actually lying right behind the rock, but when we cast to that point, our flies pass through the area of the cavity and strong turbulent flow, and then drift into the lower part of the wake where most of the trout actually live. Behind a small object this doesn't really matter, but because the cavity region is about half the size of the object above it, for a boulder that is 5 feet wide, your entire drift might be in unproductive water. In addition, to get to that spot, you might be casting your fly line over the place where trout are actually feeding, thus spooking the fish before you even get a chance to put a fly over them.

The Multiplication Factor

Objects don't exist on a stream bottom in isolation, and the macro effects of turbulence—depth, lines of drift, and opposing forces—can either augment a rock's importance to trout or diminish it. For instance, in a place where water flowing into an object is already strongly turbulent, no matter how tasty a rock looks, the force of the upstream turbulence will combine with the turbulence around the rock, negating any beneficial effects the rock itself might offer to trout. It also makes the hydraulics so convoluted that you won't be able to figure out what's happening in the vicinity of the rock. It's okay to throw your fly there—who knows? But your fly might also end up nowhere near where you predicted it might drift, and only a dozen or so drifts in the area will let you figure out just what the current is doing to your offering.

Now imagine a stretch of water with moderate flow where the main line of drift intersects perfectly with the rock in front of you. Lying right in the middle of a food highway, the stagnation point in front of that rock assumes even greater significance. And imagine how appealing that spot in front of the rock would be to a trout if, in addition to these things, that rock was located in the lower part of a wake from a bigger rock upstream, right at the point where turbulence settles down and becomes uniform. That's a spot you want to concentrate your efforts. If you are wading a small stream where you can hit every likely place, this is not such a big deal. But if you are floating a big river where you may have to row from one side to the other to hit this spot, it's to your advantage to anticipate a path that will take you within casting distance of this spot, while the less productive water in other parts of the river slips away as you float downstream.

SPECIFIC PLACES IN A RIVER

Now that we've got some idea of how currents affect where you find trout in rivers, it's a lot easier to examine parts of the river with more familiar names and predict where trout might be found.

Heads of Pools

The head of a pool is a place where water makes a hydraulic jump, where it goes from fast, shallow water to slower, deeper water. The hydraulic jump combined with the deeper water produces a reduction in current velocity, and is a place where trout can hold in the current without wasting energy. Usually there is a shelf where the water depth increases dramatically, and trout can hold just under that shelf. It's a natural place to pitch your fly, not only because these places concentrate trout, but because the faster water at the head of a pool allows you to slip your fly into the current with less chance of disturbing fish.

A lot depends on the velocity of the current. At slower flows and lower drops in altitude, not much turbulence is created at the head of a pool, so the fish may be right up against

Here is a spot that has it all: food, as evidenced by the drift line bubbles; rocks on the bottom; protection along the bank; and a moderate current without too much turbulence.

A classic head of a pool scenario. Really, trout will feed almost anywhere in this photo except in the heavy white water at the head and the downstream side of the big rock, which is too far removed from the current to provide food (unless there is an extremely heavy hatch). Trout 1 is in a little pocket of protected water but still close to the protection of the white water, which would hide it from predators. Trout 2 is in a small pocket along the far bank, just to the side of the main flow. This fish won't often get caught: drag will be an issue as you would have to cast across all that fast water to get a fly to it, and the fly would drag immediately unless you threw a lot of slack. Trout 3 could actually be anywhere along that shelf indicated by the change in color—anywhere along that edge would be a great spot. Trout 4 is in the area where the main current begins to slow, just off the far edge of the main current. It is more likely to feed there than behind the big rock because it is closer to the main food-carrying threads of current.

the shelf. However, where currents are faster or the water drops from a higher altitude, you get a pocket of extreme turbulence at the head of a pool. Although trout might dart into that water for shelter if they are frightened, the flow may be too unstable because of strong vortices, and trout will seldom hold in this nasty stuff to feed. If the water is boiling and frothy, instead of looking for trout right in the main flow, look farther downstream where the boils diminish and the water has a more predictable temperament. At high flows you can observe a seam on either side of the main flow where the velocity is minimized—this is where to find trout in the head of a pool at higher flows.

In pools with a narrow head that widens as the river progresses downstream, flow reversals are formed on each side of the current, just as they do behind a rock, but only if the river is fast enough to produce vortices and strong turbulence. In slower flows you get a nice seam at each side of the main current flow, and an area of stagnant water close to the bank where friction with the shallow stream bottom slows the water down.

However, with strong flows and large vortices, big whirlpools form on one or both sides of the head of the pool, but the velocity of this water is greatly reduced from that of the main current, so trout often lie in these places to feed. There is often an "eye" in the middle of these flows where not much food is drifting and thus trout won't be as likely. But on both sides of the whirlpool, especially the side closest to the bank, trout line up and feed heavily. This creates problems of strategy in relation to fishing the rest of the river, because although trout face into the current here, as they always do, in this case they face downstream in relation to the rest of the river. In addition, the flow just a few feet away is flowing in the opposite direction, so getting a fly to drift naturally in these places often calls for a few minutes of strategizing instead of wildly blasting casts into the current. Here, sometimes a straight downstream cast gets the perfect drift with a dry fly or a nymph.

Usually one side of the head of a pool is better than the other, depending on the angle of the shelf at the head of the pool in relation to the water velocity. But I remember one pool on the Bitterroot in Montana where the entire length was productive. I was fishing early in the morning in early fall, looking for trout rising to tiny mayfly spinners that predictably fall to the water on this river about the middle of the morning. I found a few half-hearted risers in a big, slow pool, but not what I was hoping for, so I took a walk upstream to look for more fish. I didn't find any risers, but at the head of one pool was a shallow riffle with a nice shelf dropping into deeper water just below it.

The water just screamed for a small Pheasant Tail nymph hung under a bigger dry fly to act as the indicator. Once I got rigged up, I pitched my flies into the riffle and let them slide down over the shelf. The current was so uniform that by fishing directly upstream, I could get a long drag-free float over the shelf. My first half-dozen casts on my side of the river produced four nice fish on the nymph, a mix of browns and rainbows. As I began working out into the middle of the river, I continued to take fish, though not as regularly because the drift was a little trickier and I had to mend the line to get the nymph to drift naturally.

I think I caught over a dozen fish, and didn't think much of the water against the far bank because it looked too fast and turbulent to hold trout. As I waded out into the middle of the river, I saw that the nice shelf extended all the way to the far bank, but the drift looked really tricky because my fly would drag almost immediately. I said to myself, "Forget it, why work so hard to fish that nasty spot—you've already caught a bunch of fish in this spot." But I changed my mind, and with an upstream reach cast and a series of mends after that, I managed to get some nice drifts up against that far bank. Am I glad I did, because the two nicest fish of the morning came from that spot.

This was over 10 years ago, and I think I remember that spot so vividly because the entire head of the pool held fish. Typically one side is far better than the other, so this one was a delightful exception.

Middle of Pools

At first glance, the middle of a pool looks bland, not as fishy as the head of a pool. But in many rivers the middle parts of pools are where most fish are concentrated. Why? Probably the most important reason is that the riffles at the head of the pool spew food into the water below it. Riffles are where most

The thalweg, *or the deepest part of the channel in a stream, does not always run down the center, and it can even move from one side to the other through the course of a pool. In low water like this it's important to find the* thalweg *because it channels the major part of the flow and thus the food.*

Probable location of feeding trout in a pool during moderately high spring water. The trout at 1 is off to the side of the main current in an area of cobbles on the bottom that gives it protection from the current. The trout at 2 is in the calm eddy in a little divot along the bank, still in an area of high food abundance but in slower, slightly shallower water, making it easier to feed. The trout at 3 is slightly behind a projection in the bank, again protected from the current but still near the main flow. The three trout at 4 are off to the side of the main current, at the edge of a slight shelf in the bottom.

insects and important baitfish like sculpins and dace live, and when they hatch or get dislodged, they drift from the faster water at the head of the pool to the more sedate water below it. Turbulence flattens out here, which means under the surface the currents are more uniform and predictable, and fish can find places to hold their position and feed without struggling to make a living. Just look a little harder to pinpoint likely places for trout.

Your first point of reference is the *thalweg*, the fastest, deepest part of a pool. In a stylized pool it shoots right down the middle, but pools are seldom symmetrical or so neatly arranged, so the *thalweg*, identified by the line of debris and bubbles, may wander from one bank to the other. Feeding fish won't be too far from it, and where they are in relation to it depends on the speed of the current.

If you look at a typical pool in cross-section and could see different speeds of current in lines like those of altitude on a topographic map (there is actually a word for lines of equal velocity, isovels), you would see the velocity at a maximum in line with the *thalweg* just below the surface (there is some friction with the air/water interface), with the velocity tapering off as the water gets deeper or closer to the bank. This is because of friction with the layers of dead water against immovable objects, possible because of water's viscous nature.

Where trout will be in relation to the *thalweg* depends a lot on the maximum velocity of the river in question. If the main current moves faster than a slow walk, look for trout some distance from it, as much as 4 or 5 feet. This is a typical situation during spring runoff, when the maximum velocity of the river is just way too much for the fish to handle. On the other hand, once a river settles down to normal levels, fish will move closer to the *thalweg*. In the very low water of late summer or during any drought period, you'll find most trout directly under the *thalweg*, and the places on either side of that area more than a few feet away may be barren.

Because the bottom of a river is not a shiny, polished surface, lots of objects, mounds, and trenches cover it. Each one of these slows the water even more, but stays adjacent to faster water just above it—the gravy train. You will find more fish in a cobbled bottom with lots of different-size rocks than you would in a bottom made of smooth sand or shale bedrock. Divots, humps on the bottom, sunken logs, and other structures provide a break from the current and, if they are large enough, a refuge when the fish are frightened. Thus if you are faced with a big long pool and just don't have the time or the energy to fish the entire thing, look for places with a jumbled bottom. If the water is too high or dirty and you can't see the bottom, just look for wakes on the surface that indicate objects below.

Tails of Pools

Tails of pools are by far the most difficult places to fish. They can also hold the biggest fish in a pool, or at least the biggest fish interested in feeding. Because rocks, gravel, and sand

The same pool in the low water of late summer, with probable fish locations. Notice that they have all moved into the bubble line, which offers the security of deeper water and a steady food supply. Also note that there aren't as many trout here as in high water. Some of the trout that were there in spring may have been forced to take less desirable positions and been taken by predators, or they may have moved either upstream or down, into more desirable water.

Most likely places for trout in the tail of a pool. Trout could be feeding almost anywhere in this photo as all the water is desirable, but the most likely places to find them feeding would be at 1, 2, and 3 in front of rocks, located right where the water breaks over. It's easier for fish to see food coming to them from the smooth water in front of the rocks, and the fish can dart back to the rocks if danger threatens. The fish at 4 is in a nice bowl that concentrates food, in a slightly deeper trench. Trout may also drop down into the shallow water below the place where the tail of a pool breaks over (5), especially if food is abundant.

pushed by high water settle to the bottom as the current slows down, over time the back end of a pool accumulates streambed material and both the banks and the bottom build up, forming a funnel at the tail of the pool. If you look at a cross-section of the tail in three dimensions, you see all the water coming through the pool is squeezed both vertically and horizontally, concentrating anything drifting from above. The thin, shallow water of the tail of a pool also harbors baitfish of all kinds, because they are safer from predators in the shallow water.

But tails are tough to fish for a couple of reasons. You can blame part of this on the continuity equation derived by Leonardo da Vinci, where he noticed that if discharge is constant but area is decreased, velocity goes up. This is why fish feed in the tail of a slow pool—they get more food passing by them. But the increase in velocity as water rushes through the tail makes getting a natural drift difficult because no matter

You can see the color change at the tail of this pool where the water shallows. Trout often hide along the drop-off.

where your fly lands, without some tricky antics on your part, the velocity difference between two places in the tail whisks your fly line and leader away from the fly faster than it would in the middle of the pool, or in a more uniform section of riffled water.

The water in the tail of a pool is most often smooth and the surface unbroken, so approaching fish is difficult without them spotting you, or the wake from your wading warning them of your presence. I spotted a big fish in the Battenkill one season that rose only just at dark, in a shallow, unlikely place in the tail of a big pool. I could tell he was a big fish by the deep plunking sound he made when he rose, and although he did not make showy rises, I could see the water shimmer on both sides of him, betraying a sizable head. He would let the other fish in the pool splash away happily at the evening caddis hatch or spinner fall, but he would never show himself until it was almost too dark to see.

The first few times I tried to catch him, I hurried because I was concerned about running out of light. I realized too late that I waded too quickly to get into casting range, and he stopped rising, probably spooked because of the wake my wading had pushed over his position in the smooth water of the tail. I thought I would get smart the next time and waded in below him, but because I was in faster water, as soon as my fly landed, it would get dragged downstream by the much faster water under my rod tip. Next I tried wading very slowly to a position about 50 feet diagonally upstream of him, throwing slack line plus a reach cast to avoid drag. But after one cast over him, he stopped rising. I continued to try for that fish using every trick I knew, but after a few weeks, the heavy evening hatches subsided to the point where he was not interested in rising, or else he moved, because I never saw him again.

Exactly where feeding fish locate themselves in the tail of a pool depends again on water velocity and the structure of the tail itself. Where a tail is relatively wide and the bottom shallows up slowly, fish can be almost anywhere, so in that case look for little wakes on the surface that indicate submerged rocks. These are often fairly subtle in the tail, but even a slight V-shaped wrinkle in the surface can indicate a sizable rock—and I find that especially in tails of pools, trout are more often located in front of a rock than behind one, so cast well above the disturbance.

Where the tail of a pool rises dramatically from deeper water upstream, fish will often position just at the margin of deep and shallow water. Follow the line of color change that indicates a change in depth across the tail of the pool, and you may find trout all along that edge. Just as you would in the middle of a pool, look for where the debris line delivers food to this area. Right where it crosses the change in depth, draw a mental bull's-eye and you will be able to pinpoint the best place in the entire tail.

Rock Gardens

Rock gardens or pocketwater are places that are neither pools nor riffles, but sometimes long stretches of broken water formed by fast current and a profusion of larger rocks. This kind of water presents a different conundrum—everything

It's tough to read the water in a rock garden like this, because almost every spot in this photo could hold trout. But the most likely places will be in the vicinity of the biggest rocks. The trout at 1 is in front of a large rock, in a slight trench and also with the current broken by the large rock in front of it. Trout 2 is off to the side of a large rock, where it has easy access to the main current flow for food. Trout 3 is in the same slot as trout 1, just a little closer to the sanctuary of the rock. Trout 4 is on the deeper side of a large rock, with a close place to hide yet access to the food supply, as indicated by the bubbles. Trout 5 is in a nice deep trench between two large rocks, with current slowed by the slightly deeper water.

looks good! But you'll beat yourself up trying to fish all the good-looking spots unless you have all day and are restricted to a small piece of water. Not only will you have to poke your fly into numerous nooks and crannies, but wading in this kind of water is physical, and if the rocks are slippery and the current fast and deep, it can even be dangerous. So it's best to skim the cream off the top by stepping back, getting a bigger picture, and looking for combinations of factors that indicate good feeding spots for trout.

My first piece of advice is that you ignore the banks at your peril. The water here is always slower than in the middle, often with deeper pockets between rocks than you would expect, and friction along uneven banks often slows the flow to a very comfortable place for trout. The Madison River in Montana between the outflow of Hebgen Lake and its junction with the Gallatin and Jefferson Rivers at Three Forks, where it forms the Missouri, is basically one long stretch of riffle and pocketwater for 40 miles as the crow flies and probably triple that in river miles, except where it is backed up by Quake Lake and Ennis Lake. There are virtually no classic pools to speak of. And in most of those river miles, the majority of its feeding trout are found within a few feet of the banks. In fact, I once fished it with Craig Matthews, owner of Blue Ribbon Flies and one of the most experienced anglers on the Madison, and despite the river's size and brawling nature, Craig fished all day in hip boots and barely got his ankles wet, because most of his casts were within 5 feet of the bank.

Other places to look are where the riverbed plateaus out and its vertical drop is not as severe as in other places. Just a slight change in the slope of the streambed can slow the water enough to make it more comfortable for trout, but you can't see this when you are down in the water wading. You need to walk the banks, or even drive along a river to spot these places. You will see the surface of the water smooth out slightly and will see a bit less whitewater and standing waves. These sections can be as small as a living room or as long as a half-mile, and by concentrating on them you will narrow your odds.

Another way to keep from going nuts in pocketwater is to scan a large stretch of water carefully and look for places where assemblies of rocks or a combination of rocks and a bend in the river form a miniature pool. You can find these

Guide P. J. Daley fishes some tasty pocketwater on Maryland's Savage River. His problem is that trout could be living in almost any place in the photo.

by looking for areas of smoother, darker water unblemished by too much whitewater. In some rivers there may be a fish in front of every rock, but in places where the trout population is not as dense, you need to find the bigger, better places more likely to hold several trout than that isolated rock that takes you 15 minutes to wade close to, yet only holds a single fish.

RIFFLES AND RUNS

In between pools, and sometimes forming the head of a pool, are hydraulic structures we call riffles and runs. These are places with relatively fast water but typically fewer big rocks, so the whitewater you see from the hydraulics around rocks does not form, but you see little bumps on the surface caused by turbulence with the smaller stones and gravel on the bottom. Riffles are typically wider and shallower than pools—if the water is deeper than 3 feet, the turbulence caused by the bottom does not make it to the surface, so what you have is a "flat" or actually what you might just call a pool.

The exact definition of a run is hard to pin down, because although a riffle is a hydraulic that is discussed by biologists and stream hydrologists, a run is more of a fisherman's term, and being more casual and less exacting than scientists, we don't have formal definitions for some of the river features we talk about. Typically, a run is deeper and narrower than a riffle; the water does not run quite as fast, but runs faster than the water in the middle of a pool. Being an intermediate kind of feature, one angler's run might be another's riffle or even small pool. Reading a run depends more on how riffle-like it is or how closely it resembles a pool, and it's really tough to generalize what to look for in this kind of water.

Riffles, however, do have distinct features to look for. First of all, the typical riffle, in cross-section, is more rectangular and often more symmetrical than a pool. The cross-section of most pools is vaguely U-shaped, but often with humps and valleys in places. And in a pool, the velocity differences from one place to another are often dramatic. In a riffle, the velocity is much more uniform, from top to bottom and from bank to bank. There is often a pocket of slower water close to one or both banks in a riffle, but still the current-speed differences are not as large as in a pool. This uniformity makes riffles harder to read, but I love fishing them because most anglers pass them up as being too fast or too shallow for trout. Don't make that mistake.

Your first evaluation should be to eyeball the slope of the banks and the velocity of the water. Riffles with little vertical drop and gentle current are harder to read because fish can live almost anywhere in them. The water flows at a comfortable speed for feeding, about the speed of a casual walk, and just a little baseball-size rock or a slight hump of gravel can give trout all the protection they need to live comfortably in a riffle.

Here, look along the sides of the riffle where it meets the slower water against the bank. Look for rocks that are just slightly bigger than all the other rocks. As long as the water is at least 18 inches deep, suspect trout, because although the water may look too shallow, the disrupted surface of a riffle provides just as much cover from predators as an overhanging tree would in a still pool. And since the whole surface is broken, trout have lots of places to hide. You will most likely not even be able to find a foam line to tip you off where feeding trout lie—the whole riffle, from bank to bank, is often one big foam line.

The best places to look for trout in a riffle. Trout 1 and 2 are in the slower water indicated by the slick surface and are in front of submerged rocks. Trout 3 is also in a slick and is along the side of a submerged rock. Trout 4 and 5 are also in slicks behind submerged rocks, and notice they are quite a distance behind the objects that slow the current, where the water is not as turbulent and they can see their food easier.

Deeper than a riffle and not as slow and defined as a pool, this run can nonetheless hold many fine trout, and indicated here are some of the most likely places. Trout 1 is off to the side of the main current, on a shelf where the water begins to deepen. Trout 2 is on the other side of the current and close to the shelter of a number of large rocks. Trout 3 is alongside a large rock that is perfectly placed on the seam between fast and slow water and shallow and deep water. Trout 4 is in a little slick where the force of the current lessens but still off to the side of the main current. Trout 5 is in the seam on the opposite side, in front of a large rock.

In riffles with a steeper vertical drop, trout don't have as many places to live and feed. Although this makes it easier to find the places they might be living, be aware that you won't find as many trout in this kind of riffle as you would in the more gentle variety. The seam close to the bank is an obvious hot spot in a faster riffle, but there are also other places to look.

Rocks larger than others in the surrounding streambed are also places to look for fish. And in every fast riffle, you will find deeper, slower pockets where trout will concentrate, because if you look at old Leonardo's continuity equation in reverse to the way it applies to the tail of a pool, any time the area the water flows through increases, velocity decreases. You find these deeper slots by looking for smoother, glassy surfaces in a riffle where the turbulence formed along the bottom does not get to the surface, or at least does not cause as great a disturbance as it would in shallower water. These deeper slots may also show up as darker spots on the bottom because not as much light penetrates there, so you have less of a reflection from the bottom.

Flats

Now, a flat is definitely not a term you find in a stream hydrology textbook, but in my opinion many trout streams have them, especially rivers with a gentle gradient. To me, a flat is a piece of water that is not fast enough to be a riffle or run and not defined enough to be a pool. It's flat, featureless water that shows few hydraulics on the surface to help us determine what is going on below, yet trout love this kind of water for feeding because the current is gentle enough for them to just suspend there, without any need to rely on a deeper pocket or pile of rocks to buffer the effects of the current.

The first thing to look for in a flat is the foam line. It is often not well defined, or there may be several minor foam lines running through a flat, but if you can find one, it will help you find trout. The smooth surface of a flat does not offer as much protection from predators because fish are visible from above, so in this case trout are often loosely pegged to places where they can bolt when danger threatens. These places can be a log, a pile of rocks, or even a deeper channel somewhere in the flat.

Don't always assume the fish will be right next to this protection, however. I have a favorite flat on the Delaware River on the New York–Pennsylvania border where trout, and very big ones at that, move up out of a deep slot when they feed. These fish move almost 60 feet out of that deep channel to feed in very shallow water, even in the middle of the day. How do I know those fish come out of the deep slot? Because every time I hook one, without hesitation it bolts right past me and runs downstream into that dark hole where it thinks it is safe.

In otherwise featureless flat water look carefully for the bumps and swirls that indicate submerged objects, because a pod of trout may often be pegged to these structures. The trout will most likely feed in front of and off to the sides of these objects.

When the current is relatively swift, trout will be more likely to feed on the inside of the bend, where the current is slower and easier for them to handle, as shown here by trout 1 through 3. However, if there is a little point or projection that helps break the current, you may find some on the outside of the bend, such as trout 4.

Luckily the hole does not have any logs or other snags in it, so I have a good chance of landing these fish.

Bends

Given the option of fishing water that runs in a straight line or a river with lots of bends, I will take the bendy stretch every time. In rivers with a mostly straight course, punctuated by an occasional bend, you will find more trout in the vicinity of the bend. Straight pieces of water are often too fast, or sometimes even too slow, yet when interrupted by a bend, you get both an increase in current on the outside of the bend and a decrease in current on the inside. And because of the scouring effects of water encountering the obstacle of the bend, you always have a deeper spot followed by a shallower bar downstream of the bend toward the opposite bank. Bends form pools. Some rivers offer almost no pools except where the direction of the river changes and forms deeper pockets.

Where you find trout in a bend of a river depends on the speed of the current. In fast current where the slope of a riverbed is steep, even though the outside of the bend may look better and harbor a nice undercut bank, the current against the outside may be too fast for trout to feed, unless there is a rock or log against the outside bank to break the flow. Fish in fast-water bends are usually found on the inside of the bend, on the seam where fast water meets slow current. Even though it appears that fish on the inside of a bend have no cover or protection, don't forget that it's just a quick dart to the protection of the deeper water in the middle or the undercut against the far bank.

Another reason to suspect fish on the inside of a bend in fast current is that because centrifugal force piles the water up against the outside bank, gravity forces it in an opposite direction, which pushes food from the main current back to the inside of the bend. Because the force of this current is reduced due to the change in direction, trout have a comfortable place to take advantage of it. This effect is hard to see on the surface because this change in direction happens under the surface where you can't see it. But it does affect how you should approach a fast bend, because fish on the inside of a bend often face into this flow, which cocks them 45 degrees or so downstream from the direction you think they may be facing.

This is especially important when fishing an active fly like a streamer. The typical streamer tactic is to cast to the far bank and strip back to your position, and if you are standing on the inside of the bend where the wading is easier to negotiate, by casting to the far bank and stripping back, you place the fly in a position where it is coming directly at the fish. Prey

In a slow-water bend, trout are more likely to feed on the outside of the bend because the current on the inside of the bend does not bring food at an acceptable rate.

species don't often swim like they are attacking a predator, so a trout in this case would either ignore the fly or actually be spooked by it. A better approach is to cast directly upstream or downstream in a bend, because in that case, the fly will pass broadside in front of the fish.

In slower currents, trout are often more likely found on the outside of the bend, because the inside may be almost stagnant and not offer a steady supply of food. A good rule of thumb is that if the water piles up against the outside bend and is slightly higher in elevation than the water at the center of the

In a target-rich bank like this, with lots of roughness to break the current and good cover, trout will feed in places where little indentations in the structure provide protection from the current but still enough of the main flow to carry plentiful food.

bend, fish will more likely hold on the inside of the bend. If the bend looks flat and uniform in height, a better place might be on the outside. This can change with fluctuations in flow, so don't always assume trout will be in the same place. The fish you caught during high water in May on the inside of a bend could have moved to the outside of the bend in the slow currents of mid-August.

Banks

Judging by the trout streams I have fished, I would say that no matter where you are fishing, whether it's a mountain river in Patagonia, a chalk stream in England, or a coastal river in California, you are just as likely to find trout willing to eat right up against the banks as you are to find one in the middle of a river. Brushy banks offer protection from predators, but even more important is that they offer slower, shallower water where trout find it easier to feed. I don't hold much stock in the theory that trout hold close to the banks waiting for terrestrial insects like grasshoppers and ants to fall into the water, because I have seen trout along banks happily feeding on mayfly or caddisfly hatches. I really think it has more to do with the ease of feeding than the anticipation of a random meal falling from above.

What makes a good bank? First, as always, look for the drift line to find out where food is drifting. If there is a single line of drift and it's somewhere between the middle of the river and the far bank, you can probably assume there won't be many trout on your bank, no matter how deep the water is or how many trees hang over the water. In the same light, if the main line of drift meanders from one bank to the other, as they sometimes do, look for trout along the bank where it runs closest. So the "good" bank may be on the north side of the river where you are standing, but 50 yards downstream the good bank might be on the south side.

Often one side of a river is just too shallow for trout, and they'll be found in the deep water against the far bank. Trout may slide over to the shallower side when the light gets low in the evening and lots of flies are hatching, because it's easier for them to feed on the surface in shallower water, but under most conditions they will be found up against that deep bank.

Let's say you have a long, deep bank in a pool 100 yards long and you just don't have the energy to fish every inch of it, or perhaps you are fishing a nymph or a dry fly and want to hit only the best places and not throw your fly randomly along every inch of the bank, where you risk spooking a trout by putting your fly line and not your fly on its head. Even before trying places with rocks or logs up against a bank, the first place I look for are little divots or bays, where the bank curves in ever so slightly. Trout love these places and often position themselves just above the depression, within it, or at the tail end of it. It doesn't take much either. Just a 6-inch point along a bank will often hold a nice trout. And it seems that the more irregular the margins of a bank, the more trout it will hold.

Second in importance are rocks or logs along a bank because they offer the same attractive reduction in current as the little points along a bank do. Trout will find comfortable places in the little nooks and crannies in front of, behind, and

The bank here looks shallow and gradual and might not hold fish until late evening during a hatch. But the far bank, with vegetation and a steep slope that suggests deeper water, might be a great place to find fish. Of course, the seam right in front of my friend Cole is not bad, either.

along the sides of rock piles and logs where they get both a comfortable current flow and a place to hide all in one. Trees overhanging the water also provide shade that hides trout from predators, but unless the tree offers shade in conjunction with other attractive features like submerged rocks or logs, often shade trees appear more attractive to fish than they actually are.

A tree that has fallen into the water along a bank is called a sweeper. These can be great places for trout, but they can also be disappointing. If a sweeper just brushes the surface but does not extend very far under the surface, it can be disappointing, because although it offers a lot of value in protection from predators, it does not over any reduction in current for a trout trying to find a place to hold and feed. Don't ever forget that we're trying to find undisturbed trout willing to eat a fly, not a fish huddling in fear under a branch.

The one time shallow sweepers become important is during a heavy insect hatch, because the sweeper concentrates floating insects and funnels them into a concentrated lane. At these times, look for trout in front of the sweeper where it connects to the bank, and also at the outside tip of the sweeper. The area right behind the sweeper is a dead zone during a hatch because it strains all the food off the surface.

A more sunken sweeper, one that touches the bottom of the river, offers both safety from predators and protection

Just a small projection and bay along this bank formed a great place for a large brown trout.

And here is the trout that was living there.

from the current, so these are a lot more valuable to the trout. Fish feeding on insects will again be found right at the crotch where the sweeper connects to the bank, and just on the inside of the outside edge. Also, bigger trout may live underneath or just behind the sweeper because the sanctuary of the tangled underwater branches offers a haven for baitfish.

THE PROXIMITY FACTOR

When reading the water, don't just look at discrete places or objects in the current. You should get a more holistic view because a tasty rock that offers some nice protection from the current in the middle of a shallow riffle, where a trout has nowhere else to go, might not have much value. Rocks, logs, points along banks, and riffles offer little value if they aren't somewhere close to a deeper hole or other sanctuary. A trout is more likely to hold next to a rock if it has not only that rock for protection from predators, but also a secondary refuge at the bottom of a deep pool.

I have a spot on the West Branch of the Delaware River on the New York–Pennsylvania border that consistently produces large trout for me, yet it is the dumbest, flattest, most boring piece of water you can imagine. It is only 2 feet deep at the most and offers absolutely no cover. I have never seen another angler fishing it, even in this very crowded river. The reason is that just below this boring water is a deep slot where the fish have plenty of protection, and they move up into the flat water to feed. When hooked, they immediately run downstream for that deep slot, so I know they use it as a refuge.

Look for places in a river that combine a number of attractive factors. A rock along the bank, with a log alongside it, lying right in the middle of a foam line in current about the speed of a slow walk, is a higher-percentage bet than just one or two of those features. And this is far more important as the size of a river increases. In a small stream, you can easily hit every likely spot in a pool without moving and cover every one of those places in a mile of river with just a casual afternoon's fishing. In a big river like the Missouri or Deschutes, where it might take 15 minutes just to wade into position, you can't possibly hit all of the likely spots. And the bigger the river, the patchier the distribution of trout will be. So relax, have fun, and increase your odds by choosing your spots carefully—with an emphasis on finding trout willing to feed.

Sweepers, or downed trees lying in the water, are attractive places for trout to live. Trout 1 is in the most likely spot, just upstream of the place where the thickest part of the sweeper first enters the water. Fish may also lie all along the sweeper, like trout 2, and another likely place is at the end of the sweeper, like trout 3. Trout will be more likely to feed on the upstream side of a sweeper because the tree strains all the food out of the water or directs it outward, and a fish downstream of the sweeper will not get enough food.

In big rivers where you can't fish it all, look for a combination of attractive elements. The spot indicated here is where the tail of the pool breaks over and food is concentrated; it also has large rocks nearby for protection.

CHAPTER 4

How to Approach a River

By now you have the seeds of an idea of where to find trout in a river. But even small mountain streams may run for miles, and you probably want some guidance on where to stop your car or drift boat, where to get into the water, and what to do once you get in the water. To an experienced angler, especially one with an intimate knowledge of a particular river, these seem like silly questions. But I know from answering questions on podcasts, in fishing schools, and at fishing shows, these are honest and valid questions. People can cast well and know how to tie on a fly, but the first step out of their vehicle is often confusing and intimidating.

WHAT DO I DO IF I SEE OTHER ANGLERS?

You're driving along a famous trout stream that you've been told holds a lot of nice trout. You see a big pool with a few anglers in it so you stop the car, put on your waders, rig your rod, and stroll into the water. From the road you saw three people in the pool, but what you didn't see were a half-dozen anglers sitting or standing close to the bank, either waiting for something to happen or rigging their gear. Now nine pairs of eyes are on you, and you feel like you just walked into a country redneck bar in a tuxedo. Oops.

If you see other anglers lined up like this in a pool, it is not a good idea to move in between them. Either go well upstream or downstream of them—or find another pool.

If you like fishing in a crowd, and want to fish some pools where other anglers are, hoping you'll get some good advice, I guess I can't talk you out of this strategy. Maybe you are a little unsteady on your feet and are reluctant to wade fast water without someone close by who can get you out of trouble. Sometimes you meet a friendly group of anglers who will welcome you into a pool and give you advice all day long. But not usually. You will most likely be thought of as an intruder. What's one more person in a pool? It could be that all these people are friends, members of a club or Trout Unlimited chapter, and want to fish together. Or maybe these people are all spaced out along a pool, each with his or her section, and putting one more person in the pool might crowd it just a bit too much. True, somebody was there first, but I can assure you that person did not take any kindlier to the second person as the ninth. Let me talk you into a different approach.

We go fishing to concentrate on catching fish or observing nature. Or just to get away from the stresses of everyday life. Do you really want to spend your day looking over your shoulder, worrying that you might be getting close to another angler, or spend an afternoon with strange eyes boring into the back of your head? I don't, and I doubt you do. My advice is to either drive along the river until you see a parking place with no cars, or maybe one car, or just take a hike upstream or downstream from this pool until you find a stretch of water that is empty, or at the very least has only one angler in it.

Don't tell me rivers are too crowded and you can't find a place like this. If you are willing to walk or explore in your car, you will find a less-crowded place upstream or down. I fish some pretty crowded rivers like the Missouri and Madison in Montana, the Farmington in Connecticut, and the Delaware on the New York–Pennsylvania border, and even at the peak of the season I can always find a stretch of water to myself. It may not be just where I wanted to fish, and it might not even

down, and when I told him I had planned to work upstream, he quickly walked downstream along the bank, well around the bend, until he was out of sight. Be that guy.

SHOULD I WORK UPSTREAM OR DOWN?

This is a question I get frequently from people, even from relatively experienced anglers. I suspect it's because this decision is both personal and situational, and there is never a correct answer. So let's look at the different variables that might make you choose one or the other.

Your first concern should be with spooking trout as you move. The common perception is that trout have a blind spot immediately behind them because there is an acute angle to the rear of a trout where its eyes physically can't see. In theory. So this argues for moving upstream, because you are coming up behind a fish, in its "blind spot." The problem is that feeding trout really don't have a blind spot. When they feed, they don't constantly face directly upstream because as they move around to capture prey, they often dart from side to side, and when they turn sideways they can see directly downstream. Often trout turn completely around and follow an object downstream before eating it, thus placing the angler working upstream directly in harm's way. You just can't trust those trout to do what they are shown to do in diagrams.

I have proven this to myself many times. While it is true that you can get closer to a trout by coming up behind it, something about your presence alerts them when you get too close. I regularly play a game with fish when they are just not feeding, or I've caught enough that I want to do a little research. I will find a fish visible in the water and sneak up immediately behind it. I can usually get to within 20 feet, but as soon as I get closer, even if I am moving slowly, not thinking I am making any noise, the fish will suddenly bolt for cover. So whether the blind spot is narrower than we think, or we make some kind of noise on the stream bottom that we don't recognize, or we make ripples on the surface that are imperceptible to us, I don't really know. All I do know is that theory and field observations just don't agree here.

However, you are still less noticeable when you come up from behind a trout because they don't have binocular vision on their sides and don't see as well to one side or the other as they do directly in front of them. One of the things that catches their eye and puts them on alert immediately is when they perceive movement, even in their peripheral vision. We are very cognizant of sudden movements in our peripheral vision as well, like a deer darting into the road when you are concentrating on the road ahead of you. Trout eyes are a lot different from ours, but all vertebrates respond to movement in their peripheral vision.

This argues for keeping our movements to a minimum when we are close to trout. You can't really eliminate casting motions, and those movements are pretty fast and frightening to a trout, but you can minimize what you show the fish when they are spooky by casting at a lower angle, sometimes parallel to the water, and keeping your fly line, which is highly visible moving through the air, as far away as possible from a trout. You can also move slower when approaching a fish, as the slower you move, the less likely you will be to catch their attention.

Trout are less likely to spot you when approached from downstream, but it's still wise to keep your profile low and use background cover to your advantage, as Martin Carranza is doing here.

Casting on a horizontal plane keeps your fly line low and is less likely to spook trout.

Trout have a circular window to the outside world, or I should say a roughly circular window. They see the 180 degrees above the water squished into an angle of 97 degrees because of refraction, to the point where anything below 10 degrees above the horizon is invisible, so either staying as far away as possible or keeping your profile low will make it less likely a trout will notice your movements. I say *roughly circular* because again, in the diagrams you see in books, a trout's window is circular but that's only in a pond with a calm surface. Any disturbance to the surface of the water makes the window less circular and less clear, which is why you can get very close to trout, even directly upstream of them, in riffled water. The sight line at the edge of the window is constantly

Here is a trout's window looking upstream in very smooth water at an angler that is only 15 feet away. Note that the angler's body is visible, and the rod and fly line moving through the air are quite apparent.

If the trout moves into shallower water, the window is greatly constricted, and the angler now becomes a white smudge on the horizon. If the angler crouches down, he can also keep most of his profile out of the window. You can see why movement, more than anything else, spooks a trout—if the angler were not moving, he would look just like the clouds in the sky.

In a narrow stream like this, your best option is moving upstream.

moving and swirling, so any movement on your part becomes just a part of the background movement.

You should assume, therefore, that trout can see you almost all the time, and the farther away you are from them and the slower your movements, the less likely you are to frighten them. Regarding upstream or down, let's first tackle a narrow stream, maybe the width of a double-lane highway. If you work upstream, you will spook fewer fish because you are coming in behind them, where they still may be able to see you but you will be less noticeable. If you work downstream, you will always be in their full vision when you get close to them, so you will have to both keep your profile low and move very slowly, or you will have to stay farther away from them. Staying too far away in a small stream makes your casts less accurate and puts more line on the water, often in conflicting currents, so presentation gets more difficult. Yes, you can do it, and it's possible to fish a small stream very well moving downstream. You just have to work harder to keep from spooking the trout.

You always have less leeway in a small stream for retracing your steps, regardless if you work upstream or down. Due to the narrow stream corridor, every fish you walk past will have spotted you and is likely to be spooked, unless you get out of the water, move far enough away from the water that you can't see its surface, and then get back into the water in a new spot. So it is possible to fish upstream for a while and then fish downstream, but you don't want to work back through the water you just waded through. A much safer bet is to get out of the water, walk a distance away from the water until you have placed some distance between you and the spot you left the water, and then work back downstream to the place where you left the water.

Big, wide rivers give you much more leeway. If a river is 100 feet wide, you can walk along one side of the stream, either upstream or downstream, without fear of spooking all the fish—particularly if the fish are between the middle of the river and the far bank. Fish in wider rivers also tolerate the presence of anglers better because they usually have a deep-water refuge close at hand and are less likely to be frightened by movement 50 feet away. So you can stay farther away from the trout and move either upstream or down.

In bigger rivers, a significant reason for fishing upstream or down is how strong the current is. If the current is strong, unless you want to keep getting out of the water, walking upstream along the bank (assuming that's even physically possible, as it might not be because of high cliffs or impenetrable brush), and getting back into the water, you're going to have a much easier time of it if you work downstream. You'll be moving with the current each step, not fighting it constantly as you move.

It's important to recognize all the pros and cons of working upstream or down before you even get into the water. I have a favorite run on a large trout stream that always produces some nice fish for me, but in higher flows it's a very difficult place to get to. I want to be along the far bank opposite the place I first approach the river, because the near side is much too fast and deep to wade.

I have two options for getting to this spot. One is to go about 100 feet below it and cross the river in a narrow but very swift section. It's the only place the river is shallow enough to wade, but it's still almost to the tops of my waders, and the water is fast enough and so full of slippery boulders that crossing it is always exciting, sometimes more thrilling than I like. My other option is to walk 200 yards upstream, wade into

In big wide rivers, sometimes it's just easier to work downstream.

the pool above, and cross the pool, moving through the pool at a 45-degree angle to the current on a gravel bar I've located, through water that is deep but not as swift. It's a downstream angle, so getting there is relatively easy but takes longer. Once I get to the far bank, I can wade around the back side of an island to get to my spot.

The only problem is that to get back to my car, I have a choice between a quick but dangerous crossing downstream of my spot or a safe but long slog back upstream, against the current. So before I even get into the water, I eyeball the depth and speed of the current to determine if I want to approach it from upstream or down. I still fish the same way once I get to my spot, but every time I fish it I have to determine which is the lesser of two evils. And to be honest, a lot of my decision is based on my mood: Do I want to deal with that long upstream slog, or do I want to risk the fast, dangerous crossing?

HOW CLOSE CAN I GET TO THE FISH?

When you see fish rising, or when you approach a piece of water you suspect holds trout, there is always a judgment call between trying to get as close as possible so that you can make an accurate cast, and the idea that the closer you get to a fish, the more likely you will scare it. Every piece of water is different, and in truth every single fish is different in the distance at which they suspect your presence.

Fish don't always spook when they see you—sometimes they sense a difference in the surface of the water, and sometimes they hear an underwater sound that is not part of the background noise. One fish in a pool might be in fast water at the head, surrounded by bubbles and the noise of rushing water, and will let you get 20 feet away. A fish in the middle of the pool, where the surface is smooth and quiet, might not let you get within 60 feet. And to compound it further, that spooky fish in the middle of the pool might let you close the distance to half that if it's just before dark, if it's feeding heavily, or if rain disturbs the surface. You are going to get it wrong, and you will spook fish. It's part of the game, so don't agonize over it. Move on to the next one.

One factor in bigger rivers is the smoothness of the water's surface, along with its velocity. In long, slow flats, working upstream seems to be a smarter option, because you will always be moving up behind the fish. However, when you wade upstream you push more water because you fight the current, and pushing water makes more noise and creates waves on the surface that are sometimes not so apparent to you but extremely visible to the fish. These waves distort an ordinarily smooth surface and wiggle the edges of a fish's window in a way that is not part of the normal background movement they see. They know something is approaching long before they see anything above the water.

In this case, sliding downstream carefully, working with the current instead of pushing wakes upstream, can sometimes get you closer to a fish than sneaking up behind it. Of course, in a riffle any wakes you push are immediately dissipated in all the rough water around you, so it's seldom a concern in faster or riffled water. But on a smooth surface with slow current, you can push a wake 50 yards or more upstream of your position.

One mitigating factor in your ability to get close to trout is how eagerly they're feeding. When a fish is feeding every few seconds, you can get a lot closer, sometimes right on top of the fish. This is especially true in low-light periods, but they can be less spooky even in the middle of the day. I suspect it is their inability to focus much of their brain resources in avoiding predators when food is abundant—apparently the importance of getting food when it is abundant trumps the increased exposure to predators in the evolutionary winnowing of genes that get passed on to the next generation.

It could also be a vision factor, as perhaps when their brain is focused on tiny objects close to them in the water, trout do not recognize larger objects above the water. Empirically, you see this on some rivers like the Bighorn in Montana. This rich tailwater always has some kind of food drifting in the water column, and if you have fished there, you know that the trout are seldom bothered much by either wading anglers or drift boats. Unless you walk right on top of them, they continue to feed despite the tremendous commotion produced by hundreds of anglers passing by them each day.

You might suggest that this is a conditioning factor, fish seeing people day in and day out—but I don't think it is. The Battenkill is a river that also suffers from heavy boat traffic during the summer, in this case rafts of inner tubes and canoes manned by people looking to escape the heat of the summer in the Battenkill Valley. The Battenkill is not a rich stream, offering up its insect hatches in fits and starts, and in my lifetime I have watched it go from a river where fish would be out in the open and occasionally feeding during the day to one where they stay hidden in the middle of the day and only come out to feed in the evening and early morning. Those fish may be conditioned to the heavy boat traffic, but as they are not as distracted by food all day long, they stay out of the way.

NOISE

Sound waves move five times faster and four times farther in water than they do in air. This is a scary fact, because it seems like any little motion we make in a river will alert wary trout to our presence. Luckily, there is more science behind this basic science. The most important part of this is that fish can be broadly grouped into two types with regard to hearing: generalists and specialists.

Specialists, which include carp, catfish, and shad, have a broader band of hearing and can hear noises from much farther away. They can detect both particle motion and changes in pressure waves created by underwater sounds because they use both their inner ear and their swim bladders to detect noises. Luckily, trout, bass, and sunfish do not have the specialized structures of these other fish and use only what is called near-field hearing, which is based on particle motion as opposed to pressure changes, and the near-field component

In smooth water like this Montana spring creek, stealth is essential. Keep your profile low, your movements slow, and your false casts to a minimum.

Many people believe metal-studded wading boots spook trout. It seems logical, but science does not back this up, because trout can't hear this kind of noise from more than a few feet away. And, when walking on slippery subsurface rocks, studs add a huge degree of safety and stability to the rubber soles, which are much better than felt on grass, dry rocks, snow, mud, and logs.

of noise decays rapidly. This may be why carp are so much harder to approach than trout, even in relatively muddy water.

In addition, structures in the water, like rocks and weeds, help ameliorate sound waves and any ambient noise in the water caused by riffles, and pocketwater also masks the noises we make. Deep water also allows noise to travel farther because there is less interaction between the sound waves and the bottom. So if trout can only hear sounds from a few feet away, why do they spook when wading soles with metal studs are scraped along the rocks 50 feet away? This was the question posed by John Mosovsky in a paper titled "Understanding Bioacoustics to Catch More Fish," where much of my understanding of trout hearing discussed here came from.

I have been wearing metal studs on my wading shoes for many years, and I can't say that I have noticed trout any spookier when I am wearing studs than when I am wearing felts. In fact, a number of times I have approached happily feeding trout to within 30 feet and scraped my metal studs on the rocks without noticing any change in their behavior. But I must stress that when I scraped my studs on the bottom, I was careful not to make any surface disturbances on the water at the same time. Trout are far more visually oriented than aurally oriented. I suspect that sloppy wading, pushing more visible waves on the surface of the water, or abrupt movements of your body above the water, due to studded soles being less stable than felt on some kinds of rocks, are far more risky for spooking trout than the noises you make.

But what about the lateral line? The lateral line system is a series of pores lined with specialized hair cells that are joined by a canal that runs almost the full length of a fish, especially in the head area. It allows fish to "hear" prey items in dirty water, one reason why streamer flies with bulky heads, lots of hackle, or deer hair are so effective in dirty water, because trout sense the vibrations in the water caused by these. The lateral line system also allows trout to detect changes in current flow around their bodies to help them stay oriented properly in the current. But again, the lateral line system works on near-field particle disturbances. It is not like an early-warning system radar array. A trout can't detect your Muddler Minnow in dirty water from more than a few feet away. Thus the lateral line system is not going to detect the scrape of a metal-tipped wading staff from more than a few feet away.

CHAIN REACTIONS

Sometimes, a single fish in a spot can bolt up through the entire pool and spook every other fish living there. This makes intuitive sense, because a fish seeing another fish frightened enough to swim quickly to the security of deep water, or a riffle, or a log should raise the alarm. I have seen cases where this is true, especially in the low, clear water of summer when you can see every stone on the bottom. You approach the tail of a pool, and you don't see the fish feeding just in front of a rock in the tail. It senses you and darts to the head of the pool, where deep, broken water makes it feel secure. As it swims to the head, you suddenly see a half-dozen other fish follow it to the same place. You then wonder if it's even worth it to fish that pool.

Often it is worth a try. Some other fish in the pool might have been visually isolated from the ones that spooked. Perhaps they were tight to the opposite bank in a deep slot, or perhaps some were on the far side of a rock pile and did not notice the other ones bolting. I have sometimes watched a single fish spook up through a pool and swim right past other fish that were busily feeding, and kept on feeding without missing a beat.

You can even play a fish through a pool, and despite the desperate struggles of the fish you have hooked, others seem to care less. If it's a small fish you've hooked, bigger ones will often chase it and try to eat it. It's always good practice to try to lead a fish you have hooked away from places you suspect might hold other trout, but sometimes trout, especially big ones, call most of the shots, at least in the initial part of the battle, and you have to let them churn up seemingly good water. In that case, if you feel strongly that the pool holds more fish, it's wise to rest the pool by stepping away from the water, either moving to the shallows or sitting on the bank, and giving it a 10- to 15-minute breather.

In approaching trout, I know that you want some concrete answers so that you can stalk trout confidently in any situation. I don't have any easy answers, and if anybody tells you different, they haven't studied trout behavior closely. My own observations that sometimes trout spook at the slightest insult while others seem to be more carefree are backed up by scientific studies. A team of scientists in Canada studied a group of rainbow trout and found that in any given population, there are shy trout and bold trout. The shy trout retain long memories of predator threats and spook at the slightest hint of trouble. The bold individuals seem to forget these dangerous experiences within a couple of days and concentrate more on feeding than on avoiding predators. And like all things in nature, most trout in a population probably fall on a continuum between very shy and very bold.

A similar study on brown trout in Sweden gave further evidence to the fact that trout have individual personalities. When a novel object was released into an aquarium full of brown trout, some immediately investigated the object while others fled to corners of the aquarium in fright. You would suspect that the bolder trout, who fed more often, would be the most successful in the wild, but in the Swedish study when the fish were released into the wild, it was the shy individuals that grew most rapidly. Of course, the relative success of a shy or bold trout probably varies with environment, and even in a single pool there might be places better suited to shy or bold fish. This is likely why wild populations continue to pass on genes of both the shy and bold personalities, because in any given year-class, survival of the individuals that go on to reproduce varies with the interaction of a fish's personality and the environment it chooses.

CHANGE LOCATION OR CHANGE FLIES?

What should I do if I'm not catching fish? Should I change spots or change my fly pattern? This is a question that all of us face almost every time we're on a river, and if you think this is a conundrum only for novices, you are mistaken. The choice you make here is one of those aspects that makes fly fishing—in fact, fishing in general—so fascinating and mysterious. But when you finally find something that works, it's a feeling of accomplishment that can make your day.

Much depends on how well you know a river. If you caught fish in a spot yesterday or last week or last month, as long as the water temperature or water level has not changed significantly, it might be best to stick with a place you know holds fish. However, you should temper this with the thought that the more time you spend casting over a pool, the greater the chance you have spooked the fish and put them off the feed. But if you stay off to the side of the fish-holding water and have not ripped your line off the water a number of times, you may be able to fish the same place for an hour or more. Riffled or deep water is best when you plan on parking yourself in one spot for any length of time, because fish feel more secure when the surface is disturbed or the water is deep. If you are fishing over flat, shallow water, the meter runs quicker because fish there won't tolerate as much disturbance.

Regarding fly changes, if the water is below 50 degrees and no insects are hatching, you may want to stick with a fly you know should be successful longer than you would when the water is warmer and the fish more active. This is because in cold water, you may have to place your fly in exactly the right place many times before you put it right in front of a trout that is not inclined to move. On the other hand, if water temperatures are between 55 and 65 degrees, trout should be aggressively feeding. If you are sure you have placed your fly in the right place with the right presentation more than a dozen times, it's time to try a new fly, or perhaps just alter your technique. If you are fishing nymphs, try setting your strike indicator deeper or adding a heavier fly to your tippet in case you are not getting deep enough. If you are fishing dry flies, try adding a second, smaller fly as a dropper. If you are fishing streamers, change the angle you cast relative to the current, try a faster or slower retrieve speed, or try an erratic retrieve.

If you see insects hatching or laying eggs, my best advice is to keep moving until you find rising fish or a place where you get a strike in 10 casts or less with a nymph. With a hatch in progress, it's almost certain that trout will be feeding on insects somewhere, and it's amazing how fish respond to an insect hatch in one pool and not one just above it. I can't tell you how many nights I have parked my butt on the bank of a favorite pool in the Battenkill in the evening, watching Hendrickson mayfly spinners fall to the water without a single trout responding to them, only to go to the office the next morning and discover that some of my fishing buddies were covered up in rising fish just a few miles downstream.

Even if you don't find rising fish, you might still try a dry fly or nymph in the faster water because fish may be feeding only on the emerging larvae below the surface, or they may be rising unseen in the riffles. Trout can make extremely subtle, almost hidden rises in riffles, and unless you are staring directly at a spot, you may miss them entirely.

CHAPTER 5

Hatches and Rising Fish

In my discussions with fly fishers wanting to bring their fishing to the next level, I often hear this with slight variations: "I love trout fishing, but I just don't know if I want to spend the time learning all that entomology." The entomology that you really need to be a successful trout angler is actually minimal. If you can tell a chickadee from a blue jay at your bird feeder, you can learn enough entomology to be deadly.

Trout are opportunists when they feed. Time and again, scientific studies have shown that they prefer to eat the largest prey they can easily handle, but sometimes this data just does not agree with what we see on the water. Or the fish seem to refuse fly after fly, even though we think we have an imitation that is pretty close to what they are eating. Sometimes it really is selective feeding, but often it's not the fly pattern at all but something else we're doing wrong. Let's look at true selectivity first and then examine reasons for refusals that have absolutely nothing to do with the fly pattern you have tied to your tippet.

SELECTIVITY AND HATCHES

Unless water temperatures are frigid, below 45 degrees, there is always something hatching. Insects hatch all the time, although it may be merely background noise and not enough to get fish to respond. Tiny midges hatch in slower water, a caddisfly or two hatches every hour in a riffle, or stoneflies crawl onto the bank and split their larval skin. But the hatches we're talking about are those that get fish active, that either prompt them to move a little farther for subsurface food or actually rise to the surface to pluck mayflies from the surface film. Often when it's a good time for one insect to hatch, it's also good for another, so at any given hour during the day there may be from two to a dozen different insects hatching at once. Do trout really pick one over the other?

Trout eat what is safe part of the time, and part of the time they experiment. If they didn't experiment, they would never switch from one food to another. What can happen is that one insect begins hatching before another, and the trout get "keyed into" a particular insect and ignore the others. They develop what is called a search image for one particular insect, and just ignore the others. They have to do this because they are constantly bombarded with bits of twigs and cottonwood fluff and stones in the drift, and if they didn't develop a mechanism to ignore this debris, they would use more energy in chasing junk than they would gain by eating the good stuff.

This is what we call selectivity, but it doesn't happen unless one insect is vastly more abundant or easier to capture than another. But in my experience, it's the exception rather than the rule. Most of the time trout will switch back and forth from one insect to another or from one stage of an emerging insect to another, based on whatever bug can be captured with the least effort. And that bug is usually the one right in front of their snouts. So, yes, most times you need a reasonable imitation of something they've been eating at any point from the past few hours to the past few days. But almost never is there exactly one fly pattern that will take fish, to the exclusion of everything else in your fly box.

Five anglers are standing in line in a pool, well separated but within earshot. Fish are feeding actively on the surface, but no one is hooking anything. Groans, mutters, and outright cursing fill the air. Finally, the guy in the riffle at the head of the pool hooks a trout, a nice one about 15 inches long, and as he stands up after releasing the fish, he yells confidently, "Caddis! They're eating tan caddis pupae." Everyone in line changes to a tan caddis pupa. The guy in the riffle catches three more fish, and one other guy lands a trout, but nobody else does really well.

Have you been there? Maybe you were the guy in the riffle, maybe one of the unlucky ones. But to assume that fish were eating tan caddis pupae because one guy caught a fish on a tan caddis pupa imitation is the ultimate in arrogance and stupidity. Underwater, with lower visibility and objects drifting by at a pretty fast clip, I imagine a tan caddis pupa is also a close-enough imitation of an emerging mayfly, an aquatic beetle, a drowned moth, or even a small aquatic crustacean like a scud. Only if that guy actually saw a fish eat a tan caddis pupa underwater (almost impossible to determine, even with mask and snorkel) or killed the fish and found it full of tan caddis pupae (and nothing else) can we assume he was right.

Yes, you might be able to sample the fish's recent diet with a stomach pump, but most people don't carry them, and few of us kill trout these days. So any time we catch a trout on a fly that we selected carefully, we like to think that we've figured out what the trout is eating and we have matched the hatch correctly. It's what makes trout fishing interesting. But it is seldom as difficult as we make it out to be.

That guy in the riffle was in the water where fish are easiest to catch because they have to make quick decisions, and he could probably have caught trout on a mayfly nymph, a stonefly nymph, a scud imitation, or a midge larva. Or maybe he was a little more experienced at fishing a nymph than the other anglers. The trout likely didn't care what fly they took as long as it looked like something reasonably good to eat.

THE ENTOMOLOGY YOU NEED TO KNOW

Insect	Quick ID	When Important	Hook Sizes	Colors	Insect Behavior	Fishing Techniques
Stonefly nymphs Two golden stonefly nymphs and a large black stonefly nymph. Note the thick tails, prominent legs, and lack of gills on the abdomen that distinguish them from mayfly nymphs. If you look carefully you can see the gills between the legs at the thorax on the golden stoneflies. The underside of the black stonefly nymph shows the feathery gills attached to the thorax.	Thick legs, two thick tails, and robust antennae. No gills on abdomen. Bigger species are flat; smaller ones rounder and skinny.	Any time	6 through 18; most common 10 through 16	Tans, yellows, browns, blacks	Crawl on bottom. They wiggle when drifting in the current but never swim.	Weighted nymphs fished close to bottom, dead drift
Stonefly adults A large stonefly adult. Note the long antennae, robust legs, short, thick tails, and two pairs of wings held flat along the body.	Large wings flat over body. The rest of the insect looks almost exactly like the nymph.	Windy days when adults get blown into the water. Egg-laying flights almost any time of day.	6 through 18; most common 10 through 16	Tans, yellows, browns, blacks. Large Salmonflies have orange accents.	Adults hatch from nymphs that crawl out of the water, so hatch times are of limited importance. More important when adults return to the water to lay eggs. In flight, they are clumsy and slow, and four wings are visible.	Long-bodied dry flies, often with foam and/or lots of hackle and large hair wings. Either dead drift or twitched across the surface.

Mayfly nymphs 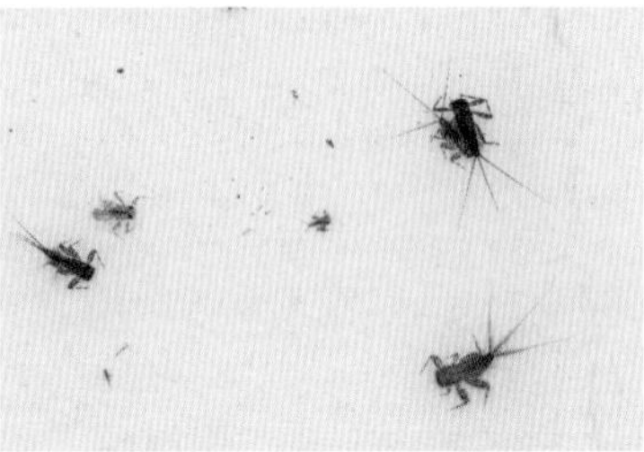 A number of different species of mayfly nymphs, all from under the same rock. Note they all have two or three long tails, short antennae, and gills along the abdomen. These abdominal gills are the best way to distinguish them from stonefly nymphs, which have a similar appearance.	Thinner legs and antennae than stoneflies. Always gills on abdomen. Flat to minnow-shaped.	Any time	6 through 26; most common 12 through 20	Dark brown, tan, cream, olive	Some crawl on bottom like stoneflies; some burrow in mud and are thus available to fish only when they hatch; some are strong swimmers.	Typically dead drift, as most do not swim, but a few species swim rapidly, so it is worth experimenting with motion.
Mayfly emerger  A mayfly caught in the act of emerging. Note the nymph shuck still hanging from the rear of the fly. When mayflies are in this helpless state, trout prefer them over the adult fluttering on the surface. 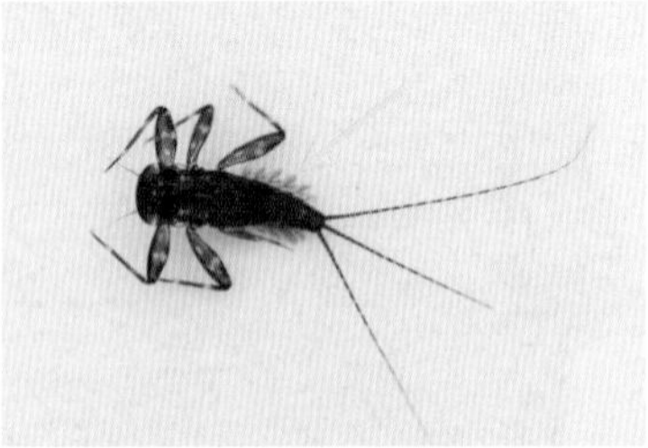 A closer look at a mayfly nymph showing the abdominal gills.	Shuck of nymph hanging off the end. Wings often seen emerging from thorax.	Only during hatches when some adults are seen on the water. Emergers are hard to spot unless you are very close to the water's surface.	6 through 26; most common 12 through 20	Dark brown, tan, cream, olive, orange, black bodies. Wings shades of cream and gray, sometimes speckled.	Flies will be just below the surface or half in and half out of the water. They make wriggling motions but nothing that can be imitated by fishing techniques.	They are trapped in the surface film, so a low-riding dry fly or floating nymph. Dead-drift presentation. Sometimes a wet fly fished dead drift will imitate drowned adults.
Mayfly dun  A mayfly dun or subimago has a robust body, relatively short tails, and translucent wings.	Tails about same length as body, ride surface of the water lightly. Distinctive, triangular wings make the insects look like sailboats. Wings are translucent.	During hatches when adults are seen on the water or in the air	8 through 26; most common 12 through 20	Dark brown, pink, reddish, tan, cream, olive, yellow, orange, black bodies. Wings shades of cream and gray, sometimes speckled.	Flies exhibit wings above the surface. They may ride the water sedately or may also twitch and wiggle on the surface. In the air, they fly in a straight line, either toward the banks or upstream.	Dead-drift dry fly with a prominent wing is most productive. In bigger species (larger than size 14) or if strong winds are blowing, the occasional twitch may help.

Mayfly spinner  A mayfly spinner exhibits a skinnier body than the dun, the wings are more or less clear (sometimes with speckles) and the tails are typically longer than those on the dun.  This is the classic view of a spent mayfly spinner on the water, with wings and tails fully spread. 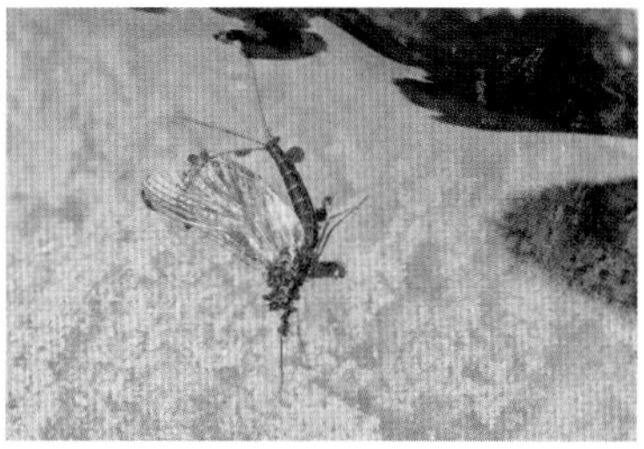 Often mayfly spinners fall with one or both wings tipped sideways, though, which shows that trout don't need an exact imitation because the naturals may be on the water in different profiles.	Tails long, up to twice the length of the body. Wings clear, sometimes with strong veins or speckles. Bodies thinner than dun, sometimes with a visible egg sac at the end of the abdomen.	A day or more after a major mayfly hatch. Mornings and evenings in hottest times of year; late morning to mid-afternoon in cooler weather.	8 through 26; most common 12 through 20	Dark brown, reddish, tan, cream, olive, yellow, orange, black bodies. Wings transparent, sometimes speckled.	Typically flying upstream in groups; faster and more agile than duns. When preparing to lay eggs, they will hover above the water (often riffles) and dip rapidly up and down. When flies hit the water, they may leave wings upright for a period but often lie prone in the surface film, which makes them hard to see.	Dead-drift dry fly; best are ones that ride low in the water, right in the surface film. Sometimes a twitch with very large (size 10 and bigger) species will help.
Caddis larva 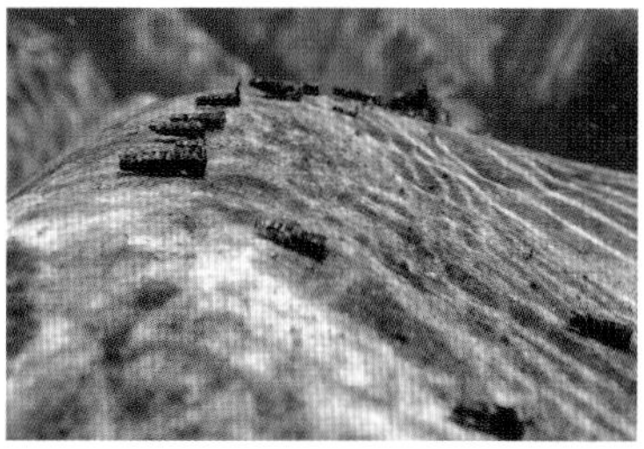 Cased caddis larvae from underwater, covering the upper surface of a rock. Because these are more exposed to strong currents, trout may see more of them than larvae that live protected under rocks.	Grub-like shape, six prominent legs, two small hooks at the end of the abdomen. Sometimes inside cases made of sticks, sand, or gravel; sometimes without a case.	Any time	10 through 22; most common 14 through 18	Cream, tan, olive, green, orange	Crawling on bottom or attached firmly to rocks. Sometimes live in nets made of silk.	Dead-drifted nymphs, close to the bottom

Caddis pupa 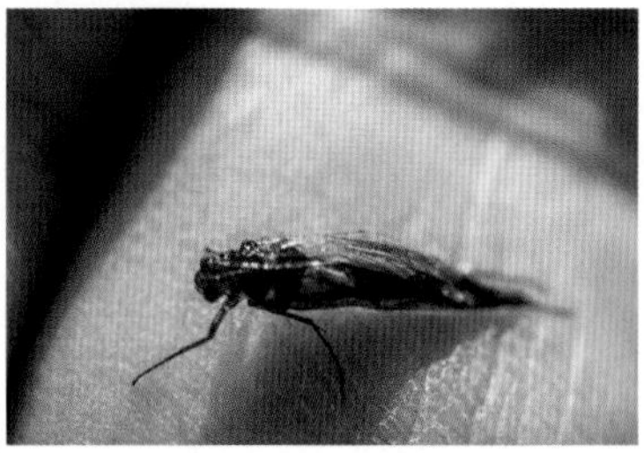 A typical caddis pupa. Most are dull brownish-gray (although a few have bright green bodies) and between a size 14 and 18. You don't need many different imitations for them—the most important consideration is how you fish them. Dead drift works best, although sometimes drawing one quickly toward the surface will provoke a strike.	Long antennae, segmented body, very distinct wing pads held underneath the thorax	Just prior to and during caddisfly hatches; otherwise unavailable as they are hidden in silken cases on the bottom.	10 through 22; most common 14 through 18	Cream, tan, olive, green, brown	Some rise slowly to the surface, where they spend much time struggling to get out of pupa case. Others rise to the surface quickly. Many species scull in the current in an erratic, jerky manner.	Most times fishing a caddis emerger dead-drift at the surface or a deep pupa imitation throughout the water column dead-drift. Occasionally swinging the fly in the current or fishing the pupa with twitches is effective.
Caddis adult  An adult caddis. Most are fairly dull-colored, in shades of tan, brown, and gray, sometimes with green or orange bodies. Caddis adults are very actice on the surface once they hatch, and trout often prefer the emerging pupa.	Long antennae, segmented body, with wings held tent-shaped over the body. No tails. They look like moths in the air.	When caddisflies are seen on the surface of the water	10 through 22; most common 14 through 18	Cream, tan, olive, green, brown, dark gray bodies. Wings typically dull tan to gray.	Typically hop and jump on the surface, sometimes skittering sideways. If water temperatures are cold, they may also ride the water with little motion.	Winged caddis dry fly. Best to try dead-drift first, but active dry-fly techniques like skating the fly may also work.
Egg-laying caddis adult 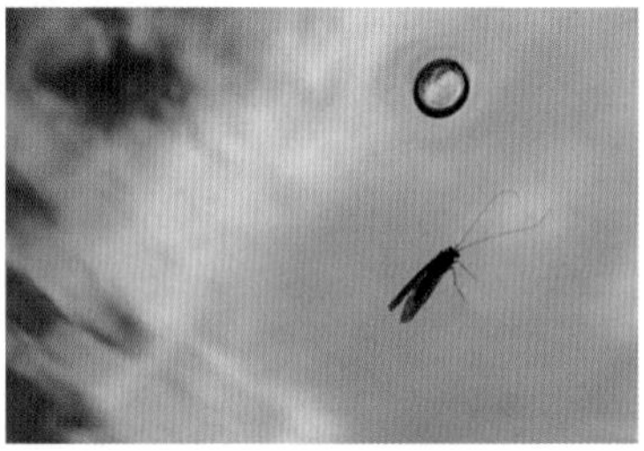 A trout's-eye view of the same caddisfly from underwater. You can see why profile is usually a lot more important than color in an imitation of an adult insect.	Long antennae, segmented body, with wings held tent-shaped over the body. No tails.	When flights of caddisflies are seen moving upstream in large numbers, then dipping onto the water's surface. Also look for adults clinging to waders.	10 through 22; most common 14 through 18	Cream, tan, olive, green, brown, dark gray bodies. Wings typically dull tan to gray.	They fly upstream in groups, often large clouds. Often they are just migrating and not laying eggs, so do not get on the water. Make sure adults are actually dipping into the water and are on the surface. Smaller adults are hard to see on the water, so look carefully.	Dead-drift, low-floating dry fly, or a dead-drifted wet fly or soft hackle just under the surface
Midge larva 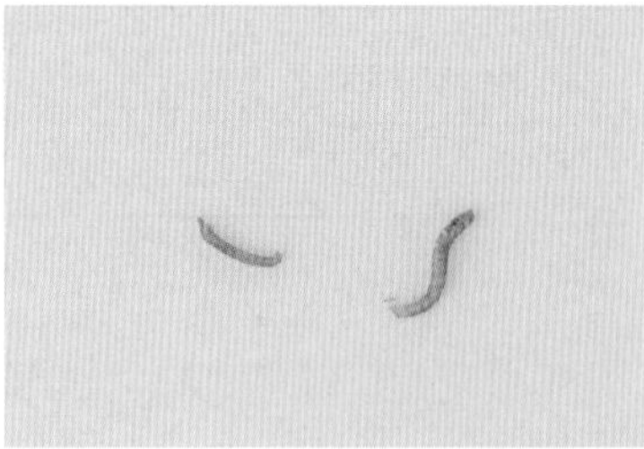 Midge larvae come in many colors, but the most common are red, green, brown, and gray. They don't look like much so they are easy to imitate with some thread, wire, or fur on a hook, but trout, even very large trout, relish them in tailwaters and spring creeks.	Skinny, wormlike, with no visible legs and small head	All the time where they are abundant	14 through 32; most common 18 through 24	Bright red, orange, cream, brown, green	They cannot swim at all and when dislodged from the bottom will drift helplessly.	Small, skinny nymphs fished dead-drift, close to the bottom. No movement at all on the fly.

Midge pupa Midge pupae are helpless when drifting toward the surface, so a dead-drift presentation and a light tippet are essential. Trout often prefer the helpless pupa over the bottom-dwelling larvae and fast-moving adults. This fat Missouri River trout was eating midge pupae in April. You ignore these tiny flies at your peril. Get a good magnifier and stop complaining you can't get them on your tippet.	Small, skinny body with bulbous thorax. Small wing pads with whitish gills at front end.	When adult midges are seen hatching	15 through 32; most common 18 through 24	Typically dull tans, grays; sometimes red	They slowly drift in current, rise to the surface, and struggle feebly to break pupa case.	Small, simple fly fished dead-drift anywhere in the water column, from close to the bottom to just below the surface
Midge adult You can often find adult midges in spider webs. They can be identified by their single pair of wings, lack of tails, and feathery antennae. This spiderweb gives you a good idea of what color and size midge to use if you suspect trout are feeding on them.	Skinny body, no tail. Single pair of thin wings. Feathery antennae.	When adult midges are seen hatching, and then when mating flights buzz over the water	16 through 32; most common 18 through 24	Typically dull browns, tans, creams, grays	They hop, flutter, and skitter across the surface.	Small hackled dry fly fished dead-drift or twitched across the surface. During mating swarms, a larger dry fly fished as a cluster of adults can be effective.

THINGS THAT MASQUERADE AS SELECTIVITY

Drag

Drag, or the movement of your fly contrary to an object on the water that is not attached to anything, is one of the primary causes of what appears to be selectivity. If your fly is not behaving like the natural, a trout won't even move toward it because it does not fit that search image pattern it's looking for. You can try every fly in your box, and you can have the perfect imitation, but if the fly is not behaving naturally, the fish will at least pass up your fly, and if the drag is really overt and the fish is nervous, it might actually stop feeding.

This is especially true when you stand in one spot and continue to rotate through all the flies in your box. If a fish is rising in the same place regularly, and you have found a position that's comfortable to you and does not disturb the fish, why should you move? Drag is often positional, and just by changing your casting angle you can eliminate drag, or at the very least you can limit drag on part of your drift. Look carefully at not just where your fly is landing, but where your line and leader are landing as well. Is there a way you can keep faster currents from yanking your fly line sideways? Is there a slower current that is holding back your line, making it yank on the fly? Can you carefully change positions without scaring the fish? Sometimes just a move of a few feet can make a difference.

Lengthening and lightening your tippet can help as well, because the more flexible your tippet, the less likely it will transmit the pull of contrary currents to your line and the thicker part of your leader. Also, a long tippet can land in loose coils, which will have to unwind before they put much pressure on the fly. It's amazing how much difference going .001 inch smaller on your tippet makes on the presentation of your fly. This is especially true with flies smaller than size 18, which don't have much mass to overcome as opposed to bigger dry flies, which have a slight amount of resistance to drag just because their size is more resistant to outside forces.

Finally, changing the type of cast you use can mitigate drag. Throwing an upstream curve by the use of a reach cast is almost always a better idea than making a straight-line cast, because the upstream curve has to invert before the fly begins to drag. Purposely throwing slack into your line and leader by making an underpowered cast, or more precisely by using a parachute or pile cast, can give your presentation an extra foot of drag-free drift—which can make the difference between a solid take and a refusal.

If you suspect drag but are not sure which tactic will work best, and it's a fish you really want to catch, I'd advise you to try all three of these at once: Change your position, change your tippet, and change your cast. If that tactic doesn't work, and you are sure you're not getting drag, then move on to the next possibility.

Spooking the Fish with Your Casts

This one took me a long time to figure out, but after fishing many years over fussy trout and observing their behavior closely, it was one of those things you slap yourself and say, "How could you be so stupid?" We all have times when we spot a feeding fish and we make one bad cast over it, which sends the fish bolting for cover. If you can see the fish, there is no doubt what happened. If the fish stops rising, you're not sure—did you scare it, or did the fish just stop feeding for some other reason?

But there is a more subtle variation. Watch the behavior of a rising fish, and if it is rising with a regular rhythm, try to get a rough idea of how often it rises. After you make your first cast, pay attention to how soon after the fish rises. If it rises shortly after your cast in the same place, you can assume that you did not spook the fish. However, if you make a cast to a fish rising every 20 seconds or so and the fish takes a full minute to begin rising again, you can assume that your presentation spooked the fish slightly, not enough to send it swimming for the nearest log, but enough to make it sink a little lower in the water column, and wait it out to see if that annoying thing happens again.

SCAN TO WATCH VIDEO 004.
Casting to a difficult riser.

A trout feeding in the surface film with subtle rises won't move very far for a fly. Placing your fly more than a few inches to either side or spooking it by getting the fly line too close may result in disappointment.

The other scenario is that the fish might not stop rising but it might move. If a number of fish are rising in the same area, this is tough to discern, but if you have only seen one fish rising and suddenly another fish rises 3 feet upstream, you may have bumped the fish out of its position. This happens more typically in slow water where fish can reposition easier, as it is tough for a fish in fast water to move to another position.

Inaccurate Casting

Are you sure you are putting the fly over the trout's head? The faster the water, the farther below its resting position the fish will feed, so if you put your cast right on the rise every time, the fish may not see it. Putting the fly a foot or two ahead of the fish is always a smart idea, and it's surprising how often even experienced trout anglers don't think about this and cast directly to the rise. I know I am guilty of this many times every season.

On long casts, it is very common to undershoot your target and put the fly well short of a feeding fish. I was fishing on the Missouri River one summer day and my friend Toby Swank, an experienced guide from Bozeman, was standing on a high bank above me, watching my presentation and generally making me feel foolish and inadequate, as he loves to do. There were a number of rainbows in the 17-inch range rising in the slow water along the bank, and I could see the rises fine, but Toby could see both the rises and the fish. The fish were across from me, and I thought my casting was right on the money, but Toby kept yelling "You're short!" Of course, he took great delight in being able to taunt both my presentation and my stature with a single phrase, but regarding the presentation I kept retorting, "I'm right over that fish." "No you aren't—you're at least a foot to this side of him," he'd reply. "The next time throw it two feet farther than you think you should."

Sure enough, on the next cast, when I cast the fly way longer than I thought necessary, the fish rose and I was hooked up, if only briefly, as the fish shook the fly loose after the second jump. I turned around and looked up at the bank above me, and all I saw was Toby turned around, head below his shoulder, shaking it slowly.

I think there are a couple of reasons for making a presentation that is too short on long casts. One is that at water's level, it's difficult to see how close your fly is to the spot a fish rose. The other is that, especially with experienced anglers, we've spooked enough fish over the years that we worry about getting too close to the fish, so we err on the short side. So if you make repeated casts without a rise and you're sure you are not getting drag, it pays to cast to what you think is beyond your target.

OKAY, SO MAYBE YOU DO HAVE THE WRONG FLY

There are widely varied opinions on how important your fly pattern is, and luckily it's a problem we will never solve because trout from different rivers behave differently. Trout from the same river even have different eating habits depending on the time of year and water flow. And even trout in the same pool show varying degrees of difficulty or selectivity depending on the exact place in the pool they're feeding, and even on their individual personalities.

Trout have personalities? Not exactly, but in the same situation one trout may exhibit different behavior than one right next to it. We all know that dogs and cats and horses have individual personalities, but they're warm-blooded and closer on the evolutionary tree to us than fish. However, my son and I have had snakes and turtles and bearded dragons as pets, creatures that aren't much more advanced than fish, and I can assure you from careful observation that even "primitive," cold-blooded creatures have "personalities."

Let's take a look at two differing opinions on selectivity, both from experienced and capable anglers. The first is from *Selective Trout*, by Doug Swisher and the late Carl Richards:

> Most anglers experience real success only when the fish are not selective, at those times when rise activity is sparse or nonexistent. During heavy feeding activity, however, some anglers are virtually helpless. Their predicament is usually due to the unrealistic appearance of standard patterns of trout flies. These patterns simply do not simulate, to the trout, their view of the naturals. But realistic and effective patterns for specific hatches make it possible to hook at release many more trout, even during the most selective rises. (Swisher and Richards, p. 13)

In other words, if you don't have exactly the right fly, you'll go home hanging your head. No amount of brilliant tactics will override this deficiency.

Now take a look at the other end of the spectrum, from another seasoned fly fisher, Bob Wyatt of New Zealand, in his book *What Trout Want: The Educated Trout and Other Myths*:

> While a good likeness doesn't hurt, I know that a fly with a good general shape and size is all I need to be in business. If the insect is particularly small, this is a real issue and practically the whole story. The Grey Hackle is a great old pattern that nobody uses anymore, but it still works as well as it ever did. (Wyatt, p. 52)

No one disputes that size is the most important aspect of fly selection when fish seem to be feeding in a selective manner. Shape is often thought to be second in line, but as

There are many mayfly species called Pale Morning Duns (PMDs) or Sulphurs. All have light gray or cream wings, a yellowish body with shades of olive or orange, and pale legs and tails. They hatch all over the world and range in size from 14 to 22.

I would use any of these various dries and emergers during a PMD hatch. A trout sees emergers, fully emerged duns, and crippled flies that don't quite make it off the water during a hatch. Sometimes trout may prefer the emerger over the fully emerged adult, but I am willing to bet that a good presentation with any one of these will catch trout during a PMD hatch.

You often have to get very close to the water's surface to see what kind of insects are on the water. What is on the water is a lot more important than what is in the air.

insects hatch, they take on all sorts of shapes and contortions, so shape is not as critical. And color, or even the exact materials used in a fly pattern, is far below the other aspects in importance.

It's often stated that trout can see color quite well and even that trout can see into the ultraviolet spectrum where human eyes can't go, so that not only do you need to imitate the visible shades of color, you also have to match an insect's UV profile. In practice, though, as long as your fly is close in shade to something the trout are eating or have eaten recently, that is probably as far as you have to go. I have experimented with pure white and pure black flies when trout were feeding on insects with their typical subdued colors of browns and creams and olives, and I have found that those extreme shades are avoided—but as long as a fly is pretty close in a grayscale tone to the natural, it will work fine if everything else, especially size and presentation, is in line.

I tie all my Pale Morning Dun, Pale Evening Dun, and Sulphur mayfly imitations in a generic shade of yellow. These are all yellowish/olivish/orangish mayflies that hatch everywhere in the world, usually in early summer; in Europe they call them Pale Wateries. Guides and other anglers have told me that I need one with just the right shade of orange for the South Fork of the Snake in Idaho or the Bighorn in Montana. When you fish the Madison, you are supposed to have ones with an olive tinge. And in Pennsylvania, they should be very pale yellow. Yet I have fished my generic yellow ones in all those places and have done as well as I could have hoped.

So size and shape and perhaps shade (light as opposed to dark as opposed to medium) are important. But there are other reasons you may have the wrong fly, and it has nothing to do, exactly, with your exact fly pattern. You may be so far off in the size of your fly, or where it is positioned in the water column, that it appears the fish are being selective. They are probably just ignoring your fly, treating it like they would a twig or stone or some other inedible junk. Check these things first before you change your fly.

What fly is on the water?

This one gets all of us into trouble. You see clouds of size 14 tan caddisflies in the air, so thick that you breathe them in and choke. Trout are rising all around you. You are blinded to everything else until you look down on the water. Surprise! You don't see a single caddisfly on the water, but you do see a fair number of size 18 mayfly spinners with a dark red body. They are a different shade and size than those caddisflies in the air, and you can flog the water with a size 14 Elk Hair Caddis until you finally catch a fish that recognized that size and shape as something it ate yesterday. But most of the fish are single-mindedly looking for a skinny size 18 bug.

It's a lot harder to bend down and squint at the water's surface than it is to look up into the bright sky and see insects silhouetted against streamside foliage. Sometimes you may even have to wade out into deeper or faster current to see what is actually in the feeding lane of the trout, as there may not be many drifting insects in the shallow water where it's easier for you to stand. And if the insects are right down in the surface film, you might not even be able to see what's on the water, and it might be necessary to put a little aquarium net in the water to figure out what is in the film.

Are there multiple flies on the water?
This one can drive you nuts. It's quite common to have more than one kind of insect on the water, especially in the evening when flies are both hatching and returning to the water to lay their eggs. Trout may be eating all the different insects at once, which typically makes them seem dumber than dirt because if they are eating a wide variety of sizes and shapes, as each insect comes by, you can probably put on any fly and catch fish as long as your presentation is decent.

But unfortunately, fish can sometimes concentrate on one of the insects and ignore the others. One insect might have been on the water first, so the fish keyed in on that one and just ignored the others if they are greatly different in size and shape. It's often the case that a few very large insects are hatching and we naturally notice them and ignore the smaller stuff because the big ones are easier to spot. In addition, we are hoping the fish are taking the bigger insect because then we can tie on a nice size 12 fly we can see instead of a teeny size 20 that disappears into the glare. Most times, though, much to our annoyance, fish prefer the smaller insect, possibly because it is more abundant.

As a general rule, if mayflies or caddisflies are on the water, fish prefer them to tiny midges, and unless all you see is midges, you probably won't have to put on a size 24 midge pattern. Trout also seem to prefer caddisflies and mayflies to stoneflies if they have an equal chance to capture them. Often you see a lot of stoneflies in the air, but due to their hatching habits, they are not found on the water as often unless they are laying eggs.

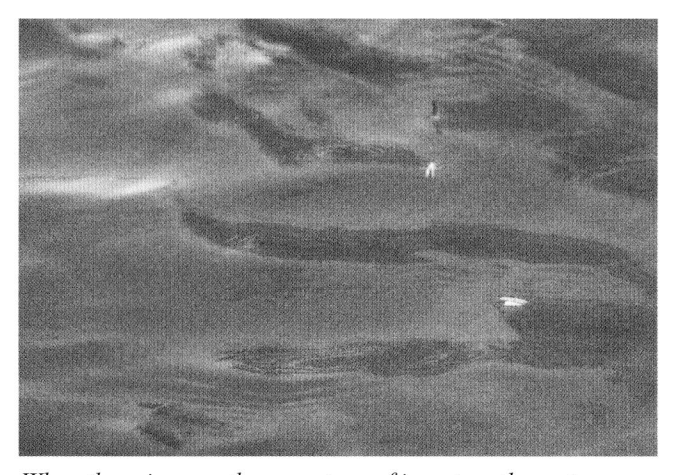

When there is more than one type of insect on the water the game becomes a lot more interesting—and sometimes more frustrating. Even in this small patch of water there are two caddisflies in the foreground and a mayfly dun in the background.

SCAN TO WATCH VIDEO 005.
What insects look like from a trout's point of view.

Trout can even have a taste or texture preference for one fly over another, but no one has figured out a clever way to determine this in natural situations. My fisheries professor, Neil Ringler, performed an elegant study in a man-made indoor stream and determined that trout preferred mealworms over fuzzy caterpillars even when the caterpillars were more abundant than the mealworms. But to do that with the myriad of natural food items trout have to choose from would keep a grad student busy for life.

What stage are the fish eating?
Just because you see mayflies in the air or adult mayflies on the surface doesn't mean trout are eating fully emerged bugs off the surface. That's what we hope for, because there is nothing more fun than fishing a dry fly to a rising fish. But trout may be responding to a hatch in a different manner than you think or hope. For instance, breaking the surface with their noses means a leap of faith, a foray into an alien environment, like bobbing for apples for a human. Trout do it because flies on the surface are, at some point in the hatch, the most abundant and easiest prey to capture. But sometimes other stages of the insect are more reliable.

Recognizing the stage the trout are eating is even more important than figuring out the exact insect they are feeding on. Fish don't always get a great look at what is drifting overhead or in the surface film, but it is easy for them to tell the difference between something riding on the surface of the water, sitting high up on its tiptoes seemingly walking on water, and an insect trapped just below the surface, either trying to push through the surface film or drifting just under it waiting to make the dramatic move to a terrestrial life. The profiles are vastly different.

Why should it matter? It does because trout often choose one form over the other, most often preferring the emerging or subsurface form to the one riding high on the water. It's annoying to us because we'd prefer to fish a fly that rides high on the water so we can see it and track its progress, making sure the fly floats in the right place and avoids drag. Trout are just not that cooperative, and when they are feeding on emerging insects, it seems that they pass up a fly with too much stuff sticking up above the surface. Sometimes you can get away with a little short parachute wing or a tuft of CDC (a soft feather from the tail end of a duck) or deer hair sticking above the surface for visibility, with the rest of the fly hanging below the surface. But if the fly rides too high, it's almost as if the trout were saying, "No way, I'm not going to rise for that bug because it's about to fly away." Ones stuck in the surface film are easier prey, it's that simple.

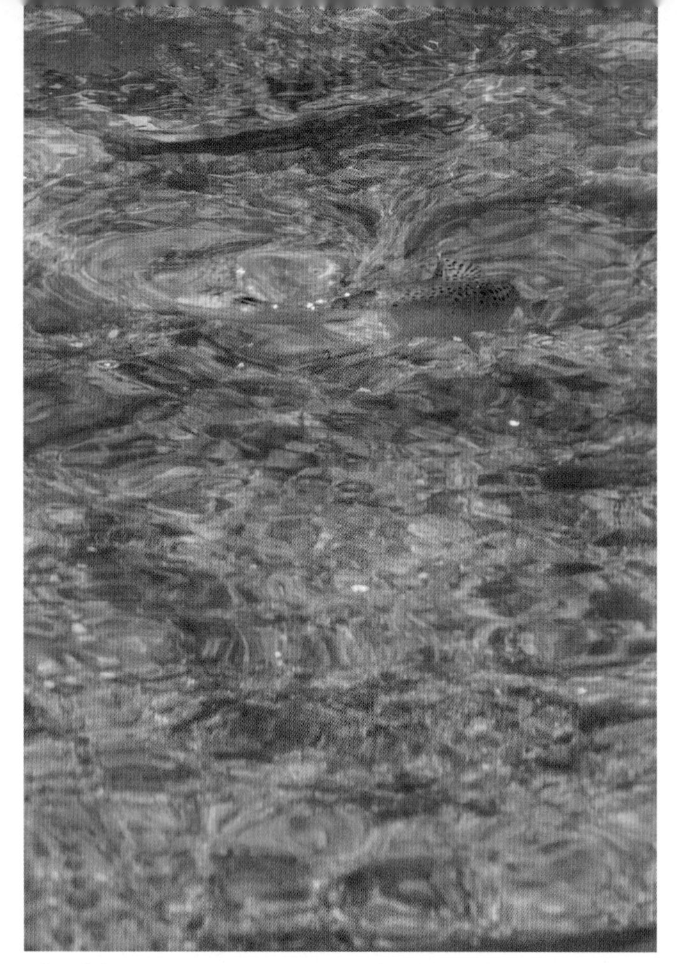

This fish rises to an insect just under the surface. Its head never comes above the surface.

It still creates a rise form because its body was close enough to the surface to make a bulge in the surface.

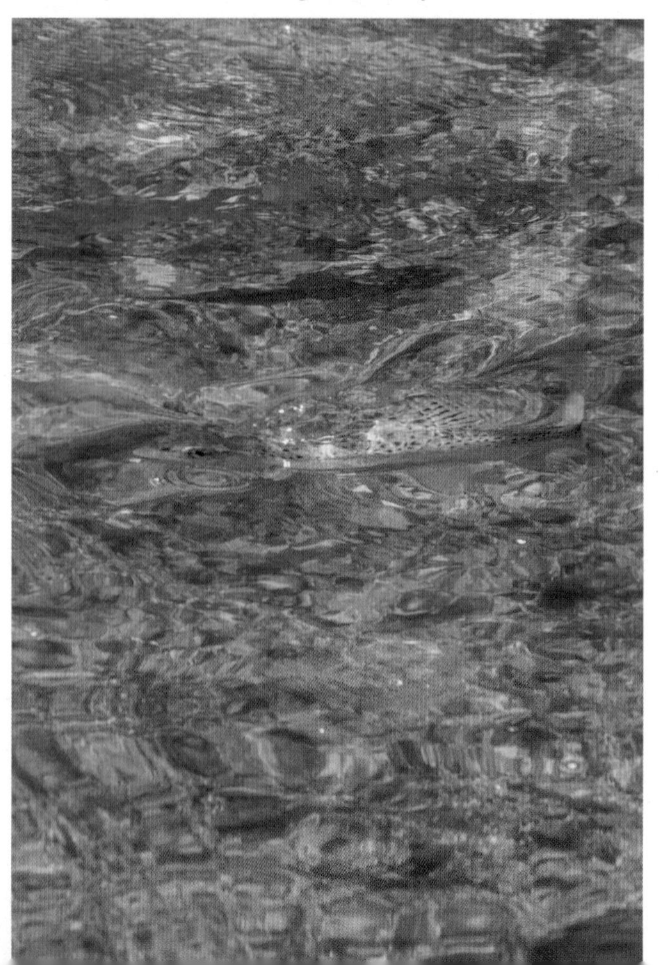

But if you look at the aftermath of the rise, you don't see any big bubbles.

One instance is when trout are feeding on insects still a foot or more below the surface, but when they move up into the water column to grab one, their momentum causes a disturbance in the surface or even a splash, like you can make when you cup your hand underwater in the bathtub and push down rapidly. It causes a disturbance on the surface, but your hand never left the water. These rises are typically splashy and violent and are more irregular than periodic because most of the time the fish does not come high enough in the water column to disturb the water. In a case like this, with splashy, irregular rises, a nymph is a better bet than a dry fly or emerger. The fish really aren't even looking at the surface, so a dry fly can go unnoticed.

A little bit trickier is when trout are eating insects just below the surface film, or half in and half out of the water. This is one of the most appealing stages of a hatch to a trout, because insects at this stage can't swim away and they can't fly away, so a trout knows its prey is an easy mark. In fact, fishing the emerger stage, using a fly that rides just below the surface or lies low in the water, is almost always a better idea than fishing a high-floating dry fly and will often work throughout a hatch.

It's often said that if you see bubbles after a rise, the trout has eaten an insect on the surface, but this is not exactly correct. A trout may take an insect just below the surface, and part of its mouth will still extend above the surface, inhaling air and expelling it through its gills. But if you see bubbles, you can bet the fish was feeding if not on the surface, at least

This trout has its eyes on a tiny mayfly on the surface.

There is no doubt that the fish took something off the surface because its head came right out of the water. However, this happens so fast the camera catches it as a blur, and you might miss it if you were not looking right at the spot.

The fish creates a big swirl after it rises.

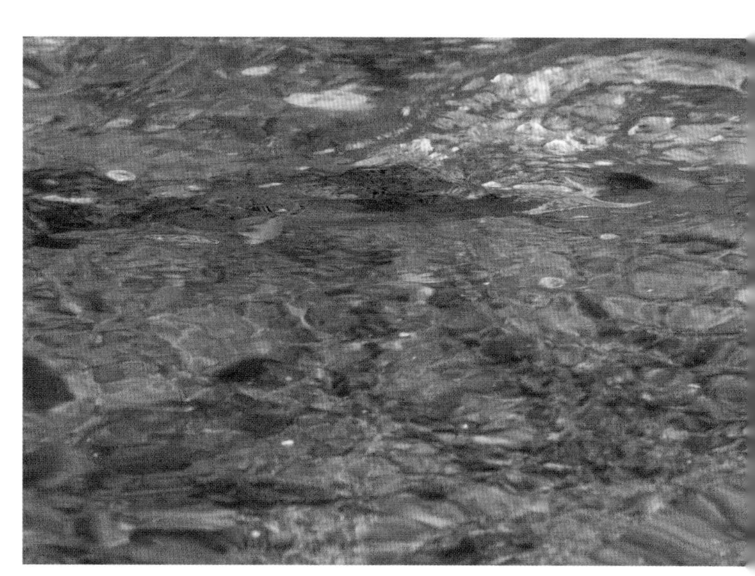

Now you can see the large bubbles that formed, a very strong indication that the fish took something right off the surface.

just beneath it. Often at the same time as this you will see fish "bulging," where you think you have seen a rise but only the back and the dorsal fin breach the water's surface. Again, it's still a rise to an emerging insect, and anyway unless you are very close to a fish or watching it with binoculars, it may look like any other rise.

I think the best course of action during a hatch is to assume trout are taking emergers rather than fully winged adults. Only switch to a high-riding adult mayfly or caddisfly if you are sure you have seen a trout take an adult insect off the surface. They will probably take an emerger anyway.

Another situation that involves both the hatch stage and multiple hatch issues is when some species of flies are hatching but others are sneaking past and laying eggs at the same time. You see a mayfly or caddisfly hatching and you try one dry fly after another and nothing takes your fly, even though the fish are rising furiously. It could be that another insect is

Mayfly duns, with their upright wings, are a lot easier to spot on the water than mayfly spinners.

falling in the riffles well above you, dropping to the water to lay its eggs, and then falling spent to the water, having used up its final burst of energy to mate and deposit eggs. These insects then drift down to where you are fishing, but they are hidden in the surface film unless you get right down to the surface and look carefully. But just as when trout are taking emergers, they may be choosing these spent forms because they are not about to get up and fly away. Trout sense this, and select for the easier targets.

I learned this lesson early in my fly-fishing life. The closest stream to my home was a rich, riffle-and-pool stream of medium size and abundant insect life. Every evening in late May and early June, trout would rise furiously for the last 45 minutes of the day. The air was filled with size 16 tan caddisflies, and you could see them hatching off the surface. The fly of choice was a size 16 Adams, which was known then, for some strange reason, as a deadly caddis imitation. Why that was so I don't know, because the Adams has upright wings that look nothing like an adult caddisfly, and it has tails, which adult caddisflies do not. But it worked, sort of. You would catch a trout every 15 minutes or so, which would mean you'd hook, on the average, three trout in that intense period while many more just kept rising.

Sometimes mayfly spinners fall to the water with their wings upright, but most of them soon lay spent on the water and are hard to see without looking carefully at the surface.

There was a regular group of anglers who fished the same stretch every night, and most nights we'd pick the same position. On successive nights I noticed two guys below me who were just tearing up the fish, almost every cast. I could see by their precise casting that they were better fly fishers than I was, but still I could manage to get my fly where I wanted it, drag-free, on most casts.

After the hatch one night I followed them back to their car, and with the innocence of a curious teenager, I asked them what they were using. "Look at your waders," one of them told me. I looked down, and at the wet spot where the high-water line of my wading remained were scores of small, very dark gray caddisflies, about a size 18 or maybe even 20. I looked up and the second guy said, "Now it might make sense what we're using." He showed me a size 18 hare's ear wet fly, the old traditional style with wings made of duck quills. "We fish 'em just under the surface because we think the trout are eating those little ones, not the bigger tan ones, and that kind of caddisfly seems to crawl under the water to lay its eggs."

So I had been blinded by the easier-to-see, bigger caddisflies in the air and had never even noticed the smaller dark bugs on my waders, which would have been impossible to see in the fading light. To this day, when trout get snotty in the evening, the first thing I do is to look down at my waders.

Mayfly spinners have also fooled me in similar ways more times than I can recount. Sometimes spinners fall with upright wings, which can tip you off, but most times spinners fall to the water with their wings pinioned in the surface film. They are then almost invisible, either with a wing spread out to each side in the classic spinner pose or with both wings tipped over to one side. After the rigors of mating and egg-laying, and because mayflies don't take any nutrition once they've hatched from a larva, they don't even have enough energy left to hold their wings upright.

I've found that trout prefer mayfly spinners over any other insect on the water, possibly because the females can be laden with eggs, but for sure because spinners are helpless prey. In fact, if I even suspect mayfly spinners are falling above me, I'll put on a spinner pattern before any other dry fly because I have more confidence in a trout taking a spinner than any other pattern.

Just because trout may be feeding on a different stage of a hatch does not mean you need a special fly for each stage. For instance, a good emerger pattern can be fished with no fly dressing at all when trout are bulging or feeding on insects just below the surface. The same fly can be dabbed with a touch of white desiccant powder if you suspect trout may prefer a fly just in the process of emerging, half in and half out of the water. If you want to get fancy, you can just dress the front part of an emerger and let the back hang in the water. I've never bothered to go that far, though, because if a trout is eating a fly that is just emerging, or perhaps emerged but before its wings have fully formed, or if the fly is "stillborn," where the adult never fully emerges from the larva case, I don't think the trout care. As long as the fly just does not look like a fully emerged adult, I doubt if they can distinguish between a stillborn and an emerging fly. I know I can't, and I have a bigger brain than they do.

I have one caddis imitation that has a simple fur body and a wing of hairs from a snowshoe rabbit foot. I fish it during the hatch as a caddisfly that is just emerging, and I fish it when I suspect trout are feeding on spent caddisflies after they've laid their eggs. The only time it doesn't work is when trout are eating adult caddisflies skittering across the surface because it sits low in the surface film and doesn't skate very well. But it's far more likely to find trout being picky about emerging caddisflies and spent insects than chasing adults across the water. And besides, I have Elk Hair Caddis for dealing with the skittering flies.

How is the insect behaving?

Most times when you fish a hatch, the Holy Grail is dead drift. Period. Few insects move with overt motions across the current, and, yes, they do hop and flutter when they hatch, but you can't imitate that with the coarse movements you can make with a fly rod. If insects are fluttering and trout seem to prefer eating the ones that are fluttering, a much better strategy is to pick a fully hackled fly that sits high on the water, because these flies dance in the current more than a low-floating pattern, and the whirl of hackle around the fly may also give it an impression of movement to the fish.

But there are times when outright manipulation of a dry fly will entice trout more readily than one that is floating sedately. The first time I ever fished the South Fork of the Snake was with an old friend, the legendary Wyoming guide Joe Bressler, and Joe had said the fish were on Salmonflies the previous week. Now, the Salmonfly is a huge stonefly, about a size 4 or 6, and it hatches for a very brief period each summer. It's more talked about than seen because it's so big, it gets huge trout excited about feeding on the surface, but because it only hatches for a few days in any give stretch of river, most visiting anglers miss it. So we didn't see any Salmonflies but the trout were still looking for them, so a big dry fly seemed like a smart plan. Besides, it's fun fishing a size 6 dry after fishing size 18s most of the time.

I started fishing my dry as I normally would, throwing reach casts from Joe's boat, trying to get a dead drift in the deep water along the banks, but when we switched places and I took the oars, Joe cast his big dry right to the bank and stripped it back like a streamer. Or like a bass bug. And the fish liked it. I knew Salmonflies were big bugs and twitched a lot on the water, but I thought the bass-bugging technique was a bit much. That is, until a few years later when I finally hit the lottery and happened to be on the Madison River in Montana at the peak of the Salmonfly hatch in the riffles just

You will find that you don't need a ton of patterns to effectively match hatches wherever you go. Here are some of my favorites, flies I would not be without anywhere, clockwise from left: PMD Sparkle Dun, Rusty Spinner, Olive Parachute Emerger, Olive Sparkle Dun—and, of course, a beetle for throwing at the fish when you have no idea what they are taking!

above Ennis. Not only did those bugs twitch on the water, they got right up on their legs and buzzed across the water, flopped, spun around, and continued across the river like a barefoot water-skier. Now I could understand Joe's technique, and it made perfect sense.

Other large mayflies like the Hex, the Eastern and Western Green Drakes, and the Brown Drake also make a lot of commotion on the water. These flies are so large that the occasional subtle twitch with the rod tip is not out of line and may actually get a fish to notice your artificial. Just watch the insects—if they're floating sedately down the river, as they often will do when the water is cold, don't move the fly. But if the naturals are putting up a fuss, then try a twitch or two. You couldn't get away with the same tricks on a size 18 mayfly, though, because these tiny flies don't move very far when they twitch, and any motion you make will be way too blatant.

Caddisflies move around on the water a lot when they're hatching. Some skip, some hop, some slide across the surface in long glides. The natural temptation is to move the fly, but do this with caution, especially if the flies are small and your motions may be too obvious. I've also seen that it's usually the smaller trout chasing active caddisflies, while the adult fish seem to prefer the emerging pupae or stationary adults. However, moving a caddisfly is an excellent option for fishing a dry fly when there is no hatch, when fish are not actively eating on the surface but might notice a fly skating across the water. I'll discuss some of these techniques later, when we look at methods for fishing a dry fly when there is no apparent hatch.

PICKING FLIES FOR HATCHES

You will notice that I haven't recommended any specific fly patterns for fishing hatches. Patterns come and go, and for me to recommend specific fly patterns that might not be offered by the time you read this book would be dating it. Even more important is that I could recommend Diddy's Fabulous All-Purpose Killer Emerger and you could search high and low and not find any, so you'd toss my book in disgust. There are always tons of hatch-matching patterns available, and better ones come out each year. Get a bunch of popular flies that imitate mayflies in the dun, emerger, and spinner stages; caddisflies in emergers and adults; and stonefly adults (you don't need emergers for stoneflies, just egg-laying adults) in a few sizes and shades and have at it.

The chart earlier in the chapter will give you an idea of what kind of flies you might need if you were to fish anywhere in the world, without any help from local sources of information like guides or fly shops, or without any research on the Internet. But that's still a huge selection of flies to carry. In practice, you'll learn your local hatches and which flies and what stages are important. When you travel you'll buy or tie flies according to what hatches you might expect. Hopefully you'll always have leftovers after a trip, and you'll soon find that despite the multitude of flies in your box, you'll see that the sizes and colors and stages you need are not that different from river to river, even if you fish California in the summer and Chile in the winter.

And don't be afraid to modify. You can trim all of the hackle from the top and bottom of a standard dry to make a spinner. You can trim the wings off a dry to make an emerger. Scissors are a very handy item to have during a hatch, and I wouldn't fish anywhere without a nice sharp pair. The scissors from a standard pocketknife work just fine as long as they are sharp, but when I've found myself without a pair of scissors, I have found that I can hack most materials away with my leader snips. It's not pretty, but I doubt if the fish care.

CHAPTER 6

Fly Selection and Fishing Strategy—Winter and Early Spring

Now that you have some guidelines on where trout might be in a river, how to approach them, and what bugs they might be eating, your next decision is what fly to tie on. At this point you don't even know whether to start with a nymph, a streamer, or a dry, much less the exact pattern, but would you believe me if I told you this is the least important decision you will make all day?

It's a lot different for anglers who fish the same waters year after year. Not only do they know where most of the fish live, they know what flies have worked in the past and they confidently rotate through these proven patterns until they find one that lights up the fish. But you are faced with an unfamiliar river. Maybe you are on vacation and trying a new river for the first time. Maybe you have not done much fishing at all, and you've been skunked every time you fished this particular river. Already your confidence is lower than that smart local upstream who always seems to pick the right fly, even though it's probably more of an issue that he knows exactly where to fish and how to present the fly in that exact spot without spooking fish. And he has confidence in his fly, so he fishes it carefully and methodically.

Even if you have done your homework and looked on the Internet for a fly selection tailored to this particular river by a reliable fly shop, they probably recommended a mixture

In mid-winter with clear, cold water, the best course of action is to find a slow, deep pool and work it slowly and carefully with nymphs and an indicator.

of nymphs, dry flies, and streamers. Which one do you pick first? The type of fly you should pick has much more to do with prevailing conditions than some kind of magic formula that says, "If the water is 1 foot higher than normal, the water temperature is 55 degrees, and it is 3 o'clock in the afternoon, fish a size 14 Lightning Bug nymph." I know you want those answers. Sorry, as much as you want them, no one will be able to give them to you because they don't exist—there are so many variables in a dynamic environment like a trout stream that the best we can do is propose a few generalities. Beyond that, it's trial and error. But isn't that why we love fly fishing? Because there are no easy answers, and the thrill of discovery is often just around the next bend.

I was working on a TV show one season and one of the lessons I wanted to get across was that often not only are there a multitude of flies that will work on any given piece of water at the exact same time, but there are even multiple fly types that work. I was on a stretch of the Gallatin River I had never fished, never even looked at before, and I wanted to try to catch a trout on a nymph, a dry fly, and a streamer from the same pool within minutes of each other. The water temperature was about 58 degrees, a near perfect temperature; it was late afternoon; and the water was just slightly high with a tinge of color in it. Small cream mayflies and some bigger caddisflies were hatching. Those are all good conditions.

I started out with a Pheasant Tail nymph at the head of a small pool, and after a few casts was into a 12-inch rainbow. One down. Then I swung a Woolly Bugger streamer through the tail of the pool (I could go back and forth in this pool because the water was not clear and relatively fast, so the fish were not very spooky) and connected to a small brown trout. I survived round two. Next, I fished an Elk Hair Caddis up along the far bank and in the middle of the pool, and after a length of time that made me slightly nervous that I wasn't up to the challenge, I noticed a fish rising along a log and managed to catch that brown trout. The sequence never made it into the final TV show, but I think you get the point: If fishing conditions are good, you can catch trout on any type of fly you feel like using.

That's what happens under ideal circumstances. If the water had been 2 feet higher than normal, if the water temperature had been 40 degrees, and if no insects had been hatching to get the trout active, it's quite likely that I would not have caught any trout. I might have gotten one to take a fly, and I would have been quite proud of myself under those conditions, and most likely it would have been on a nymph or streamer fished slowly and close to the bottom. So right away you can see that under less-than-ideal conditions, some kinds of flies are better than others. And, yes, there may have been one fly pattern that worked better than others—but don't ever let anyone tell you a particular fly pattern is the only thing that will work on a river.

With all the fly pattern information available to us today on the web, I think it's silly for me to suggest specific fly patterns to you. I have no idea where you like to fish or where your travels will take you, and there are far better and up-to-date sources of information on seasonal and regional favorites available to you in a few seconds with a search.

Where I do think I can help you is to suggest fishing tactics for various water conditions you may find throughout the year in your travels. So let's take a seasonal approach to picking the best techniques for fishing those flies. I've found, surprisingly, that even given the relative temperature and altitude differences between high-mountain streams in the West and lowland rivers on the East Coast, there is actually not much difference in the way you approach rivers at any given time of year, except that runoff in the West usually happens much later than it does in the East or South. (Even though a southern river like the White in Arkansas and a western one like the San Juan in New Mexico seldom have spring snow runoff, they do have rainy periods in the spring that produce about the same conditions.)

DEAD OF WINTER, WATER LOW AND CLEAR

Winter is not an easy time to catch a trout on a fly, but your best hope is low, clear water. In streams not fed by the outflows of dams (tailwaters) or primarily by groundwater flow, in other words what we anglers call "freestone" streams, trout may

Steve Seinberg (top) and Dave Grossman from Southern Culture on the Fly *magazine attempt to create some open water on a delayed harvest trout stream in the mountains of North Carolina. Winter fly fishers will go to great lengths to get their fix.*

spend a great deal of their winter without any activity, almost in a state of suspended animation. In very cold water, many trout find a place with low-velocity current—not dead-calm water but pretty close to it—and they will likely be tucked into a root wad, muddy bottom, or deep pool full of big rocks. All they need to do is stay out of heavy current, where ice jams may float down, or shallow water, which might freeze to the bottom and where predators can find them. Think of a cozy place with the covers tucked over your head.

If you plan on fishing in extreme cold, it is possible to catch trout on days when the water warms up a bit, but you may be disheartened to find that slow, easy water the trout should be sheltered in is covered with ice. I was in the foothills of the Blue Ridge Mountains one February when North Carolina hit record lows, dropping below zero at night for a few days straight. Dave Grossman and Steve Seinberg of *Southern Culture on the Fly* magazine had promised to take me fishing, and because I hadn't fished in over a month, I was not going to let a little cold weather slow me down.

We headed to one of their favorite delayed harvest rivers (delayed harvest rivers are those stocked with fish, sometimes large ones, but catch-and-release is practiced during the colder months). When we got to the river, it was a solid sheet of ice except for a few small open spots where the water ran fast enough to prevent freezing. "No problem," they said. "We'll just break the ice and come back in ten minutes, and the fish will be relaxed enough by then." Having lived in the North all my life, I wanted to tell them that by the color of the ice, it looked like you could drive an 18-wheeler over it, but I let them try to stomp through the surface.

After 15 minutes we gave up and drove to a stream that was lower in altitude. We still had to fish narrow channels between icebergs, but the trout, being hatchery fish, were inclined to eat nymphs even under those extreme conditions. Wild trout seem to be less inclined to feed during extreme cold weather, so one tip I can offer in these conditions is find a stream with hatchery fish in it, even if you are normally a wild trout snob.

In spring creeks and tailwaters, the water is likely quite a bit warmer than the air because the bottoms of deep reservoirs and groundwater reflect the mean annual temperature of an area. Fish in these waters may feed daily and may feed from dawn to dusk with a peak in the middle of the day. Trout in freestone streams invariably feed from noon until late afternoon when the water warms up, and it only takes a few degrees increase to get them out of their torpor and feeding. None of these winter fish feed aggressively and it is rare for one to chase a fly, so your main focus is to get your fly as close as possible to a fish. This means fishing close to the bottom.

A lot of authors and teachers recommend that you fish "low and slow," and fishing slowly makes sense in a lake, but in running waters this means fishing your fly dead-drift, just as fast as the current is flowing. Any faster than the current makes your fly look unnatural and like something that is trying to get away, and trout are unlikely to chase anything under these conditions. If you try to fish slower than the current speed, your fly will look just as unnatural, plus trying to fish a fly slower than the current will make your leader tighten, pulling the fly off the bottom and up toward the surface, as it will if you just try to hang your fly in the current.

It helps to imitate something the fish are accustomed to seeing, because those types of flies arouse the least suspicion. Yes, you could try something totally oddball and perhaps interest the rare aggressive fish, but your chances are better with a familiar shape and behavior.

So what do they eat this time of year? Midges are the primary food during the winter in most streams. Midges hatch 12 months a year, even on some of the coldest days, and if a trout is feeding at all, you have about an 80 percent chance that it is eating midge larvae or pupae. Larvae get kicked up by the current or by other people wading and drift helplessly. Pupae drift in the current and head toward the surface most often in late afternoon, although I have also seen them hatching in the morning and at noon. Both of these stages have absolutely no swimming ability, and it is harder to make a tiny fly drift naturally than a bigger fly because it has little mass of its own and is at the mercy of the tippet movements, so trying as hard as you can to get a dead drift is more critical here than in any other circumstance.

You may be lucky enough to see a mayfly hatch, especially of small, size 18 to 22 olive mayflies with a brownish tinge to the body and bluish-gray wings. These flies are not as common as midges during the winter and tend to hatch on cloudy days that get above 40 degrees air temperature. They even hatch in late-season snowstorms, the kind with large, wet flakes. These olive mayflies may actually get trout feeding on the surface in slower water and back eddies, and they are more likely to provide surface action than midges. Trout will rise to adult midges on the surface but not as often as they are tempted by the olive mayflies. The problem with the olive mayflies is that you don't see them in every river (they are more common in tailwaters and spring creeks during the

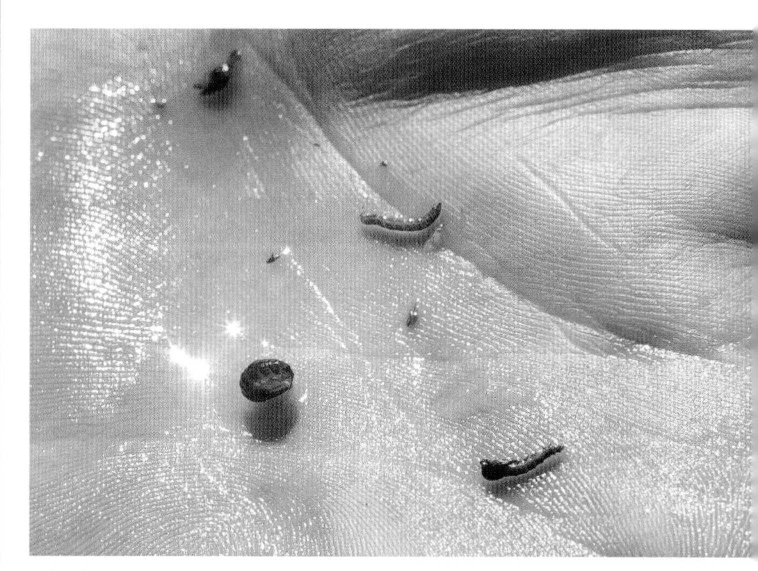

Clockwise from top: a midge larva, a midge pupa, and a scud (curled up). These are some of the mainstays of winter and early spring fishing, and imitations of them should always be in your fly box.

Scuds, small freshwater crustaceans, are available to trout all winter long because they live their entire lives underwater and never hatch.

These sow bugs and scuds all came out of the same trout's stomach. When they die, or when they are subjected to digestive juices, they turn pink or orange. The sow bugs, third and fourth clockwise from the top left, look like they were eaten more recently than the scuds.

winter), so the opportunity to catch one of their hatches in the winter is a rare treat on most rivers.

Even if the trout don't respond to adult flies on the surface, though, just the presence of these flies get them on the feed because the nymphs are actively leaving their sanctuaries under rocks and in aquatic vegetation, drifting in the current and rising to the surface. Thus if you see a few of these mayflies on the surface, you can fish a small, slim nymph like a size 18 Pheasant Tail in likely places, and if you get the fly in the right place and at the trout's level, you should pick up some fish. This is also a rare winter circumstance when a nymph can be gently twitched toward the surface or swung in the current on a tight line.

Another common insect you will see along trout streams in winter is a small black stonefly, often called the snowfly because you see them crawling on snowbanks close to rivers. They don't hatch on the surface of the water, as with most stoneflies, but crawl into the shallows and climb out of the water on rocks and logs. I have sometimes seen them on the water, and whether they hatched there or got blown there by the wind I am not sure. What I am sure of is that I have never seen trout take the adults off the surface. I have heard of other people who have reported they saw trout eating adult black stoneflies in the winter, but I wonder if there were midges or olive mayflies on the water at the same time and the trout were eating those. A size 18 dark, slim nymph will imitate nymphs that might get dislodged from the bottom and eaten by trout, but I would not bother with trying to imitate the adult insect with a dry fly.

If you don't see midges or olive mayflies on the water and the water temperature has risen a few degrees, don't despair. There are many other critters down there that trout eat that never hatch, so you won't see any indication of them above the water. These include freshwater crustaceans like sow bugs and scuds, small pale creatures anywhere from a size 12 to size 18. These little shrimp are available all winter long, and I have even seen trout rooting through aquatic vegetation to dislodge them at dawn in winter, but that was in a spring creek where water temperatures are tolerable to trout even early in the morning. Aquatic worms and earthworms that get dislodged from their terrestrial habitat will also be found in winter trout streams, and although I have not found imitations of them to be as productive as small nymphs, it would not hurt to try a worm imitation if nothing else works.

Most baitfish bury themselves in mud and dead submerged leaves and other debris during the winter and are not as active or available as you might think. Still, streamer patterns sometimes work in the middle of the winter, especially when fished dead-drift or with small strips with long pauses in between, to imitate a cold baitfish that doesn't have enough energy to swim strongly in the current. I would expect that just like trout, baitfish are more active when the water warms up a few degrees. Just remember that trout are ill inclined to chase a fly very far in the middle of winter, so don't expect fish to chase a streamer retrieved with constant foot-long strips, and don't expect them to follow a streamer as far as they would at warmer times of the year.

High-Stick, Close-In Nymphing

By far the most reliable way to catch trout in the middle of winter is to use a high-stick nymphing technique, which keeps the fly drifting close to the bottom and at the same speed as the current. This kind of fishing is only effective close to the angler, within a few feet of the end of the rod tip, so it requires a moderate current to keep yourself relatively hidden from the fish. Although trout are not as spooky in the winter as they are at other times of year, you still won't be able sidle right up to a trout in slow current in most rivers when the water is clear.

You may have heard the term European nymphing, or Czech or Polish or French nymphing. These are all methods that came out of tournament fishing, which is dominated by European teams and requires that you catch as many trout as possible in as little time as possible. So the methods, although where in a river you can perform them is limited, are abso-

This colorful little brown trout, taken on a small scud imitation, is the one whose stomach contents you see in the previous photo.

lutely deadly. The differences between each of these methods are probably more than you want to know. I know they are for me. If you really want to study each one of these specific methods, I recommend you read George Daniel's *Dynamic Nymphing*, which is the most complete and authoritative work on the subject—and it's clearly written and illustrated.

The term high-sticking is an American term for a method that is similar but somewhat less precise than the European methods. In the European ones, fly line never touches the water, and a long leader goes directly from the rod tip to the fly—or sometimes just a bit of fly line extends beyond the rod tip. In the American high-sticking method, the leader is shorter and more line is out beyond the tip, and often up to 10 feet of fly line actually touches the water. The European methods utilize a very tight line where the angler is in touch with the flies throughout the drift, while in the high-sticking one sometimes the line is tight and sometimes not. With high-sticking, a strike indicator might be used or not, depending on the whim of the angler and the conditions.

One major difference between the European style and American high-sticking is that in high-sticking, the angler uses a conventional fly cast and retrieves line as it comes back to the angler to take up slack. In the European method, the flies are merely lobbed back upstream and line is pinched with the line hand and not retrieved. Regardless of whether you slant toward the European or the less precise high-sticking method, this kind of fishing requires intense concentration and quick reflexes, plus an ability to visualize what is going on under the surface.

No matter which method you use, the main purpose is to have the portion of the leader between the fly and the surface of the water as vertical as possible. This is the best way to get flies to the bottom quickly and to let them drift, if only for a few feet, exactly as fast as the current. Your flies are only fishing effectively for about 25 percent of the time they are in the water, typically in the middle of the drift, not at the beginning, as they are sinking or at the end when they begin to rise toward the surface.

Let's take a look at a couple of instances of using each of these techniques. There is no reason you can't drift your nymphs European-style on one drift and with a high-sticking method the next, and you might even use a modified version that is halfway between the two. Once you understand the purpose of these methods and what they do to make your flies drift naturally, the mechanics eventually become automatic.

High-Sticking

This method works best for longer distances, where you can't wade to a place where you can fish right under your rod tip, and is also better for fishing to an area upstream of your posi-

High-sticking a nymph on a misty morning on the Savage River in Maryland. Note that none of Art Noglack's fly line is touching the water, and he is following the leader and fly through its drift.

tion. It's also better for spooky fish because you don't have to wade right up to them.

With a weighted fly, or two weighted flies, or a fly with weight on the leader, cast at an upstream angle with a tuck cast. The tuck cast, developed by George Harvey and Joe Humphreys at Penn State, is a way to allow your flies to sink vertically on a slack line, which is the quickest way to get them to the bottom. Initiate your forward cast as usual, but when the rod tip first comes into view, squeeze your thumb down and the three fingers beyond your index finger up, which pivots the tip of the rod down quickly. Keep your rod at this high position; don't follow through as in a normal cast. The flies will tuck under the fly line and get momentary slack, enough to let them drop to the bottom, or at least deeper than you would by completing a normal cast.

Keeping your rod tip high, begin slowly taking in slack, just as quickly as the current brings it to you, so that there is no slack in the line and just a slight bow in it because of the effect of gravity on the line. Strikes will show up as either a twitch in the junction of the fly line and leader, or an unnatural tightening of the bow of fly line between your rod tip and the water. Once the fly gets close to you, raise the rod tip a bit higher and pivot your arm, following the place where the leader enters the water as the flies drift past you.

Joe Humphreys can't stand strike indicators, and I know it's heresy, but you can also use this method with a strike indicator, keeping as much fly line as possible off the water and keeping a tight line to the indicator. Because of the weight of a heavy nymph or pair of nymphs and the air resistance of a strike indicator, the nymphs tuck under the indicator quite nicely, and this way of fishing may be more comfortable for someone who has learned nymph fishing with indicators. Sorry, Joe.

This method can be used at many different angles, from directly upstream to across-and-downstream. The more you aim your cast upstream, the longer the drift, because your flies will be at an effective level almost up to your rod tip. As you begin to cast at more of a cross-stream angle, you'll get a good drift until your flies get just downstream of your position. At this point, the line will come tight and will begin to pull your flies off the bottom. This is not necessarily a bad thing, because if you can reach your arm way out so that the rod tip is as close to the current lane that the flies are drifting in as possible, the flies will rise to the surface straight up, rather than sliding across the current. When aquatic insects emerge, most of them are not strong swimmers so they cannot glide sideways in the current, so rising straight up is a more natural motion.

European-Style Nymphing

European-style nymphing is merely high-stick-nymphing with a very short line and heavy flies. You'll hear all kinds of grumping that it is nothing new, that people were fishing this way in the 1930s in California or Colorado, and although it is

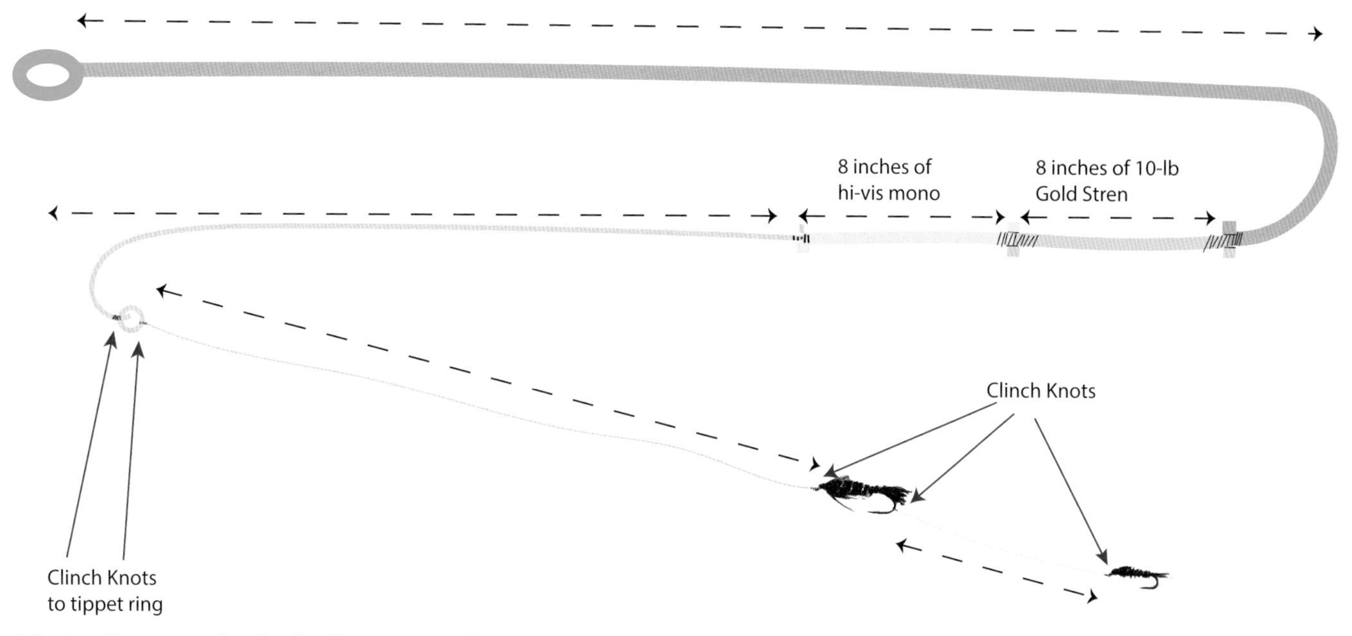

A basic all-purpose leader for European-style nymphing. The formula is from George Daniel's book Dynamic Nymphing.

hard to believe that people who fished with nymphs using a high rod didn't occasionally make casts right under their rod tips with heavy flies, I'll leave it to others to decide whether it was developed in Czechoslovakia or Colorado. There is no doubt, however, that competition fly fishers in Europe refined the technique and developed some specialized leaders and flies to make it more efficient.

And European nymphing is just that—efficient. The casting is not pretty, it's more a quick lob, and the method is best used within 10 feet of your rod tip and is best suited to riffled water. Let's look at how you can do this with your regular trout rod and leader, and then see how the modifications that competition anglers developed makes this method even more deadly.

Take a standard 9-foot 4X nylon leader and add a 5-foot tippet of 4X fluorocarbon. At the end of this tippet, add a 20-inch section of 5X fluorocarbon with a surgeon's knot, but use enough material so that you're left with tag ends that are about 8 inches long. Snip the tag ends that point up toward the butt section of the leader, and also the lighter tag end that points to the terminal end of the leader so that you are left with an 8-inch dropper. To this, tie a small unweighted nymph or soft-hackle. Next, at the end of the 5X piece, tie on a heavily weighted fly—the heaviest you can find in your fly box, maybe something with a large tungsten bead, or, better yet, one with two tungsten beads.

Find some fast, moderately broken water that is between 2 and 3 feet deep just beyond your position. It's important that you get pretty close to where the fish are lying, which is why precise wading to put yourself into the right position and careful movements so that you don't disturb the water are key to this type of nymphing. What you will attempt to do is to let your flies go quickly to the bottom and then keep in constant touch with them as they drift naturally. The long

European-style nymphing is most effective in fast, choppy water like this run at the head of a pool on Montana's Rock Creek. You need to get very close to the fish, and in quieter water you may spook them before you can get close enough to fish effectively.

High, cold water doesn't just present obstacles to catching fish, it also makes wading very tricky.

tippet is necessary because the heavier the material, the more resistance it offers to the water and the more it will try to pull your flies downstream and off the bottom. The ideal device would be a thin piece of wire that does not bend at all and goes straight down to the flies. But wire is too stiff and would not let your flies drift naturally, so we use the next best thing: thin fluorocarbon. Thin so that it offers as little resistance to the current as possible, and fluorocarbon because it sinks better than nylon.

With just a few inches of fly line outside of the tip-top, flop this rig into the water and let it drift downstream until the line is tight to the tip. With your rod hand in front of your body, lift with the rod while your flies are still anchored in the current, and flip or lob the flies about 45 degrees upstream (when compared to a line that would go straight across the current). Keeping all of your fly line and as much of the leader as possible off the water, begin to raise the rod tip until the leader points in a straight line to the flies, with no sag or slack in it.

Keep your line hand at a normal position, and don't strip in any slack. Instead, as the flies move downstream, raise your rod and pivot your arm and body, keeping just a slight amount of tension on the flies. You should be leading the flies downstream, and your rod tip should be just downstream of where you suspect the flies are drifting. You will get the feel for just how much tension you want, but it should be not enough to pull the flies downstream but tight enough that you are in constant contact with the flies. If you feel any resistance on the flies, set the hook with a short jab downstream. You may also see the place where the leader enters the water just hesitate a bit, as if something is holding it back. Because you are in direct contact with the flies, you don't need a strong hook set, and if that resistance was only on the bottom, your flies will sink back down and continue to drift.

Getting the feel for this requires practice, and you will set the hooks into plenty of phantom strikes before you finally connect with a trout. You will eventually be able to discern by both touch and sight when your bottom fly ticks along the bottom, and will be able to distinguish the softer, firmer pull of a trout inhaling the fly. You will watch the spot where the leader enters the water and will recognize what angle means a nice dead drift and what angle means something has taken hold of your fly. You will miss many strikes, you'll hang up on the bottom, but eventually you'll be rewarded with a pulse and heavy weight on the end of your line, the kind that brings a silly grin to your face.

DEAD OF WINTER, WATER HIGH

I don't think there is any better scenario for getting skunked than trying to fish with a fly in cold water that is in flood. Most people don't attempt it. I'm regularly asked for my tips for fishing under these conditions, and I wish I could offer some clever ideas that will turn the trick in a frigid flood. Even fishing with a live nightcrawler close to the bottom is a long shot here, so you can imagine how difficult it is with a fly.

Nymph Fishing in High, Cold Water

Not only is the water too cold for trout to be very active, but the high flows will compound the difficulty of getting a nymph down deep to the fish. As flows increase, the velocity of the water close to the bottom, where the fish will be, is no different than it is when the water is low. But now you have doubled or maybe tripled the depth through which your leader has to pass, and you will likely have greatly increased surface velocities. If you threw some weighted nymphs in the water (I mean literally threw them into the water, right from your fly box without attaching them to a leader), they would eventually get to the bottom and drift naturally. But the minute you attach a leader to them, you have big problems. The long length of leader between your fly and the surface will catch the current and quickly whisk your fly away from where it is supposed to be—if it can even get there in the first place.

More weight can help, maybe using two heavily weighted flies plus some weight on the leader in the form of split shot crimped on the leader above the dropper knot. You might get a few inches of drift, but with the water high and probably dirty, you have a couple of other problems. Visibility will be impaired, and for that very short drift you will need to place your fly right in a trout's face to get it noticed. But even worse is that the floodwaters have probably loosened ice flows along the bank and may also be carrying logs and other debris. This physical assault on the trout will move them to shelter under logs, way inside undercut banks, and other places where debris can't slap them in the face—but also where you can't place a fly.

What about sinking lines? A fast-sinking line should be able to get your nymph down to the trout, right? Yes, a sinking line can, but sinking lines are still influenced by the drag of the current, whisking your fly quickly away from the trout in an unnatural manner in most places. The one spot you may be able to fish a nymph on a sinking line at times like this would be a large, slow backeddy or a slough where a tributary comes into a larger river. These areas of slower water are probably deep enough to shelter trout from the insults of high water, with a flow that is moderate enough to help you get your fly down. With a sinking line you will have a difficult time getting a dead drift, but that's okay because in this slower water there may be dragonfly and damselfly nymphs, which swim quite rapidly, plus some swimming mayfly nymphs, scuds, or tiny baitfish. All these can be imitated by a nymph, and because you are moving the nymph through the dirty water, fish will not mistake it for a drifting twig or piece of weed.

In the clear water of late spring, you could and probably should do all kinds of fancy line manipulations with your presentation because most of these places have a counter-circulating eddy with the current of the side farthest from the main flow of the river moving upstream, after which it comes back around and meets the main flow and mingles with its currents. With a sinking line, which is pretty clunky anyway, I think the best approach is to just fire the line across the entire eddy if that's within your casting ability, pause for a few seconds before retrieving (mends are nearly impossible with a full-sinking line, so you can't use one to help your fly sink), and then begin a steady retrieve, with quick, 6-inch strips. If that doesn't work, experiment with all different kinds of retrieves, from very slow and steady to rapid foot-long pulls. You are really not trying to imitate anything in particular, but just finding a retrieve that attracts a trout's attention and looks enough like a recent meal to make the fish inhale it.

A full-sinking fly line is your best bet in situations like this, but if the water is shallower than 3 feet, you may find a sink-tip line useful. The advantage of a sink-tip is that you can mend the floating portion, so you can get a little more precise with your drifts and retrieves because you can cast well above where you want the fly to ride, and then mend the floating part of the line upstream a few times to get the fly down precisely where you want it. The disadvantage of a sink-tip is that after a few feet of retrieves, the floating portion begins to pull the fly back toward the surface and it moves out of the zone most likely to hold trout. But for shallower and smaller streams where you don't have as much deep water to cover, a sinking-tip line will do. For even smaller or shallower streams, all you may need is a sinking poly leader, which will get your fly down a foot or two.

Fishing Streamers in High, Cold Water

In the dead of winter, in most cases nymph fishing is your best choice of flies and techniques. Trout in water below 45 degrees are not inclined to chase a fly, and they will also be disinclined to eat a large meal. They instinctively know they won't be digesting a meal very quickly and attempting to digest a large baitfish in cold water might utilize more energy than they can spare. But in times of high flows and dirty water, a streamer might be the only thing to catch a trout's attention because much of the objects drifting in the current are inedible pieces of debris that have gotten swept into the flow. So a streamer, with its larger size, often brighter colors, and movement against the current, is something that can't be mistaken for a piece of leaf or a twig.

This is not a high-percentage game, but then nothing really is with a flood in the middle of winter, and consider yourself lucky to catch even one trout under these conditions. Streamer fishing is more active than nymph fishing so that

A good streamer for winter trout—not too big, nice contrast in any light because of the combination of dark and light tones, and material that provides a lot of wiggle. Rubber legs, soft marabou, and soft hackle all contribute to a lifelike impression, even in the slow water preferred by winter trout.

may help keep you warmer, and just the thought of pitching a bigger, brighter fly out there may give you more confidence. But resist the urge to put on something too big or too bright. Black seems to be the most visible color in dirty water, and I have not had success with anything bigger than 3 inches in very cold water. A black Woolly Bugger, Conehead Muddler, dark leech patterns, or even small Clouser Minnows in dark colors are all good flies to start. A size 6 is about as big as you want to go, and my bet in most rivers under these conditions would be a size 10.

For fishing a streamer in this kind of water, two things are helpful: weighted streamers and a sinking-tip line. What you want to create is a fly that darts upward briefly, and then falls as it drifts. You want to catch a trout's attention but you don't want the fish to expend much energy in capturing, so a quick dart, fall, and then drift will give your fly motion without making it cover a lot of territory. Weighted streamers get the fly down quickly and they fall when you stop stripping; the sinking-tip line keeps the fly relatively deep but allows you to mend line and manipulate the fly easier than a full-sinking line would.

Make your cast well upstream of where you think a trout may be lurking, and either make an aggressive upstream mend right after the fly hits the water or use a reach cast so that your cast falls to the water with an upstream loop already formed. Make another mend or two as the fly drifts downstream. When you suspect the fly is just upstream of a trout's position, give a foot-long strip and then stop. Don't keep stripping. Just let the fly drift for a foot or two, so that it drops down toward the bottom again. Make another strip, then another drift. Keep doing this until the line tightens below you, then pick up and make another cast.

Most trout take the fly on the drop, and you may see your line suddenly tighten or else you will feel the trout as you make your next strip. It's important to try to strip-strike here rather than raising the rod tip. If you feel a fish or think one has taken your fly, just make one long strip with your line hand, only raising the rod tip once you feel a firm weight on the line.

In most variations of streamer fishing, one or two casts in each spot is usually sufficient because in clear water trout always see your fly and either eat it or ignore it (or just do that annoying thing and follow it without eating it). In this case, the water is cold, so you need to put the fly right in a trout's face, plus the water is dirty, so they can't see it from very far away. If you see a spot that looks fishy, don't be afraid to give it a dozen casts or more, changing your casting angle or casting position slightly each time so you cover the water thoroughly. I wouldn't change flies unless you just can't stand it. In these conditions, finding a willing trout is the most important mission, so once you feel you have covered a spot thoroughly, look for the next place. Don't try to cover all the water—just skim off the cream and work the water that looks tasty.

SCAN TO WATCH VIDEO 006.
The strip strike and streamer fishing.

EARLY SPRING, WATER LOW TO NORMAL AND CLEAR

This is the season when daylight finally seems to be longer, when you can even fish in early evening, and when there may still be some snow around but it is restricted to higher peaks. Think of it as when bluebirds begin to investigate tree cavities and nesting boxes, when you hear the first tree frogs mating, or when the first spring flowers and buds on the trees appear.

Eggs

Rainbow trout, cutthroat trout, and suckers spawn at this time of year. This provides a high-energy source of food for those trout that spawn in the fall, brookies and brown trout, but it also provides a source of food for the very fish that are depositing eggs in the river. Any egg that rolls free of the gravel and does not get firmly covered with gravel within the redd is wasted energy, and spawning trout are programmed to pick these up as they drift in the current. Regardless of how you feel about fishing for trout while they are spawning, trout eggs will be in the water and all trout will eat them, so you shouldn't feel guilty or dirty if you decide to fish an egg fly. You are matching the preferred food of the moment.

Not all trout streams have naturally reproducing rainbows or cutthroats, but most have suckers and suckers are spring spawners and their eggs are an important food source in early spring. Suckers spawn from April through June, and choose coarse sand or fine gravel in relatively shallow water to lay their eggs. Unlike trout, suckers do not build nests in the gravel, so once the eggs are laid, they fall to the bottom or drift downstream, where the eggs stick to the bottom substrate. Because they don't build nests, and because the eggs are broadcast more widely than with trout, you may not notice suckers spawning but you can be sure that their eggs are somewhere in the current.

White sucker eggs are a pale yellow to golden, and some even have a touch of green in them. They are smaller than trout eggs, so many imitations of them are of clusters of eggs. I wouldn't worry too much about matching the exact color, as the eggs change color once they have been in the water for a few hours, thus there may be sucker eggs of many shades drifting in the current and trout are probably not specifically looking for eggs of a distinct color. In streams with wild rainbows or cutthroats, eggs of many shades could be present, from pink to orange to white and every intermediate shade in between, so the most important condition for success is to match the rough shape and behavior—or lack of it—of drifting eggs.

Eggs don't swim and they don't hatch, so all your efforts when fishing these flies should be to get your fly down close to the bottom and keep it there. High-sticking or the European

This little cutthroat fell for a typical early spring fly—a combination of a pink worm and an orange tungsten bead. Some people look down their noses at flies like this, but my philosophy is that as long as I can tie it with typical fly-tying materials and thread, it's perfectly legitimate. And deadly.

nymphing style will still be the best in most situations because it is the surest way to get an absolute dead drift. But those methods really limit you to fishing riffled water, and water quite close to you. There will, however, be places where you may not be able to get close enough, for example in a seam in a riffle 40 feet away or in the middle of a wide, deep pool with slower water. Once you get more than about 30 feet away from a location, you'll have to resort to long-line nymphing, which is the way most people have experienced nymph fishing—with a strike indicator and weighted flies, with or without added weight on the leader depending on how deep you need to get.

Indicator Fishing with Nymphs

When I was a kid, I used to fish a worm hung below a bobber for sunfish and perch. When I first began, like most kids I just threw it out there and waited until the bobber went under and then yanked like hell.

One day I was fishing from a high dock in clear water and was able to watch my worm as it settled under the bobber. I noticed that often the fish would take the worm as it was fluttering down, before it came tight to the bobber, which would make the bobber just twitch or move sideways. Then I noticed that once the worm hung suspended below the bobber, the sunfish were more likely to take it when a boat wake disturbed the bobber, because the worm would twitch seductively as the bobber rocked gently in the waves. After that day I spent more time watching the subtleties of bobber behavior (or as subtle as an eight-year-old can get), and from that day on I tried to imagine what my worm was doing under the surface instead of just watching for the bobber to go under.

In the same way, when we first learn to fish indicators with nymphs, we throw a bobber and a nymph or two out there and strike when the bobber (okay, the indicator) makes a blatant move. We don't pay much attention to where our rig goes in relation to different current threads, and we don't really think about what is going on below our indicator. It's not so much about missing strikes, because it's best to strike whenever the indicator does anything different than what the bubbles alongside it do. It's really more about using the indicator as a *drift* indicator to estimate where your flies are drifting, and in extreme cases when you have a large indicator and a pair of heavily weighted flies or weight on the leader, the indicator becomes a suspension system.

The process begins with the placing of the indicator and flies. Notice I said *placing* instead of *casting*, because placing insinuates that you put your rig in a specific location for

SCAN TO WATCH VIDEO 007.

How to identify spawning trout.

SCAN TO WATCH VIDEO 008.
Various nymph fishing methods in action.

a reason. But before that, I recommend that you drop your flies into a piece of quiet water right next to you to see how fast they sink. Then figure out where you think a trout might be lying, and cast your flies far enough upstream so that they will be at their maximum depth when they drift past the fish.

How far should that be? There are no simple answers. The faster the water, the farther upstream you need to place your flies. But the current speed changes with every situation and so should the weight on the end of your leader, so this is something you will have to discover empirically. And you will discover this either by catching a fish or catching the bottom. There will be times, later in the season, when your flies will be effective in the middle of the water column or rising toward the surface on a tight line, but at this stage in the season you are best assuming that trout are glued to the bottom and not in a frisky mood.

And even those are not the only variables. If the current where you place your flies has a choppy but uniform flow, with no swirls in it, your flies will sink quicker than if you see a lot of miniature whirlpools that indicate turbulence in all directions. Those sideways swirls of turbulence snatch your tippet and move it sideways and even up, whereas in a nice, steady, uniform flow there is not as much impeding the sink rate of your flies. One of the best ways to ensure that you get a good drift is by using two indicators. Casting is even less fun with two bobbers attached to your leader, but by lining up both indicators, you have an even better indication of whether you're getting a dead drift or not. When the indicator farthest from your flies moves downstream much quicker than the lower one, you know that you are about to have a problem with drag.

Here is a basic setup for fishing two indicators: Start with a 9-foot knotless tapered nylon leader one X size larger than the tippet you intend to fish. Tie on a piece of tippet to the end of this—I like to begin with between 2 and 5 feet of fluorocarbon, going longer for water over 3 feet deep and shorter for shallower water. Tie a fly onto the end of this tippet, and if you are using two flies, tie the second one to the bend of the first fly with a foot of tippet, either the same size as you tied the first fly or sometimes one size lighter.

In the early season I like to use two flies with tungsten beads, hoping I can get deep enough without adding more weight to my leader. Weight can be added later about 8 inches above the first fly. I like to use tungsten sink putty because it is easy to move, does not usually get hung up, and if it does hang up, it just slips off the leader. It is sometimes hard to keep in

Using two different colors of indicators on your leader gives you an option for spotting one of them when light conditions change, but even more important is that you know where your fly is in relation to the leader, because you know which indicator is closer to your fly.

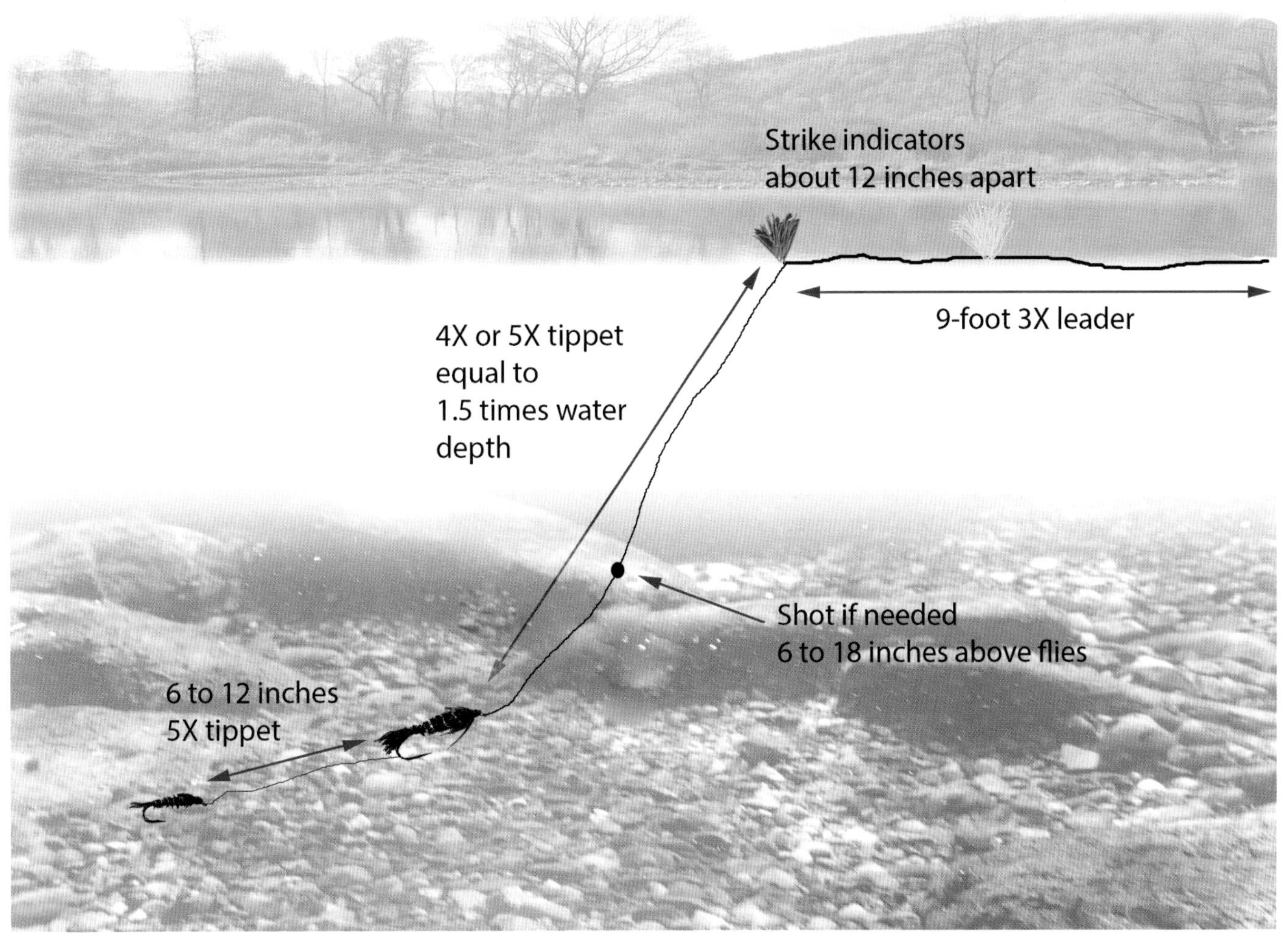

This is my basic two-indicator rig for most water types. When the yellow indicator gets downstream of or even with the red one, it's time to mend to avoid drag. The optimum mend will move only the yellow indicator, placing it back upstream of the red one, because that way you only move the leader and line, not the flies.

place, but you should not be doing any false casting with this rig, so it should stay put at least for a number of casts.

Of course, you can also crimp some split shot to your leader in the same place. It helps to have a knot in the leader to keep the weight from sliding down, but I have mixed feelings about that. I feel that the long fluorocarbon tippet helps sink the flies quickly, so if I use a knot to keep the weight from sliding, it has to be an extra knot in my leader—and knots are always a weak point. If you feel you need a knot, just cut your tippet about 10 inches above the first fly and reattach the tippet with a surgeon's or blood knot. You just have to balance the annoyance of having the weight slide down to a point where it gets too close to the first fly with the risk of putting another knot into the system.

Now estimate the depth of the water you intend to fish and place your first strike indicator one and a half times the water depth up from your lower fly. Put the second indicator 10 inches above this one. Hopefully the water is not so deep that you have to put your second indicator too close to the fly line. The farther your indicators from the end of the fly line, the easier it is to mend right to the indicator, which is what you should do to get the best drift.

You may be accustomed to using the plastic-bobber-type strike indicators. They are simple to attach, easy to move, and they never sink. They are also not much fun to cast, and they are not a terribly sensitive indicator of either your fly's drift or a strike. A fish really has to inhale your nymph before they show much movement. On the other hand, yarn casts much nicer, it is far more sensitive, and if the fish are at all spooky, it makes very little disturbance when it lands on the water. True, you have to add paste floatant to it before you start, and when it starts to get waterlogged, it helps to dip the yarn in desiccant powder, but I think these minor annoyances are worth the effort. It also helps to use indicator yarns of two different colors. If light conditions change, one may be more visible than the other, and by using two different colors, you know which indicator is closest to your fly. This becomes important, as you'll see shortly.

Cast into a likely spot, and using either a reach cast or a quick mend (or both) as soon as the indicators hit the water, place the second indicator just upstream of the first indicator. As your rig drifts down in the current, the second indicator will move faster than the first because the first is more directly connected to the flies, which drift slower than the indicators because the water below the surface is slower than the water at the surface. So the first indicator will lag a little, and the second indicator will slowly catch up to it. When it gets even with the first indicator, mend again to get that straight-line relationship between the two, and continue this through the drift. By keeping them in a straight line, perpendicular to the current, and not allowing the upper indicator to get downstream of the lower one, you will avoid sliding your fly across currents, which is more important than the flies moving slightly upstream or downstream faster or slower than the current. Natural insects sometimes move slightly faster or slower than the current in the same downstream lane, but they don't have the power to move across current lanes, which is a more unnatural movement.

The nymph pattern you try in early spring is far less important than getting your nymph in the right place with a dead drift. Some flies will be starting to hatch at this time of year, and it's always a wise move to try to imitate the insect that is most active at any time of year. The flies you'll see hatching most often in March and April, size 18 Blue-Winged Olives and scores of different kinds of midges, are small, yet in my experience a larger nymph is just as effective, if not more effective, than the smaller patterns in most rivers.

The last time I was on the Missouri River in April, the water was covered with midges and tiny olive mayflies, and although few fish were rising to the adults, I knew they must be gobbling lots of stuff under the water. I started with a midge pupa, and to get the size 18 nymph down quickly without resorting to weight on the leader, I tied it to a larger size 14 Pheasant Tail nymph with a big tungsten bead to get the little midge down. But I kept catching trout on the much bigger fly. A few took the nymph, but I would say three-quarters of the fish were taken on a fly bigger than anything I saw hatching. I even pumped the stomachs of a couple of fish, and sure enough, they were full of size 18 to 24 midge pupae. But they continued to hammer the bigger fly.

Of course, there are bigger mayflies and caddisflies and stoneflies in the Missouri, and the trout there may see a few of them in the early season when they get dislodged from the bottom or break free during the diurnal drift cycles. You would think the fish would be quicker to recognize what is actively hatching subsurface, but as study after study shows, trout are more opportunistic and less selective than we think, so a larger fly is always a safe bet in early season. Not being much of a betting man, though, I'll continue to hang a smaller fly off the end of the big one just in case.

EARLY SPRING, WATER HIGH AND DIRTY

High water in early spring is a fact of life. Snow often remains on the higher peaks, and a rainstorm or even just an unusually warm day can bring rivers up close to or over their banks, with water the color of coffee with heavy cream. This is seldom a good thing. Everyone wants to find the magic bullet that makes these conditions fun and easy to fish, but if that bullet exists, no one has found it yet.

High water later in the season, when trout are actively feeding all the time, is a different story, but the early-season stuff just makes life miserable because the water is cold and the fish will likely be glued close to the bottom, where you can't get a fly to them because of all that heavy current above

Nymphs can be effective in early spring high water. Just make sure you use heavily weighted flies or lots of weight on your leader, and use a high-sticking technique to keep your flies running slow, deep, and drag-free.

them. Even if you could get a fly down to them, you would have to put it right in front of their faces for them to see it. Add to this all the heavy current above yanking on your fly line and leader, pulling the fly away from the fish in a split second.

The first thing to do is look for softer water, where the raging current is slowed by some kind of obstruction like rocks, logs, or the banks. Look for places where the water is slow and smooth rather than places behind rocks where standing waves form, because these are tough places for trout to survive. Look at the water well below a standing wave where it flattens out and the current becomes slower and more uniform. You will also find softer water on the slower, usually shallower side of a riffle or on the insides of bends in the river.

Nymphs in Cold, Dirty Water

What techniques can you try? You are basically restricted to either nymphs or streamers, and if you decide to try nymphs, don't bother with small midges or mayfly imitations, even if you see these bugs in the air or on the water. Trout just won't be able to find a size 18 midge larva in all that dirty water. Fish big nymphs, size 6 through 10, imitations of large stoneflies or crayfish, or try bright red or orange worm flies or egg flies. Fish them dead-drift, using whatever technique suits the water in front of you best. In other words, if you can get close to the soft water, like that on the inside of a bend or riffle, try European nymphing. If the water you want to fish is more than two rod lengths away, you are probably better off using an indicator.

In this kind of water, it is more important than ever to use heavily weighted flies, or lots of weight on your leader. The quicker your flies get close to the bottom and out of the heavy current above, the more likely a fish will see them, and regardless you will get a relatively short drift in the right spot. If you don't know exactly where fish might be lying, either from past experience with the same water or advice from a guide or knowledgeable angler, fishing nymphs in high, cold water is tiresome and more like work than fishing, because you can only cover about a foot of bottom properly on each drift.

Streamers in High, Cold Water

Streamers are what most fly fishers stick with in high, dirty water, because you can cover a lot of water with a streamer and it's a big enough fly for trout to notice, even in very muddy water. You can experiment with white or bright colors, but the go-to colors that seem to produce this time of year are black and dark brown. Whatever streamer pattern you choose should get down to the bottom fast, so it should be heavily weighted with wire under the shank or a large tungsten bead or cone at the head. In all but the smallest, shallowest streams, you will also want either a sink-tip line or an extra-heavy poly leader, and you should add about 2 feet of 2X tippet or larger to the end of the sink-tip line or poly leader.

Find a place where the water looks a little slower and softer, out of the main current. Get upstream of it to one side and cast downstream-and-across in very fast water, straight across in medium-speed water, or upstream-and-across in slower water. Let the fly sink and begin to swim, then as the fly swings into the place you suspect a trout may be, try to keep it in that spot as long as possible by mending repeatedly so the fly swings slowly across the spot that looks fishy to you.

The most reliable fly for fishing in cold, dirty water is a streamer. This brown trout took a large brown Woolly Bugger on the Bitterroot River in Montana.

It also helps to hold your rod tip higher than normal to slow down the swing of your fly, because the less line on the water, the less the force trying to sweep your fly across the current. You can gently pulse the tip of the rod to make the fly look like a baitfish that is struggling with the current. Your efforts here should be to keep the fly moving so a fish notices it, while keeping the fly as long as possible in the sweet spot.

Once the fly swings directly below you, don't just pick it up and cast again. The sinking line or leader will get the fly deeper, so let it hang there for a few seconds. Sometimes a trout will follow the fly across the river and hang below it, and by making a few strips and then letting the fly just hang, then making a few more strips, a trout that followed the fly may stay interested and inhale it. This last part of the swing, with the fly directly downstream of you, can be the best part of the entire presentation, and if you can wade just upstream of the soft water, try the same technique but concentrate more on the water downstream instead of water that is across the river from you.

Streamer fishing like this can be especially productive in early spring in rivers with wild rainbow or cutthroat populations. Spawning trout, both males and females, are hard-wired to attack smaller fish that hang around their redds, because smaller trout and sculpins are notorious egg stealers, and if these sneaky little guys are frightened away or attacked, more of the eggs will survive. Cutthroats and rainbows are normally not as piscivorous as brown trout, which is immediately apparent when you look at their teeth: You can usually put your finger in the mouth of a large rainbow or cutthroat without much worry, but sticking your finger in the mouth of a large brown trout is sure to draw blood. Those nasty teeth are there for one purpose—to tear apart smaller fish, frogs, mice, and crayfish.

In this type of fishing, a fly rod longer than normal is a big advantage because you can reach out over water you can't wade into and still let the fly hang downstream. Ten-foot rods or even 11-foot switch rods, even in small streams, can be a big advantage because not only can they let the fly hang below you in more places, they also help to keep more line off the water so your fly gets a slower swing and is able to hang in the sweet spot longer.

THE HATCHES OF EARLY SPRING

With a few exceptions, the hatches of early spring are surprisingly similar regardless of geography. Small brownish-olive-colored mayflies with gray wings, commonly called Blue-Winged Olives, *Baetis* (the scientific name of the genus), or Blue Quills, hatch almost every day, very sparsely on sunny days and heavily on dark, rainy, or snowy days. You can find them on the water in April everywhere from Washington State to northern Georgia. They are very common on the streams in Europe. And even in the southern hemisphere in their spring, typically in October and November, you'll find flies hatching in the same color and size, with the same behavior.

You may also find these flies almost anytime going forward in the season, as they supposedly have more than one brood per season. I have not seen this proven scientifically, and perhaps there are different species or some of them in the same species just hatch later. Doesn't really matter. You'll see them all season long, but later in the season they are often overshadowed by bigger and more tempting insects. Needless to say, I never leave home without olive-colored dry flies in sizes 16 through 20, brownish-olive nymphs in the same sizes, and a couple of emergers in the same color and size range.

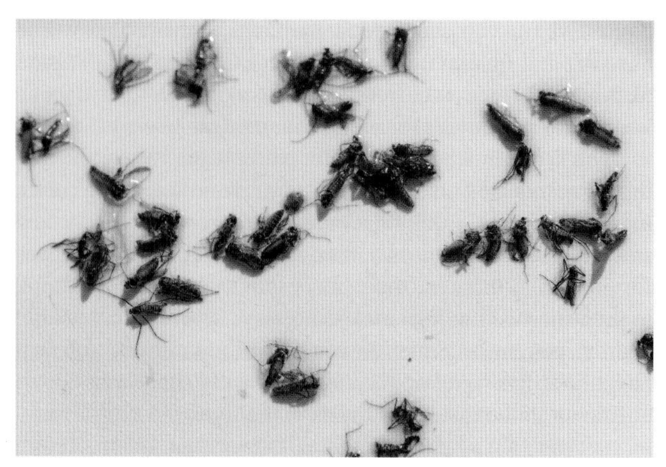

These midge larvae and pupae all came out of a single trout's stomach in early April. Trout have to eat a lot of midges to get full, so the more often they feed, the better your chances of catching them.

Midges in any color from black to white and also in many shades of gray, brown, cream, and green will hatch on every trout stream in the world as far as I know. In faster, freestone rivers they are relatively unimportant, but in the slower currents of tailwaters and spring creeks, where it is energetically efficient for a trout to eat many tiny insects, midges can be the predominant food throughout the year—and especially in early spring.

You would think trout would concentrate on the midge pupae and larvae, as these stages should be easier to capture than the adults actively skittering across the surface. In some rivers that is true, but I've also done stomach analysis of trout in the early spring and have been surprised to find an equal amount of the subsurface stages and adults in their stomachs. One of the times trout really pounce on adult midges is when they mate and form balls of multiple insects that clump together on the surface. I've watched trout in the Bighorn River in Montana ignore single midges, inhale doubles, and actually move off their feeding lanes for clumps of three or more.

Although midges come in a wide variety of colors and sizes, most experienced anglers don't pay too much attention to the exact kind of midge on the water. When the flies are emerging, most use a drab brown, black, or gray pupa, and when the adults are on the water, the fly of choice is often either a Griffith's Gnat or even a small, size 18 or 20 Parachute Adams. Because the fish may be looking for the bigger clumps of adult midges, a fly much larger than the individual naturals may be greedily inhaled.

If you see midges or have seen them on the water in the last 24 hours but you see no surface activity at all, try fishing a pupa or larva imitation (or better yet, one of each) relatively close to the bottom using one of the dead-drift nymphing techniques. If you see the occasional swirl but rises are inconsistent, probably the best approach is to fish a pupa with no weight, either with a small indicator or using something like a size 16 Griffith's Gnat in a dry/dropper combination.

If trout are slashing at something on the surface and all you see are midges, you might try skating a midge imitation, which works surprisingly well when trout are really active on midges. Tie on a size 16 or 18 Griffith's Gnat, treat it well with either powder or paste fly floatant, and then grease your entire leader with paste floatant. Start by casting across and downstream, and let the fly swing in the current, dragging it like you have been told 1,000 times to avoid with a dry fly. If that does not work, start with a reach cast, move your rod tip upstream until the fly twitches upstream a bit, then drop the rod tip and follow the fly to get a dead drift in between. Either method may work, or sometimes one will be better than the other.

With the bigger flies of early spring the rivers east of the Mississippi behave much different from the rivers in the western part of North America. In the East, although you may occasionally see larger stoneflies hatching in March and April, trout seem to ignore them. There is a black stonefly that hatches in the East—it's skinny and about a size 18, and in my experience the fish totally ignore it. In 50 years of fly fishing, I have never seen a trout eat one. I have pestered many of my friends about this fly and have never had one admit to actually seeing a trout feed on an adult black stonefly on the surface. Sometimes black stoneflies hatch at the same time as the early-season Olives, and they admit that the fish they saw feeding were eating Olives. My friend Tim Flagler, a world-renowned videographer of fly-tying videos and a very serious fly fisher, says that he thinks he saw a trout once eat an adult black stonefly on a hatchery-supported stream in New Jersey. But I have seen hatchery trout inhale cigarette butts. No joke.

So although you may see these bugs very early in the spring and it's a nice sign that dry-fly fishing may soon be upon us, I wouldn't rush out to buy a bunch of dry flies that imitate black stoneflies. I know I won't be tying any. In a similar vein, there is a larger brown stonefly that hatches a bit later in the Eastern season, in late April. It often hatches about an hour before the famous Hendrickson mayfly on sunny days. I have sat on the bank and watched thousands of these stoneflies over the years drift in a teasing manner, whirling and twitching in the current, and have never seen a trout eat one. Yet an hour later when the Hendricksons begin to hatch, trout suddenly appear surface feeding in a greedy manner. I do catch trout on large brown nymphs early in the season, and they may take these for the nymphs of that stonefly. They just don't seem to like the adults.

Along with midges and olive mayflies, the first insects to really get trout feeding on the surface in nearly every Eastern stream are the Quill Gordon and Hendrickson mayflies. Both are about a size 14, and the best methods are fishing an emerger in the early part of the hatch and a fully-winged adult about an hour later. Dead drift is the game here, and any drag seems to put you out of the game, unlike the tactics you might use with midges.

The Hendrickson mayfly is a large, handsome fly that to Eastern fly fishers ushers in the best dry-fly fishing of the season. In most rivers in the East and Midwest, it hatches in early to late May, promptly at 3 p.m.

Quill Gordons typically hatch about 1 p.m. for a few hours in the afternoon and seem to prefer cloudy days. Hendricksons come a little later, typically around 3 p.m., and in some rivers they are incredibly punctual, although in high water on warm days I have seen them hatch as early as 10 a.m. Quill Gordon spinners have never seemed very important to me, as I have never seen one of its spinner falls heavy enough to interest trout. But Hendrickson spinners are probably more important than the duns. They fall anywhere from late afternoon until dark, and the fish go completely crazy over them. In many Eastern rivers, the Hendrickson spinner fall in early May is the best time of year to catch a large trout on a dry fly.

On Western rivers it's a totally different scenario in the early season, and honestly I have never been able to determine why. Where I would never prospect with a dry fly in April in the East, just randomly fishing a dry in places where trout should be located, in the West it can be surprisingly productive. Much of this behavior, I think, is due to a stonefly called the *Skwala*. I don't know the Latin name of the bug and

Skwala *stoneflies are one of the best early season hatches in the Rockies. Most times, any big brown dry fly with a long body will draw trout to the surface.*

don't really care. It's a big brown stonefly that hatches from the Rockies to the West Coast any time from late February through April, and it seems to have no Eastern counterpart. But surprisingly it brings Western trout to the surface, even in the cold water of late winter, where the early stoneflies of the East are a non-starter.

Skwalas seldom hatch in great numbers, and it's rare to see trout rising steadily to them, or even to see more than a few trout rise to them during a day of fishing. But don't you believe fish aren't looking for them. Blind-fishing a dry fly in likely spots will often bring unseen fish to the surface, because these stoneflies either taste great or struggle for a long time in the surface film where trout can grab them. It's a trout's first Big Mac of the season, and they are on the lookout for these brown bugs if any are around. One of the best ways to find cooperative trout is to use a dry/dropper arrangement with a high-floating *Skwala* imitation, maybe something with a foam body, with a size 10 or 12 weighted *Skwala* nymph hung below it.

The first hatch of a large mayfly also happens in March and April in the western United States, the March Brown. Unlike the Eastern March Brown, a larger species of mayfly that looks similar to the Western one but hatches from mid-May to mid-June, the Western March Brown really does hatch in March. (The reason for the confusion on the Eastern bug is that it resembles an English mayfly that also truly hatches in March, and because much of our early dry-fly fishing tradition comes from England, the name stuck despite the calendar inconsistency.)

Like *Skwalas*, trout love March Brown adults, but they also eat the big, meaty nymphs with abandon, and because the nymphs get active and migrate to the shallows just before the hatch, lots of them get dislodged and are thus available to trout. The old standby hare's ear nymph is a near-perfect imitation of the nymphs, and the Adams, Parachute Adams, or any brownish-gray mayfly imitation will work. You may also

The Mother's Day Caddis hatch is often so heavy that you can't get away from them.

need an emerger, especially on sunny days when the adults leave the water quickly, so make sure you have some kind of brownish emerger or soft-hackle in size 14.

The last big Western hatch before the trees really bloom and everything breaks loose in the trout and insect worlds is the Mother's Day Caddis. It typically hatches well before Mother's Day, mid-April to the first week in May, and it's just another instance of how fly fishers don't seem able to read a calendar—or perhaps they tell non-anglers it happens on Mother's Day so they have an excuse to get out of the house when their mother is visiting.

Mother's Day Caddis are grayish brown, about size 16, with green bodies, and they invariably hatch in huge numbers, all at once. Yet they are sometimes disappointing. The air can be full of them, the water blanketed with bugs, and the legs of your waders squirming with hundreds of adults. But on some days trout ignore the adults, and very few fish are seen rising. Other days the trout flip over the adults on the surface. There seems to be no predicting how the fish react to the adults, but you can be sure that the fish will be eating the emerging pupae all the way from the bottom to just under the surface. A pupa imitation, therefore, will almost always produce when a dry fly is sometimes effective and sometimes a waste of time. Regardless, it's one of the few heavy hatches in early season, and it does get the fish moving to bugs and looking at the surface. Eastern rivers get similar blanket hatches of closely related

A nice rainbow caught on a caddis pupa pattern during the Mother's Day Caddis hatch. Even though adult flies may cover the air, water, and surrounding landscape, trout often prefer the pupae.

caddis that look similar, but these hatch later in the season, well into May, when many other aquatic insects are emerging.

Fishing Caddis Hatches

A dry fly is the most fun but the least useful type of pattern during caddis hatches. These insects can fool you, and being savvier about their hatches is a big step toward upping your game in trout fishing.

Because they are tremendously abundant on trout streams and often hatch in great numbers, caddisflies are usually the first thing you notice. The adults of many species twitch and skitter across the surface when they hatch, catching your eye, but there are often more sedate mayflies lurking among the caddis. And because most mayfly species ride the current longer than caddis, trout seem to prefer them because mayflies are easier to capture.

Added to this is the longer life of an adult caddis. They can live for up to a month after hatching (as opposed to just a day or two for an adult mayfly), and often the caddis swarms you see on the river are merely clouds of adults migrating upstream and never touching the water. So it is important to recognize the two stages when caddisflies are available to trout and easy to capture: when the pupae are trying to break through the surface film, and when the adults—finally—give up the ghost, mate, lay eggs, and fall to the water to die. Both of these stages make use of a "damp" rather than a dry fly, along with special techniques.

The first instance is when caddis pupae begin to drift in the current just prior to hatching. They have been sequestered in a

There are scores of different patterns that imitate caddis pupae—and new ones come out every year—because trout seem to be unusually snotty when eating caddis pupae. It's probably more a question of presentation than it is pattern, and some days the fish just seem easier to fool than others.

pupal case glued to the bottom for weeks, mostly unavailable to trout, but they slice open the case and rise to the surface. Some rise quickly, others drift slowly upward, and yet others swim through the water column with a sculling motion. You probably won't know what the pupae are doing down there because it's nearly impossible to observe without donning scuba gear, as Gary LaFontaine did back in the 1970s, so it's best to try a couple of techniques.

The first one, and probably the most useful overall, is the dead drift. Pick a caddis pupa imitation roughly the same size as caddisflies you've seen along the banks or on window screens, and fish it with either a strike indicator or in the European nymphing style. Be careful to get a completely dead drift as long as you can. Hedge your bets by using two different colors—I don't think color matters all that much, and the color of the adult may be different from the pupa, but you might as well play the odds. I'd start with a green one and a brown one.

If this doesn't work, and especially if you see a few trout slashing on the surface, try a more active method. Remove any weight on your leader, get rid of the indicator, and go with a single fly that is unweighted or lightly weighted. Sometimes a soft-hackle or old-fashioned traditional wet fly works better than more modern, fancy emerger patterns.

I have not had as much success with flies tied to each other with a piece of tippet connecting the two, as you would normally do with deep nymphs, but if you want to fish with two patterns, it is definitely better to attach the upper fly to the leader with a dropper. In other words, tie on a new piece of tippet but leave the heavier tag end about 6 inches long. Attach one fly here and the other to the standard place at the end of the tippet.

I have also found that a bead-head nymph, or any heavily weighted nymph, does not work as well in an active presentation as an unweighted or lightly weighted fly. I am not sure why—this is just empirical observation—but for some reason, when you swing a fly the weighted flies do not look as realistic.

To fish the nymph more actively, cast across and upstream to let the fly sink. Keep your rod tip high, and follow the point where the leader enters the water with your rod, swiveling your arm across your body. When the fly gets to a position that is quartering downstream of you, just stop moving the rod tip. Keep it stationary. This puts a sudden tension in the line and leader and makes your fly rise to the surface, in a manner similar to an emerging caddis. You might even try twitching the rod tip slightly as the fly rises to imitate the swimming motion of some species of caddis, but remember that you're imitating a tiny little critter that can't move very fast, so make these movements of your rod tip small and subtle, not overt as you would with a streamer. You may have heard this described as the Leisenring lift, named after a noted Pennsylvania angler who first wrote about the technique in the 1930s.

Of course, it helps if you have a target for this. If you see a trout swirl or splash, without big bubbles in the rise form, the fish probably rose off the bottom to catch an emerging caddis and its momentum carried the fish close to the surface, even if it ate the insect 6 inches below the surface. Position yourself just upstream and about 30 feet away from the rise (if you can get that close). Cast so that your fly sinks well above the fish and rises a foot or two upstream of where you saw the rise, because the fish was likely positioned upstream of where you saw the rise and was pushed back by the current as it rose to the insect.

Honestly, this technique sounds deadly, and you would think it would work every time. It doesn't. I have often been disappointed and frustrated trying to catch trout taking emerging caddis, and I don't think it has much to do with the fly pattern. It's just one method you can try.

Another way to fish when caddisflies are emerging, especially in bigger water, is to just swing a caddis pupa or wet fly in the current. Here, you cast straight across to a little upstream and just let the fly swing in the current until it hangs below you. If the water is very fast or if currents are tricky, try mending the line as soon as the leader hits the water, or even better, start out your drift with an upstream reach cast. This will slow down the swing of your fly and is typically standard procedure except in very slow water, where you don't want to slow down the swing of your fly and may even mend downstream to pick up its speed.

If you see many fish feeding on the surface, I am still suggesting that you resist putting on a high-floating dry fly. Try something without hackle that sits very low in the film or an emerger pattern that drifts half in and half out of the water. If you don't have one of these emerger patterns, cast your dry fly well above a feeding fish and pull the fly under by stripping line. It helps to avoid false casting when you do this, or even rub your fly in some mud or underwater so that it sinks just below the surface. You will probably still see a rise, even if the fish takes your fly a couple of inches below the surface.

And okay, if you want to fish that high-floating Elk Hair Caddis, be my guest. But if the fish ignore it or splash at it without connecting, you know what to do—go back to fishing a fly in the film or just under the surface.

CHAPTER 7

Fly Selection and Fishing Strategy—Mid-spring through Early Summer

Sometime between mid-April and June, depending on geography, altitude, and seasonal variations in temperatures and precipitation, conditions on trout streams change dramatically, as we've seen previously. Trout disperse into shallower water to take advantage of the ease of feeding on the insect life produced in riffles, water temperatures are at near-optimum for trout, and their metabolism is in high gear so they may feed almost constantly, from dawn to dusk and even after dark. This is the glory time for trout streams, when places that seemed barren of fish a few weeks ago can seem alive with trout.

It would be silly to go into detail on all the insect hatches that you might find during this time, and I won't even attempt to. Sometimes they are important and sometimes they are disappointing in terms of producing actively feeding fish, for reasons only the bugs and the fish understand. The importance of the Green Drake or Pale Morning Dun hatch varies not only from region to region and from river to river, but literally from

In late spring, foliage bursts from the trees and aquatic insects are in full activity. It's about the best time to be on trout streams. Trout are now found everywhere, from the slow deep pools of early spring to the faster water in riffles and runs.

day to day. You go fishing when you can and take what the river offers. The key to getting to the next level in your fly fishing is not so much learning all the names of the insects, but in having a bunch of strategies in your back pocket so you can take advantage of all kinds of conditions.

SPRING AND SUMMER, WATER LOW TO NORMAL AND CLEAR

These conditions are a major blessing offset by just a minor curse. The curse is that when water is clear, fish are a bit harder to approach because you are more easily spotted, and they might be just a touch fussier about fly pattern and presentation. But I'll take that minor hardship any day because with clear water I *know* fish will see my fly if I get it close to them. With cloudy water you may be fishing water that holds trout but you never know if they actually see your offering. Eliminating that one variable gives me confidence that if I change my fly pattern or presentation, at least I'll know if the fish approve.

Pay Attention to Your Leader

One of the most important shifts in tactics you should make is to pay a lot more attention to your leader. The leader that served you well in March and April just won't cut it as the water drops and gets clearer, because fish get spookier and you won't be able to stand right next to them as you could earlier in the season. With higher and dirtier water, fish feel safe and are not nearly as spooky, but as the water drops and they move into shallower water, you must do everything you can to keep that fly line away from them, whether you are fishing nymphs, dry flies, or streamers.

Most people start their fishing with a 9-foot leader in the spring and stick with the same length for the rest of the season. I know that because I'm privy to sales figures for leaders and I know what you buy. This is a big mistake, and I feel that the correct leader, both in length and tippet size, is more important than what rod you are using, what line you fish, and even what fly you pick. If you spook a fish, or if your fly looks like it is attached to a piece of rope, the best gear in the world can't help you.

Why do you want a longer leader? Get underwater with a face mask on a hot day and have someone cast a line and leader on top of you. From above, it seems like the line and leader make about the same disturbance, but from underwater you'll see that the fly line plunks down much harder, throws more waves, and probably even makes a louder sound. Plus it's opaque and much more visible from underwater. I actually don't think the opacity of a fly line floating near fish is a big problem because fish see twigs and leaves floating in the water all the time. But the splashdown is overt and frightening. When an object, whether it's a small branch or fly line, lands near trout, they spook and stop feeding for a while.

This is what it looks like from underwater when a light fly line (a 4-weight) hits the water on a delicate cast. Is there any wonder a fly line landing near a trout will scare it?

You already carry spools of material to replace your tippets, but it also makes sense to carry a spool of material that matches the butt section of your leader if conditions warrant a longer leader. The leader package will indicate the butt diameter of your leader as well as the tippet size so you know which diameter to carry. Adding a few feet to the butt of your leader will not adversely affect its ability to straighten.

Imagine casting directly upstream to a fish, or upstream-and-across. You know you have to place your fly somewhere above the fish when fishing a dry or nymph, and sometimes you don't know exactly where the fish is lying, so every place your fly line lands is potentially a zone of spooked fish. The longer your leader, the shorter that zone is during any given presentation and the longer your effective drift distance. When fishing downstream, with a short leader you are still placing your fly line close to the fish—and for that matter, upstream of the fish, where it will notice the fly line more—so even when streamer fishing with a floating line, which is the way most people fish streamers once the water drops, the longer your leader, the greater the range your fly swims over a fish that has not had a fly line dragged over its head.

When fishing nymphs with an indicator, it's important to have some leader between your fly line and your indicator, because lifting the leader when you mend your cast is much easier and causes less disturbance than lifting fly line. So let's say you are fishing along successfully in a 3-foot riffle with a 9-foot leader and catching fish, but you come up on a nice pool that you know must hold trout. The pool looks to be 6 feet deep. You know you need to set your indicator about one and a half times the depth of the water, at least to start; but with a 9-foot leader, that puts your indicator right at the end of the fly line—not a great situation. With a 12-foot leader you would have another 3 feet of leader to play with, allowing you to place your strike indicator farther from the fly line.

This doesn't even mean you have to go out and buy 12-foot leaders. I've found that you can add 3 feet of heavy nylon at the end of a 9-foot leader and still have one that casts beautifully. In leader design, the most critical part of the taper happens in the middle, or transition sections between the butt and the tippet. You can play with both the butt and tippet end, within reason, and still have a leader that casts as well as a store-bought 12-footer. I did this with my bonefish leaders for years because I think that in many places a 9-foot leader, pretty much the standard for bonefishing, is too short and spooks bonefish in heavily pressured waters. Later I found that it works just as well for trout leaders.

One sunny afternoon on the West Branch of the Delaware River showed me how extreme you need to go with leader length when fish are pounded with flies all day long. I had been fishing on the lower river without much success when I found out some buddies were on the upper river having great fishing during the Sulphur hatch. The pool they were fishing is shallow and flat, but the trout would line up in the afternoon taking emerging and crippled duns, and some of them were surprisingly large for such thin water.

The day was sunny and achingly bright; the fish kept rising, but they were ignoring my flies. I knew I had a good imitation. It's a sparse emerger with a wing of snowshoe rabbit foot and a trailing shuck, tied on a curved hook so the rear half of the body hangs in the water like a mayfly trying to escape its shuck, and it hardly ever fails me. I got into a position where the sun was just right and I could see the fish respond to my fly, and every time I cast, the trout would shiver a bit and sink slowly to the bottom, where they would stay for a minute or so.

That wasn't going to work because if a trout stops rising every time you present your fly, it's hard to get a hook in its mouth. I was not getting drag; I was making a nice reach cast, but still no luck. I waded over to the bank to sit and think about this situation for a minute when one of my more successful friends also sat down for a smoke break. When I complained about not having touched a fish yet, he said, "Oh, I should have told you. A few days ago we were having a tough time as well and kept lengthening our leaders, and we found we had to go to 18-footers before we stopped spooking fish."

I added 5 feet to my butt section and another foot to my 12-foot tippet, waded back out with the same fly, and finally managed to catch some fish. I won't say I tore them up that day, but I did catch a few and it was a lesson I will never forget. You may not ever have to go to that extreme, but on days when you are frustrated by the fish and spend half your time switching fly patterns, try a leader modification instead.

Here's how to do it: On the leaders you buy, you will see the butt diameter stated on the package. Buy some nylon of the same brand, so that the stiffness factor of your new leader butt is about the same, in either the same diameter or .002 inch bigger than your existing butt section. For instance, if your 9-foot 5X leaders state .021″–.006″ on the package, get a spool of either .021″ or .023″ nylon and carry it with you, or modify your leaders at home before you go fishing. Remove the existing leader from your fly line, cut off the loop, tie a perfection loop in a 3-foot section of the new butt material, and connect them with a three-turn blood knot (you don't need or want five turns on this heavy stuff). Connect your expanded leader to the loop on your fly line, and you are good to go.

You will probably also find you can straighten a longer tippet with this new leader. Unless it's windy, this is good practice because the tippet lands even lighter than the rest of the leader and a longer tippet, with its lighter mass, will give you a few extra seconds before drag sets in. I have found that often when I am having problems with a fly dragging over the fish, just adding 2 feet to my tippet gives me a few more inches of drag-free drift—enough to fool a difficult trout.

Nylon vs. Fluorocarbon

Both nylon and fluorocarbon have their place in your fishing vest or pack, and I would never head to a trout stream without spools of both. Understanding when and where to use each of them will put you a few steps ahead of the average angler because most people don't truly understand the differences.

Nylon is your basic material. In trout fishing, all of your base leaders should be made from nylon, but tippet is a different story and there are times you may want to switch to fluoro. The important physical attribute that distinguishes fluoro from nylon is sink rate. The specific gravity of water is 1, nylon is 1.1, and fluorocarbon is 1.78. Fluoro is denser than nylon; in fact, just sweat or fly dressing on a nylon leader keeps it floating pretty well, whereas impurities that get onto fluoro won't retard its sink rate much. In practice, regardless of the numbers, fluoro sinks about three times as fast as nylon. Now, this is only a difference of a few seconds over the course of a 30-second drift, but when fishing with nymphs, where it is essential to get your fly down as quickly as possible, those seconds can make a difference in your presentation.

Two Copper John nymphs tied to 4X tippets. The top one is tied to a nylon tippet and the bottom one to a fluorocarbon. Although in some light conditions fluorocarbon is less visible (because its index of refraction is closer to water than nylon), fly fishers more often use the more expensive fluorocarbon when fishing below the surface because fluoro sinks quicker than nylon and is more abrasion resistant. But at half the price of fluoro, many anglers use nylon for all types of flies.

So I carry fluorocarbon strictly for nymph, wet fly, and streamer fishing, but only for the tippet. Other than streamer fishing or swinging a wet fly, having an entire leader made of fluorocarbon makes it harder to mend and harder to float a dry fly. It also causes more drag because a leader floating lightly on the surface is less likely to yank a fly in an unnatural manner than one that is below the surface and subject to more conflicting currents. But as a tippet added to a nylon leader, fluorocarbon excels when fishing nymphs or wet flies. I've proven it to myself numerous times, and if you poll the guides on any difficult trout stream in the world, I am pretty confident 80 percent of them would recommend fluorocarbon when fishing nymphs.

There are other qualities of fluorocarbon that make it theoretically better for fishing nymphs as well. Its index of refraction, at 1.4, is closer to that of water (1.3) than nylon, which is 1.6. So fluoro should be less visible to fish than nylon under the surface. The jury is still out on whether it is truly less visible underwater than nylon—it should be, and it seems to be when you put both of them in a glass of water. But I think any animal that can see and eat a midge smaller than anything we can imitate with our hooks can see even a 7X fluorocarbon tippet. It may be less visible and thus ignored by the fish, but I don't think you can call it invisible.

In any given diameter, fluorocarbon is harder than nylon. This gives it a slight edge in abrasion resistance, which is why many saltwater fly anglers use fluorocarbon leaders and even commercial tuna captains use it between their braided line and their lure. I don't think it is a huge advantage, but when combined with its other properties, it makes a compelling case for fluorocarbon with subsurface flies.

Other qualities not related to fishing properties directly:

- Fluorocarbon is three times as expensive as nylon.
- Fluorocarbon does not degrade under UV light but nylon does. This is good in that fluoro tippet that is 10 years old will be as strong as it ever was, but bad because it never biodegrades, so you need to make sure you save all your leader scraps and dispose of them in household garbage. I replace all nylon tippet spools after two years because I don't trust its strength after a couple of years.
- Fluorocarbon is harder to knot than nylon because of its stiffness, and its knots are slightly weaker. However, nylon absorbs water, which weakens a tippet, whereas fluorocarbon does not, so it is probably a wash regarding knot strength.

One final word on tippet materials: You'll hear people say that you can't combine nylon with fluorocarbon in a leader, but this is pure bunk. You can, and people do all season long. I would not combine two materials that have more than .002 inch difference, and any knot in fluorocarbon is harder to tighten than one in softer, slipperier nylon, but by tying a good triple surgeon's knot, five-turn blood knot, or Orvis tippet knot, you can get these materials to combine just fine in a secure knot. Also make sure you lubricate these (and any) knots with saliva before tightening. Lubrication helps knots slip together properly, and it also helps reduce the brief heat buildup caused by friction when you tighten a knot.

To Mend or Not . . .

In my opinion, most fly fishers over-mend. There are times when a quick mend is the only way to restore a drift back into its proper aspect, but I kept track over a two-year period on my success in nymph fishing between casting with a normal overhead cast and then mending versus placing the fly properly at the outset with a reach cast combined with a tuck cast. What I noticed was that after a mend I hardly ever got a strike, unless the water was very fast and deep or the fish were aggressively pursuing hatching insects and had thrown all caution to the wind.

I am not certain why this is so, but I suspect it is because either the plop of an indicator as it is placed on the water (in theory, when you mend you try to mend the leader and line just to the indicator without moving it, but in practice, that only happens about half the time) spooks the fish, or that when we mend we move the fly into a different position in the water column even though it seems to be drifting the same as it was before the mend. This does make some sense, because you work so hard to get your fly close to the bottom where the current velocity is lower, and when you mend you lift the fly just slightly, enough to place it in the faster water just above the bottom, where it gets caught and remains until the line tightens at the end of the drift and the fly gets pulled right up to the surface.

When fishing from a drift boat, where you may sometimes have a drag-free drift for 100 feet or more when the boat is drifting at the exact same speed as the current and if there are no squirrely currents between the boat and the fly, you can effectively mend because after you mend, the fly has plenty of time to settle back down to the bottom. But when wading, your effective floats are much shorter, and I just think the fly does not have a chance to get back into position.

When fishing a dry fly, you're presented with a different set of problems. I think you can mend effectively if you mend when the fly is well upstream of the fish, and if it truly extends your drag-free float. Too often a mend moves the fly, pulls it under, and does nothing to lessen the drag on the fly anyway. And if you mend when the fly is in the vicinity of the fish and the fly happens to move, occasionally it's effective, at times when moving the fly is desirable, but in most cases it does you no good at all. Again, placing your dry fly with the right cast, with plenty of slack as the line hits the water, is much more effective than slapping the line around.

The Reach Cast and Its Subtleties

Knowing how to execute a reach cast properly, and adjusting it to fit every situation you encounter, is a big part of putting you in the big leagues when it comes to trout fishing. The reach cast is highly effective because it places the fly over

SCAN TO WATCH VIDEO 009.

What happens when a fly drags, and how to counteract the effects of it.

the fish before the leader or fly line. But just as important, it is used to get a better drift with either a nymph or dry fly in tricky currents, with less drag on a dry fly or nymph and a better sink rate on a nymph rig.

A standard reach cast the way most people do it, without much thought to the shape of the line on the water, is fine in uniform currents. If you have a fish straight across from you in uniform current between you and the fish, you probably know that if you make a straight-line cast, the fly line moves downstream faster than the fly and leader because it has more mass, and just the slightest downstream bow in the line yanks on the fly and causes it to drag. Basic stuff. By making a reach cast, which is merely placing a mend in the fly line by reaching your arm upstream just before the line hits the water, you form an upstream bow that has to become straight or inverted before the fly drags. And as we know, it also places the fly over the fish before the line and leader.

But now let's separate the puppies from the big dogs. Let's say you are standing in slow water, there is a fast current in the middle of the river, and a fish is feeding in slow water on the other side of the fast current. If you make a standard reach cast, with an elongated bow between the fly and the tip of your rod, the fast water in the middle quickly forms a tight bow in the line, but the fly line in the slow water where you are wading holds it back. Something has to move—namely, the fly on the other side of the fast current. Ideally, what you would want is a reach cast that just places the upstream bow over that fast water, leaving the rest of the cast in a normal position. There is a way to do this, and it requires a bit of practice, but after a little work, it becomes second nature.

If you experiment when making a reach cast, making the reach earlier and later in the cast, you'll find that when you make the reach very early in the power stroke, as you first start to see your rod tip coming forward and then returning the rod to a normal follow-through, you'll see that the upstream hook lands at the far end of your cast. Conversely, if you make the reach very late in the cast, just before the fly line hits the water, you'll put the upstream hook closer to your rod tip. Every time you move you are presented with a different current scenario, but if you learn to put that upstream hook over the fastest part of the current, you'll have much better control of where your fly drifts. After all, you only have a finite amount of line to work with, and by placing the upstream bow where it is most effective, you make the best out of the reach cast

To further fine-tune your reach casts, always have some loops of line held in reserve with your line hand. As you make the reach, let line slip through your fingers; otherwise, you'll land short of your target because a curve takes up more linear distance than a straight line. This is a simple matter that you would think most people would do, yet I constantly find myself not remembering to do it, and thus not getting my fly properly over the place I either see a trout or think one is lurking.

A variation of the reach cast that is more difficult to perform but can get you out of tight spots is one that you cast over your off shoulder (in other words, a right-hander would cast over the left shoulder). Suppose you are facing some water where the current flows from right to left. To get the upstream hook needed for a good drift, you make a normal reach cast, casting over your right shoulder as usual, and everything works fine. But suppose you cross the river and fish to the other side, where the current now runs left to right, and when you try a reach cast as you did on the other side, you find that it's a lot tougher to get the hook to go upstream because you have to reach across your body instead of just reaching off to the right side. It can be done, but I noticed on a recent trip, in a pool where the current ran left to right and there was a strong wind blowing downstream (left to right, same as the current), I found that I couldn't get a good reach and the wind kept dumping the fly line almost on top of the fish I saw rising. I corrected by casting at an angle over my left shoulder and combined that with a reach to the left, and this was enough to defeat both the wind and the current. I wasn't even aware of what I was doing, and probably do this more often than I realize. In fact, if I had not been in the process of writing this section at the time, I would have totally missed it.

In very tricky conditions where multiple currents make figuring out where to put your line bows more of a math problem than a nice fishing outing, you can combine a bounce cast with a reach cast. A bounce cast is merely shocking the line with your rod tip so that the line bounces back toward you, introducing little wiggles of slack line that give you further insurance toward a long float. To combine a reach cast with a bounce cast, initiate your forward cast, make the reach, but at the end of the reach, add a quick bounce of the rod tip, moving in the same direction as the reach, enough that the line bounces back against it before hitting the water. Immediately after making the bounce, return the rod to the position it would normally be at the end of a reach cast. The upstream hook is now bolstered by some slack in the line and leader, and all those little coils have to straighten before the fly drags.

Now that I've shown you the hard way to eliminate or lessen mends in your presentation, I'll tell you the easy way: Make shorter casts. Regardless of whether you are fishing a nymph or a dry fly, the best way to keep control of the fly line is to put less of it on the water, and the closer you are to your target, the less likely some swirly currents will yank your fly line downstream. This, of course, has to be tempered by how spooky the fish are and how deep you want to wade. I think it's always better to get close to fish, even if they are spooky, because line waving around in the air, mends, and more line landing on the water could spook fish as much as wading close to them. And it's never an easy decision: Do I creep forward 2 more feet to get a better cast and risk spooking the fish, or

SCAN TO WATCH VIDEO 010.
Ways of performing the reach cast.

In high, dirty water in late spring and summer, all is not lost. Water temperatures will keep fish more active, so they may chase streamers, and you may even find trout rising in slower water along the banks.

do I make a longer cast knowing my presentation won't be as great? Only a few blown opportunities will give you a hint on how close you can get to the trout on any given day.

SPRING AND SUMMER, WATER HIGH AND DIRTY

High water in spring and summer is not as much of a challenge as high water when the water is cold. You still retain the problem of getting a fish to see your fly, but the high note here is that because water temperatures should be at optimum levels for trout metabolism, trout want to—in fact, they have to—feed as much as they can. Trout growth is much slower from late summer through early spring, and the fish need to put on weight and grow while insect food is abundant. So although high water can be frustrating any time of year because you probably won't be able to fish the way you really want to, it can still be productive.

In high water fish move more often into the shallows and along the banks than they do when water is colder. So the same nymph techniques work, you just have to search for shallower water or water along banks where friction with the land slows down currents and lets them rest and feed easier. You can probably get away with nymphs one or two sizes larger than you would in low-water conditions, and of course you can use a heavier tippet because visibility is so poor. That's a good thing, because you'll need that heavier tippet to land fish in the faster currents you're faced with. Nymphs with some flash, like ones with brass beads, often work well in dirty water, as do large black nymphs because black seems to be more visible to fish than lighter colors in dirty water.

Often insects hatch heavily in high water, and by carefully looking along the banks and in slower, shallower pools, you may find trout rising to insects. It is truly amazing how trout can spot insects on the surface in dirty water, but believe me they can. I have given up on dry-fly fishing too many times, only to spot fish feeding happily in slower water when I slowed down to take a close look. I have even seen fish rise to tiny olive mayflies in water with only a few inches of visibility. How the fish know the bugs are there, and how they can pick them out among the debris high water brings, I have not been able to figure out—but they sometimes do.

Of course, the larger the insect, the more chance trout will respond to it, and I have seen amazing activity on large mayflies like March Browns and Green Drakes in high water. I have also found that if big insects are around, fish may even be lying in the shallows waiting for them, unbothered by the skinny water because predators cannot see them in the dirty water. One day on the Beaverkill in New York State I saw a number of March Browns hatching in dirty water and

Large trout—especially large brown trout—love streamers because they eat larger prey. Streamers are best fished when light is low and are less effective on bright sunny days.

happened to spot a fish rise along a slow bank. I never saw another fish rise that morning, but by working up the bank I was able to catch a half-dozen large trout on March Brown dry flies that must have been waiting for the big duns to float by. Everybody else I saw that day was slugging streamers, and I felt pretty smug.

Streamer Time

Dirty water in spring and summer just screams for a streamer, and it is definitely an exciting way to fish. Even though the water is dirty, most of your strikes will be visual—either big swirls just below the surface or trout actually leaving the water in their desire to catch that minnow or crayfish that is trying to get away. In my experience, the best time to fish streamers is when the water is on the rise, so timing is everything.

As the water first begins to fill normally dry gravel bars and creeps up the bank, lots of food gets washed into the river and minnows and crayfish get dislodged from their normal haunts and swim around frantically, disoriented, trying to find a safe haven. Once the water has been up for a few days, the fishing does not seem to be as productive, probably because a trout that eats a half-dozen baitfish needs to rest and digest those big meals before it feels compelled to go on the prowl again. Although I have heard other people say dropping water is better, that has not been my experience, but every river is different and perhaps different rivers produce well at different stages of high water.

This is not the time for a slim, elegant streamer. Trout can see in the dirty water, but they also use their lateral line sense to pick up the vibrations of a struggling piece of food, so the streamer you pick on a rise of water should present some resistance to the water to help fish find it. The palmered hackle along the body of a Woolly Bugger or similar streamer, the cone-shaped deer hair head of a Muddler Minnow or the wedge-shaped head of Tommy Lynch's Down & Dirty, or the trimmed yarn head and heavy rabbit fur of Schmidt's Junk Yard Dog all seem to fit the bill. Don't go too small either. A 4-inch streamer is not too big for a 14-inch trout, and is much more attractive to a fish much larger.

Streamer fishing is best in rivers with brown trout. Browns become mostly ambush feeders when they get to a size over 16 inches, and although rainbows, cutthroats, and brook trout also eat streamers, they are not as likely to inhale a streamer as a large brown trout—just look at the teeth on a brown trout compared to the teeth on any other trout to see the advantage they have over other trout species. I have scars on my thumb and first finger to prove that big brown trout have larger and sharper teeth, much better for attacking baitfish. Rainbows and cutthroats remain mostly invertebrate feeders no matter how large they get, but some very large browns switch to eating the bigger stuff with backbones and may only deem to sample insects during very heavy hatches of large bugs when they just can't resist. So a rise of water and the abundance of big helpless food is a rare opportunity to catch one of those large browns you never see rising.

The small river in my backyard supports wild brook, brown, and rainbow trout, and I mostly fish it with dry flies in the evening. The average fish I catch is around 8 inches long, and for years I knew there were large brown trout right behind my house because the state would electroshock the river every couple of years and would invariably pull out a 4-pound brown. But I never saw any of these large fish rising. Ever. Then one night the river went up after a thunderstorm and I walked down to it with my wife and son and dog, with a single streamer tied to my rod and no other tackle or flies. Within three casts near a tangled logjam, a brown trout the weight of about seven of the trout I usually catch grabbed the streamer, and although I didn't get a picture, I have witnesses. It's never happened again, but I must have caught the rise of water just right, when that fish was out and on the prowl.

How do you fish a streamer during a rise of water? I am not sure it even matters as long as you keep it moving, because a fish that is on the loose looking for a big meal will do everything it can to capture its prey. Upstream, downstream, across-stream—it seems to be just a matter of covering a lot of water, either in a drift boat or by wading constantly, only making one or two casts at every likely spot. You should not be afraid to retrieve your fly as fast as you can possibly move it. Not all the time, but sometimes a streamer moving very quickly elicits a reaction strike from a trout, and I don't think you can move a streamer faster than a trout can catch it. But probably the best approach is to vary your angles and retrieve speeds until you find something the fish like—even then, don't get into a set routine because every pool and every location within a pool sets up different currents.

Other Times to Fish Streamers

Streamers are not quite as effective if the water has not risen, but there are still other times to fish them. Early morning is one of the best times to fish streamers, because night-prowling fish may still be looking for a last morsel, and to your benefit you will be able to see where you are casting and wading. By early morning, though, I am not talking about having a light breakfast and getting on the water as the sun rises. This is crack-of-dawn fishing, which means you should be on the water and ready to fish a half hour before sunrise, and will probably quit fishing streamers after about an hour of fishing, after which you should switch to nymphs. Those meat-eaters will retire to their lairs as soon as the sun touches the water, but the smaller fish picking off the last remnants of nocturnal drift will sometimes feed well into the morning—and if there is a morning hatch, they may feed until early afternoon.

Those bigger fish may also prowl the shallows in the evening, just before dark and, of course, well into the darkness. I was recently fishing the tail of a pool on a favorite river after sunset; mayfly spinners covered the water, so there were many fish feeding. I had already caught a few nice ones when I noticed what looked like an unusually violent rise, not like the quiet sip of a trout taking a spent spinner, then another violent rise slightly downstream where I saw the first one. Then a serious wake rolled over the tail of the pool into the riffle below, and the fish began slashing back and forth in the riffle. It was obviously a larger trout trying to pick off the smaller fish feeding on insects.

You probably think I'm going to tell you that I wisely cut back my tippet, knotted on a streamer, and caught the biggest trout of the night. Wrong. I didn't feel like changing my tippet, so I continued to fish to the risers and enjoyed the show, watching the big trout charging smaller fish. But I have no doubt that if someone had tossed a streamer in front of that fish, it would have snapped up the fly like a Labrador retriever diving after a hot dog that falls off the table.

Dark days in general are best for streamer fishing, and even if the water is low and clear, you might have success fishing a streamer during one of those low-ceiling days when the entire landscape seems shrouded in cloud. A drizzly rain makes the fishing even better because the fish are bolder and less suspicious under low light. Even a driving rain is good for streamer fishing, although I would not put on a streamer right at the onset of a rainstorm. I have watched feeding trout as rain begins, and initially the surface disturbance puts them off the feed as they seem to wonder what is going on, but within 5 to 10 minutes, they adjust to the surface disturbance and begin feeding again.

Rigging Streamers

The easiest way to rig for streamer fishing is to merely cut your leader back to about 3X. If you are using a knotless leader and unsure of where you are in the taper, just pull a spool of 3X tippet material from your pocket and eyeball it alongside your leader. This works most of the time, especially on dark days with water temperatures in the optimum range (55 to 65 degrees), but there are other methods to try that may work when the tried-and-true routine falls short.

On bright days, you can try a streamer in the middle of the day and you can sometimes interest a fish, but stripping a streamer in the typical aggressive manner is not as productive as slowing down on your retrieve. One way to fish a streamer on sunny days is to scale down to a size 10 or 12 streamer like a small Conehead Marabou Muddler and fish it upstream, just keeping enough tension on the line that you can feel a little resistance at the end of each strip, but basically just keeping up with the current. Your fly darts downstream a bit, then drifts with the current, then darts again. It may look like a crippled baitfish or perhaps a sculpin that was flushed out of its hiding place beneath a stone in a riffle.

Not all of the baitfish trout eat are large. Sculpins are a favorite prey of trout because they aren't as fast as other baitfish, and some of them are quite tiny. When trout are spooky, sometimes it makes sense to scale down your streamer patterns.

"But wait a minute," you protest. "I thought trout are suspicious of prey coming at them, that they always want to see their prey swimming away." This may be true in a lake or in the ocean, but when a baitfish is crippled it has only one way to drift, and that's with the current, downstream. I have observed sculpins closely for hours in the little river in my backyard, and when one is flushed from beneath its hiding place under a rock or log, it invariably swims downstream. Sculpins are designed to hug the bottom, not slip upstream with ease, and the only way they can pick up any speed to avoid a predator is to move with the current. So trout, facing into the current, see plenty of baitfish coming at them. And if those theories don't convince you, let me add that I've caught many trout by casting a streamer directly upstream, too many to count as random events.

A small Muddler of some sort makes a decent sculpin imitation. The deer hair head of a Muddler simulates the profile of the broad head and large pectoral fins of a sculpin, and the squirrel tail and mottled turkey wings of the artificial give the fly the same mottled pattern as a sculpin's back.

A deadly streamer technique that is not used often is to fish a streamer, or a pair of streamers, or a streamer and nymph combination under a strike indicator. Here you don't want to move the streamer at all, because by moving the streamer you also move the strike indicator, which can make a noise only a largemouth bass at dawn would love. So this is truly fishing a streamer dead-drift, just as you would a nymph. I was shown this technique on the Madison River by guide Chris Eaton, and we fished streamers on a hot July afternoon with the sun beating down and caught trout. In fact, we caught more trout by fishing Woolly Buggers under indicators than we did fishing big dry flies, streamers in a conventional stripped retrieve, or small nymphs. I am not sure whether trout think a dead-drifting streamer is a helpless, almost dead baitfish; a crayfish drifting downstream; or a large stonefly or hellgrammite nymph. Regardless, the technique works when other streamer techniques don't, so it's worth a try on slow days.

In water 3 feet deep or shallower, during the late spring and early summer, you don't need to worry about where your fly swims in the water column. Fish will see it and will either ignore it or grab it. However, in deeper water it makes sense to try to get your fly deeper—even in low water if a pool is deeper than 3 feet because trout might not be able to see it, or aren't inclined to chase it if they are 6 feet down and your fly is riding just under the surface. There are two philosophies about getting a fly down: either fishing a weighted fly on a floating line, or fishing an unweighted fly on a sink-tip line. Both work well, but sometimes one approach works better than the other.

In smaller streams, where pools might only be 30 feet or less in width, you need to get your fly down quickly and don't have the luxury of setting up a drift by casting well upstream of the fish, so a weighted fly makes sense. The weighted fly gets down right away, as opposed to a sinking line, which needs some time to get through the water column and actually needs a few strips to pull it down deep enough to be effective. This is especially true in pocketwater, where deep mini-pools behind and in front of jumbles of boulders create pockets that are not practical to cover with a sinking line, which often gets caught in the rocks between you and the fly.

In bigger and smoother water, though, a fly, either weighted or unweighted, fished on a sink-tip line will stay in the deep water longer because when it is retrieved, it stays deep, unlike a weighted fly fished on a floating line, since after a few strips the floating line draws the fly toward the surface. If you don't want to bother with switching fly lines, a nice alternative is to use weighted poly leaders, which loop onto the end of a floating line and give almost the same presentation as a sink-tip fly line. In this case your fly can be weighted or unweighted, and there is no clear answer as to which type will work best. Some anglers argue that baitfish swim freely and thus an unweighted fly makes more sense; others argue that baitfish like sculpins, which are poor swimmers, do make quick darts to the bottom as a weighted fly does. Regardless of which streamer type you experiment with, you don't need a tapered leader on these—just a 2- to 6-foot piece of 2X or 3X tippet looped to the loop on the end of a sink-tip line or sinking leader.

Now, you can use a weighted fly in combination with a sinking line or leader, but most of the proponents of this kind of streamer fishing prefer unweighted flies, streamer specialists like Mike Schmidt of Ohio and Tommy Lynch of Michigan. They prefer unweighted flies because they feel they get better action on the fly by using lots of flowing materials in its construction with no weight added. Some of the flies they use also sport wedge-shaped deer hair heads, which give the fly a great diving action but tend to raise the fly to the surface if not ballasted down by a sinking line.

So besides water types, you may choose a style of streamer based on what you want the fly to do. Weighted flies bob up and down with a jigging motion, which may imitate a sculpin or a crayfish diving for the bottom. Unweighted flies exhibit more of a darting motion, more suggestive of baitfish like small trout, dace, chubs, or young whitefish. Of course, you may not know if a river has more sculpins than mid-water swimmers like chubs and dace, so the best plan of attack is to try both. Start with a weighted fly and a floating line in a few pools, and if that does not produce, try switching to a sinking leader and unweighted fly to see if one type of action appeals more to the trout than the other.

If you really want to push your game, try fishing two streamers at the same time. Try a big one for the upper fly and attach a smaller streamer on a piece of tippet the same size as your main tippet (not a lighter tippet as you would when fishing two nymphs, because the tendency to tangle is greater when stripping streamers). Try a light one and a dark one. Try a slim one and a noisy one. But be aware that this method has its drawbacks and should probably not be part of your standard routine. First, you need a heaver rod, at least a 6-weight and more likely a 7- or 8-weight. This is not a fun combination to cast, so fish at closer distances than you would with a single streamer. Also, fish may make a pass at the upper fly, and when you strike you may foul hook them with the second fly. Some days it happens more than others, so if you foul hook more than one fish in an hour of fishing, either wading or from a boat, I suggest you go back to a single fly.

Some days trout just flash or boil at streamers and don't often connect. It may be a territorial response, your fly might be too big, or perhaps they are just overly cautious that day. It can be frustrating, but at least you have located a fish to come back to another day. You probably did nothing wrong because a fish that wants a streamer is hard *not* to hook, but you might try either slowing down or speeding up on your retrieve to see if a change in speed alters their mood. Just don't worry about experimenting with too fast a retrieve, because you can't strip faster than a trout who really wants to eat your fly can swim.

THE FRUSTRATION OF HATCHES

Most of what you'll hear about regarding hatches is fishing to a hatch, or matching your fly to an adult insect riding on the surface. Yet this stage of the insect is not as important to trout as just when the insects break through the surface film and also when they fall to the water, spent after mating and laying eggs. The reason is simple: At these times, the insects are easier for trout to capture and less likely to give the trout a mouthful of air as it rises to the surface and opens its mouth just as the adult insect flies away. Insects trying to emerge from subsurface to above the water get trapped in the surface film—it's hard work breaking through that layer, as the old grammar school trick of floating a needle on the surface of the water shows. It's also why our heavier-than-water dry flies float. And those spent flies, well, they just aren't going anywhere—ever—until they sink to the bottom and die.

Large streamers like the Drunk & Disorderly (center) and Junk Yard Dog (bottom) present the large profile that often entices large brown trout—the kind that are hardly ever caught on a fly. The bulky heads create vibrations in the water, there are lots of feathery materials and furs to make the fly wiggle, and they are often tied without weight and fished on a sinking line to keep them in the strike zone longer. At the top is a standard size 8 streamer for comparison.

The frustration around hatches is almost a cliché. You see adult insects on the water, so you pick the fly in your box that looks like the insect you see riding the water or the one you have swiped from the air with your hat. And the fish either ignore your fly or they swipe at it, making a splash but leaving you with a slack line when you expected to feel weight on the end when you set the hook. What most people do then is to try a different fly pattern, thinking that the fish are being very selective today. Now, perhaps there are other insects on the water that you don't see, or perhaps your fly was dragging a bit, looking unnatural to the fish. But I swear to you that switching to a fly that rides just in the surface film is more often what turns the tables, as long as you are certain your fly is not dragging.

When fishing emergers, it's not so important to have exactly the right fly pattern as it is to have one that presents the right helpless profile to a fish. In fact, most of the emergers

I use double as imitations of mayflies, caddisflies, and even emerging midges when tied small enough. Any fly that has a wing that sits right in the surface film, a body that hangs down into the water, and something that looks like a shuck hanging off the end to imitate the larval shuck that the insect is trying to release itself from will most likely do the trick. The size has to be right and the color should be in the ballpark, but other than those aspects, the flies themselves all look about the same because an insect emerging from a shuck does not have the clean lines and silhouette of the newly hatched adult. They're a mess.

The Quigley Cripple is a goofy-looking fly that does not look like a typical dry fly—until you see it on the water.

Once you add fly floatant to the front half of the Quigley Cripple, it makes the perfect profile of an emerging mayfly. The wing stays upright like an unfolding wing (and helps you track your fly on the water), yet the rear half hangs down in the surface film like a nymph trying to struggle out of its shuck. Any good emerger pattern should have these qualities: something for you to track above the water and something just below the surface film that imitates an insect trying to get out of its shuck.

We seldom fish emergers as much as we should for a couple of reasons. One is that most dry flies are tied to imitate the adult insects we see flying in the air or riding the surface. The other is that emergers are just plain harder to see because they ride so low in the water, and if you can't see your fly, even more important than not seeing the strike is that you don't know if your fly is drifting right over the fish, nor can you tell if your fly is dragging.

There are ways to make this easier. You can pick an emerger pattern with a little white foam tab on top. You can also try an emerger with a wing of either deer hair or rabbit's foot hair, both of which are easier to spot on the water than an emerger made from CDC. Or you can try a parachute pattern like a Klinkhammer or Parachute Adams where the body rides low in the surface film but the fly has a highly visible upright wing so you can track it.

A further variation, based on the famous fly called the Quigley Cripple, developed in California by Bob Quigley in 1978, is a pattern where the wing is tied out over the eye at about a 45-degree angle, combined with tails of soft material that does not float as well. This fly sits in the water with the body hanging below the surface but with a wing that sits more or less upright, and that body hanging below the surface seems to be enough of a trigger to interest the fish. Quigley originally tied this fly to imitate a mayfly that was "crippled" or stuck in its shuck, but I also find the pattern to be an excellent imitation of an emerger, and flies of this style have been deadly for me over the years.

I have honestly not had as much success with parachute flies as true emergers when fish are snotty. I think they do notice the wing riding high above the water and thus think it's an adult instead of an emerger. But it's worth a try before going to a less-visible emerger pattern.

Yet another trick is to use two dry flies. Pick a fly with a highly visible white wing like the venerable Parachute Adams or even a big foam dry fly like a grasshopper or stonefly imitation. Tie a piece of tippet, about 2 or 3 feet long, to the visible fly and tie your emerger pattern to that. Now you have something to track, so you know where your emerger is at all times and can tell if it is in the right position even if you can't see it.

This arrangement has a couple of drawbacks: One is that it does not cast as easily as a single fly, and it might be hard to put your fly in the exact position you want it. The other is that sometimes trout will come up for the bigger fly, refuse it with a splash, and then you foul hook the fish on your trailing fly when you set the hook. Still, there are times when trout surprise you and grab the bigger fly with authority.

The Mystery of Spent Flies

Spent insects, whether they are caddisflies, mayflies, or stoneflies, are a mystery to many anglers because they often fall to the water quickly, under our radar, and we're surrounded by rising fish but can't see anything on the water. Mayflies aren't so bad because if you get your noggin close enough to the

Emerger flies that sit low in the surface film are some of the most effective dry flies during insect hatches, but they are devilish to keep track of on the water. One approach is to tie a small emerger to the hook of a much larger, highly visible fly that you can see under any *light condition. Follow the progress of the larger fly, and if you see a rise anywhere near it (or the large fly suddenly gets pulled under), set the hook. You'll also sometimes be surprised by fish taking the big dry when you don't expect it.*

surface, you can usually pick out mayfly spinners in the film. But when a size 18 dark gray caddisfly hits the water in a riffle 100 yards upstream of you and drifts down to the fish feeding in front of you, there will be little warning and no visible indication of what the fish are eating. Just as bad is when trout eat those tiny spent caddis while a big mayfly hatches in front of you. You can see the mayfly plainly and you keep switching fly patterns while those sneaky little caddis drift right under your nose, feeding the trout.

Just as with emerging flies, often a high-floating dry fly does not present the right profile to the fish. It's true that some mayfly spinners ride the water for quite a distance before falling prone to the water, but most mayflies and caddisflies are stuck down in the surface film, presenting no profile above the water and making it extremely difficult for you to spot them. And as with emergers, the fish sometimes refuse flies where the wing sticks up too high.

You can choose spent flies with some kind of upright wing and sometimes it works, but I have noticed that when I try to get clever and put an orange post on top of my spent patterns so I can see them, the fish seem to be less eager to inhale them as when the whole fly sits low in the film. The solution here, as with emergers, is to tie a spent mayfly or caddisfly behind a highly visible dry fly, or just cast into the darkness and strike whenever you see a rise somewhere near where you think your fly is. I typically choose that latter approach simply because many flies fall spent to the water just before dark, and I hate the thought of having to unravel a tangle of two flies with just a few minutes of light left.

How do you tell when you have a spent fly scenario? One way is to check the riffles, especially if you can get the sun behind the riffle, because when you look into the sun, you

When mayfly spinners fall to the water with their wings flat on the surface, even a large fly can be hard to spot from more than a few feet away. The only way to spot them is to bend down and get a close look at the surface, preferably in the same current lane as the feeding trout.

A good spent caddis imitation should float low in the surface film and should not have palmered hackle on the body like the Elk Hair Caddis on the right. You can turn an Elk Hair Caddis into a better spent caddis (or emerging caddis) imitation by giving it a haircut, like the one I have modified on the left.

can often see the shimmering waves of insects in their mating dance that suddenly become invisible when you change your angle and look at a riffle with the sun at your back. If flies are still very high above a riffle, you probably have plenty of time to get to a good spot in a pool. But if they are just above the water or you actually see them hitting that water, timing is critical. Get to a place you suspect holds trout right away, as sometimes these spent insects fall en masse in a matter of a few frantic minutes, and the fall can be over before you know it.

The Elk Hair Caddis on the right is fine for times when fish are chasing adult caddisflies skittering across the surface. But during most caddis hatches, lower-floating flies that sit in the film, like the Eck Caddis on the left or the generic soft hackle on top, will get you more trout and fewer refusals because spent or emerging caddis are trapped in the surface film and are easier for trout to capture.

Spent caddisflies are a little sneakier because they migrate for weeks every night before finally deciding to mate and lay eggs. So you might see caddisflies in the air, but if none of them hit the water and you don't see them bouncing on the water to release their egg masses, nothing may happen that day. One sure way to know when caddis are spent on the water is to look at your waders. Many species crawl underwater or onto rocks and vegetation to lay their eggs, and during a fall of spent caddis, you sometimes see them clinging to your waders before you see anything on the water or even any fish rising. Then it's an easy task to pick a fly from your box the same size and general shade as that fly and tie it on.

One thing you might have to do, because not many fly shops carry spent caddis patterns, is to trim any hackle from the fly so that it floats low in the water. You may even want to thin out the wing a bit, especially in a fly like the Elk Hair Caddis. Commercial versions of this popular fly are tied way too heavily for the more subtle profile you need for a spent caddis, because that fly is tied to imitate the fluttering of an adult caddis's wing, not a half-drowned caddis lying helpless in the film.

Another option is to fish a soft-hackle upstream, just like a dry fly. You won't be able to see your fly, but soft-hackle flies are typically tied without any weight so the fly drifts just below the surface, close enough that when a fish takes your fly, you will see a rise or perhaps just a swirl. Strike gently when you see a disturbance anywhere near where your fly might be.

What if you can't see your dry fly?

Fishing a soft-hackle just under the surface brings up a point that may help you get to the next level of your fishing. Tiny flies, flies just under the surface, and almost any kind of dry fly at last light in the evening are difficult to see. I always hear of people giving up in one of these circumstances because they can't see their fly. Now, I'll give anything to be able to see my fly, and will also sometimes use a fly that is not quite right but more visible than an exact imitation, but there are times, such as when fishing a flush-floating spent imitation just before dark, when you just won't be able to see your fly. Even anglers with the best eyesight possible don't always see their flies, but they don't give up.

Estimate where you think your fly might be, put it over the fish, and strike to the rise. There are times when fishing an evening fall of mayfly spinners or spent cadis, the fish go crazy. You might cast to a spot where three or four fish are rising every few seconds, in very close proximity to each other, and you could potentially have a strike on every cast you put over them. In this case, the drill is to cast, wait until you think your fly is over the pod of fish, and gently strike on every cast that does not go awry. Fish in this situation are seldom very spooky, and you can probably get away with repeated strikes without bothering them. It's really the only way—just have faith in your fly and your presentation and keep at it. You might strike a dozen or more times over the same group of fish before you finally connect. I know it's not as satisfying as seeing a fish take your dry fly, but it's also pretty satisfying when you finally connect almost into the darkness. Often a fish like this is the biggest one of the day, and you might have to remove the hook after dark using your flashlight.

Prospecting with Dry Flies

Prospecting with dry flies, sometimes called blind-fishing with dry flies, becomes an effective strategy in late spring, when lots of insects are on the water all day long. The waters also get lower and clearer, so the fish can always see insects floating on the surface, and it is not so much of a struggle to rise to the surface to take a floating insect. This way of fishing works better on rivers with a sparse food supply, like mountain streams and freestone rivers not interrupted with a dam. It is less effective on tailwaters and spring creeks until later in the summer, because these fish are so well fed on their rich food supply that they can afford to wait for the abundance of a hatch before coming to the surface.

But it can work even in rich streams at times. I was fishing a very rich tailwater river in May in the late afternoon, waiting for the Rusty Spinners I saw hovering over a riffle to drop to the water. The spinners fell, and for a brief flurry the fish rose and I was able to catch a few risers. The spinner fall was short-lived, though, and after an hour I saw few spinners on the water and no rises. I already had a Rusty Spinner tied to my tippet and a whole riffle in front of me, so I decided to work the riffle blind, as I would have done in a freestone river—even though I didn't think much of my prospects. I was pleasantly amazed when I plucked a half-dozen fish from the riffle in an hour. I never saw any of them rise, yet they must have still been on the alert for one last spinner. The other possibility was that they actually were rising sporadically, but I couldn't see them. Regardless, if I hadn't blind-fished that riffle, my day would have been nowhere near as productive.

The Parachute Adams is the most popular fly in the world, and sometimes it seems like the pattern imitates any kind of insect, even though it looks like very few of them. There is just something about this fly that appeals to trout interested in surface food, and it is one of the best patterns to try when prospecting with a dry fly.

So your first option when prospecting with a dry fly is to show the fish something they ate a few hours ago or yesterday. The other option is to go with two dry flies—perhaps a big foam pattern that just has to catch their attention, along with a smaller fly more suggestive of a recent hatch. Sometimes the fish come up to look at the big fly, decide it's too much, but drop back and eat the more subtle fly. But I would seriously not sweat the fly pattern too much, and if at a loss as to what to begin with, a Parachute Adams in size 14 or 16 is always a good bet, anywhere in the world. Because there is no hatch going on, at least not one that brings the fish to the surface, it's more a matter of reading the water and putting something that looks like food into places where a trout is comfortable rising to the surface.

This type of fishing is best in moderate to fast current, in water less than 4 feet deep. Gentle riffles, fast water at the head of a pool, and pocketwater are the best places to prospect with a dry fly. In these places fish have to make a quick decision, and even if the fly is not the pattern of the moment, if it looks buggy, it is probably close enough.

Great water for prospecting with a nymph or dry fly. Not too deep, enough riffle to make the fish feel secure and to mask your presence, and fast enough that trout have to make a quick decision on whether to eat your fly.

This would be very tough water for prospecting with a dry fly. The fish can see your movements, and the water is slow so that they get too good a look at your fly and deeper so they may be reluctant to move to the surface. Better to save this kind of water until trout get preoccupied with a hatch.

In the same light, when prospecting with a dry, I would pass up big wide flats, slick tails of pools, and deeper water in the middle of a pool. Fish there are tougher to approach and less inclined to come to the surface, and if you don't know exactly where the fish live, chances are blind-fishing over them will place the fly line over more fish more often than placing the fly in exactly the right place, so you will end up just spooking those fish. Save them for times when a hatch is on and they are visibly feeding on the surface so you can get more precise targets.

Nymph Fishing in Spring and Summer

Nymph fishing is even more productive all through the spring and summer than it is in winter and early spring, and the techniques are pretty much the same. As the water gets lower and some spots in a river get really shallow and slow, though, if you continue to fish with a strike indicator, you probably want to concentrate on more riffled water, where fish don't get quite as good a look at your fly, where the immature insect larvae live, and where a strike indicator landing on the water doesn't spook them.

Getting very close to the bottom is not as much of an issue now, because insects hatch daily and trout are able to handle the current better and will range throughout the water column taking their food instead of staying glued close to the bottom. When a hatch is just beginning or in progress, you may even catch trout when your nymph starts to drag at the end of the drift because trout chase emerging nymphs right up to the surface. A plastic or cork strike indicator is fine in the heaviest water, but for shallow water or slower currents, you may want to switch to yarn indicators because they land softer and are less likely to spook fish.

Additionally, because fish are spookier in clear, shallow water, you should pay attention to your mends and make them a little less aggressive to avoid disturbing the water too much. One strategy that helps is to make sure both the tip of your fly line and the butt section of your leader stay floating and don't hover below the surface, because mending right to the indicator is noisier and more difficult when you have to drag them up to the surface first. The tips on all fly lines eventually begin to sink when they get dirty, because the lighter-than-water plastic coating at the tip of a fly line

Keeping the butt section of your leader floating helps mending when fishing a nymph, helps keep dry flies floating, and lessens drag because on the surface there is less force on the leader than there is when it is under water. Yes, the leader will cast a shadow, but so does everything else floating in the surface film.

is thinner than it is farther along the line where the line is thicker. Therefore, frequent cleaning of your line, especially the last 15 feet of the line before it connects to the leader, is essential.

Fly lines should be cleaned after each trip (notice I said *should* because I'm not as diligent at this as I should be, and I know you'll be smarter than me) so that they float right on top. Merely strip your line into a bucket or sink filled with warm water and dish soap for a few minutes, then run the line through a soft cloth or paper towel with firm pressure. Do this until you stop seeing a gray streak on the cloth so you know your line is clean. In a pinch you can run your fly line through your shirttail while you are fishing if you notice the tip begin to sink, but be aware that for some reason these streaks on your shirt won't come off in the wash. Most of my fishing shirts are covered with little gray streaks from this practice.

To keep the butt section of your leader floating, apply some kind of grease or fly dressing to it between your fly line and your indicator. I have used paste fly dressing (my favorite), ChapStick, and even butter once when on a camping trip. Nylon's specific gravity is so close to water that all it takes is a light coating to keep it floating, and I wouldn't worry about its shadow spooking fish, as you will sometimes hear. Fish see all kinds of floating junk on the water that cast shadows on the bottom, and unless your leader is greased right up to the fly, in which case it is more apparent that the fly is connected to an object, I don't think it bothers the fish one bit.

Close-in nymphing with the European technique also works well in summer, although it can be problematic because in this technique you must be close to the fish, and in lower water you can't always get close to the fish. But in the heavy water at the heads of pools and in deeper riffles, this technique can be deadly, and these are sometimes places that you can't fish effectively with any other method unless trout are actively rising to a fly. You can stick with the traditional method, but another option is to use a drop-shot rig, similar to the way conventional bass and walleye anglers fish with plastic worms. It requires tying a couple of droppers to the end of the leader.

Start with a 12-foot 4X leader and tie a 12-inch piece of 4X tippet to this with either a blood knot or surgeon's knot, but leave one tag end 4 inches long and don't trim it. With the blood knot it doesn't matter if it's the original tippet on the leader or the second piece, but for the surgeon's knot make sure you begin with a long tag end from the original piece attached to the leader and not the new tippet. You want this dropper to point down toward the end of the leader, not stick

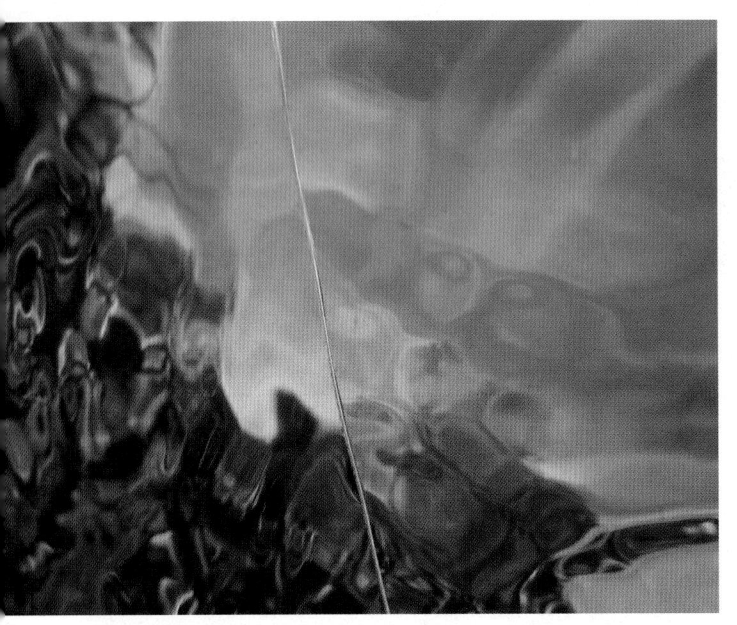

In very still, smooth water, a floating leader butt is quite apparent from underneath, so you may not want to use a greased leader butt in this kind of situation.

But in the normal broken water we usually fish, the visibility of the leader from underwater becomes a non-issue. The reflections of the bottom from the broken surface and the bubbles and swirls make a floating leader much less obvious.

up along the standing part of the leader because it will tangle easier this way.

Now tie on a 12-inch piece of 5X tippet to the long part of the 4X you just tied on. This time make sure you leave the tag end of the 4X tippet long because this is where you attach your second fly, and the stiffer, heavier piece is less likely to tangle. Tie about four half hitches in the terminal end of the 5X piece—this is where your weight will go, and the knots at the end are merely to keep your weight from slipping off.

Next, attach a split shot or two or three to the very end of the tippet, right above the knot, and tie on two flies in the droppers above. The advantage of this system is that your weight bumps along the bottom and almost never hangs up because there is no hook attached to it. The two flies ride just above the bottom and should not hang up unless you steer them into a big log. And if the weight does hang up, it usually just slips off the end of the leader and you can tie on more, without having to replace your valuable flies. Because this system is designed to lose weight occasionally, I recommend you use non-lead shot or tungsten putty so you avoid leaving lead on the bottom of the river—in fact, in some states like Vermont it is illegal to use lead shot anyway.

You can fish this rig with a more traditional leader and use a high-stick method, keeping your casts short and most if not all of your fly line off the water. Or you can go whole hog and use a much longer European-style leader with colored sighters. You will and should feel the drop shot bumping along the bottom, and you will soon learn to tell the difference between the shot bumping along the gravel and the longer, firmer stop when a fish or a snag grabs the shot.

What kind of floating line do I need?

Spring and summer are the seasons when all you will need on most trout streams is a floating line. There are a number of confusing choices, but you really can't go wrong with any floating line. The differences between the types are relatively small, and you can adjust your techniques to work with any kind of floating line.

The decision is based on what kind of fishing you do most often. Fly lines are constructed on a taper, including a level tip section (where you attach your leader), a front taper, a belly, a rear taper, and a running line. You see taper diagrams all the time where these sections are exaggerated, but honestly the differences are quite minor, and any high-quality fly line will cast well and present a fly just fine. When looking at the multiple types of floating lines available, many of the differences are just price points, with the most expensive lines offering more durability and a slicker surface for better line shooting. My advice is to buy the best fly line you can afford, because a good one will last you from two to five seasons, depending on how much you use the line and how much wear and tear you give it.

The more expensive lines come in both smooth and textured finishes. Textured finishes shoot better (the texture acts like dimples on a golf ball and reduces air resistance) and are best for longer casts, but they make a little noise when they run through the guides, which bothers some people. If you fish larger rivers and make a lot of long casts, you'll be better off with a textured finish, but there is also no downside to the textured finish on smaller waters as long as the noise doesn't bother you.

Your most important choice should be what kind of taper you pick. The two basic taper choices are weight forward and double taper. It's often said that a double taper, which has a much longer, heavier belly and no running line in the middle, will bend a rod more and slow down its action, but this is

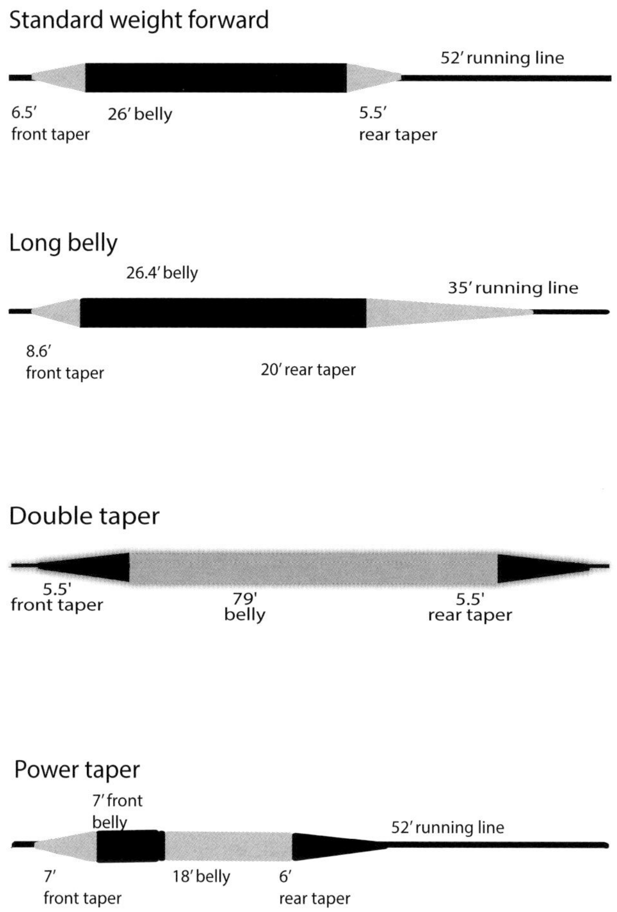

Standard weight forward

52′ running line
6.5′ front taper
26′ belly
5.5′ rear taper

Long belly

26.4′ belly
35′ running line
8.6′ front taper
20′ rear taper

Double taper

5.5' front taper
79' belly
5.5' rear taper

Power taper

7′ front belly
52′ running line
7′ front taper
18′ belly
6′ rear taper

Exaggerated diagrams of floating line tapers, highlighting the differences noted in the text.

only true beyond 35 feet. What most anglers don't realize is that weight-forward and double-taper lines have exactly the same taper for the first 35 feet. Weight-forward lines quickly slim down after that to a thinner running line, which provides less resistance when shooting a lot of line. Double tapers keep their belly diameter throughout the entire middle of the line and then taper down at the end in a mirror image of the front section. In fact, they are designed to be reversed after a lot of use—when one end wears out and begins to crack, as fly lines inevitably do, the line can be reversed.

Double-taper lines are not as much in favor as they used to be, but I have trouble understanding why. Most trout are caught within 40 feet, and both weight-forward and double-taper lines are the same over this distance, so why not just get a double taper and get a line that lasts twice as long? I have a feeling they are not as popular because most of us like to show off occasionally with a long cast, and weight-forward lines do allow you to cast farther because you can shoot more line at the end of the cast.

But double tapers offer other advantages. They make long roll casts easier, because the thin running line of a weight forward does not have as much mass beyond 35 feet and roll casts tend to collapse. And if long false casts are something you use often, they also hold more line in the air, because a thin running line hinges once a false cast gets beyond 40 feet. However, there are not many actual fishing situations where a false cast over 40 feet is practical, except for dry-fly fishing in very large rivers.

Why are weight-forward lines so popular? They offer as much delicacy as a double taper up to 40 feet, roll cast in short just as well, and when you want to reach out there, it is a much easier matter to shoot line to get distance. So they are a great general-purpose line, offering delicacy in close when you need it and the ability to fire a streamer to the far bank should you need to. Their one drawback in practical fishing situations is that the thinner running line does not mend on long casts as well as a double taper. This is because when you lift up the rod to mend line, it's better to have more mass to move, and you can mend farther because the heavier mass of the belly transfers the energy along the line better.

There is one type of compromise line called a long-belly weight-forward or easy-mend line. These extend the belly farther than a standard weight forward but not to the other end of the line like a double taper, so you still have the ability to shoot line on very long casts but also retain the ability to mend line easier up to about 50 feet. These are probably the most useful line and should be more popular than they are, because the compromises are minimal and they do everything well with the exception of very long casts, like 80 to 90 feet. But few trout are caught at that distance anyway.

One type of weight-forward line, sometimes called GPX, Bank Shot, or Grand, is a whole or half size heavier than the rated size on the package and has more weight distributed up front, with a shorter tip and front taper. These are designed for casting large streamers or large indicators when nymph fishing. They don't offer as much delicacy as other lines, so as an all-around line they are less useful: If you fish a lot of streamers and big nymphs with a lot of weight, you probably want one of these and also a more standard line for times when you aren't throwing flies and nymph rigs with a lot of mass. The heavy front eliminates the need to do much false casting, as you typically just pick up the line and fire a new cast, shooting any line you need for additional distance.

CHAPTER 8

Fly Selection and Fishing Strategy—Midsummer through Fall

As water levels get lower and temperatures rise, summer and fall fishing call for more of the same, smaller and lighter. This is the time of year that sorts out the casual fly fishers from the true diehards, so if you want to up your game, don't hang up your rod after the major hatches end in early July.

There is a difference in the impact of a 6-weight versus a 4-weight on the water, and because of the low, clear water, fish are spookier because they often don't have as much water over their heads. Even riffles are not as concealing as they were a month ago, because in the slower flows the surface disturbances smooth out. So trout may remain closer to overhead cover and shade because their biggest threats come from above. At the same time, though, don't assume that trout will always be hiding in the shade or in deep water. When food is plentiful, during a hatch or when a swarm of flying ants cov-

In late summer, food is not as plentiful and sometimes the best places to fish are shallow riffles. Insect food is produced in riffles, and fish in shallow water are sure to be eating, not just resting.

ers the water, fish will move into places where it is easiest to capture that food, even if it means lying in a foot of water out in the bright sunshine.

I've always found that fish in shallow water, away from cover, are actually easier to catch than fish lying in deep water at this time of year for a couple of reasons. One is that you know the fish in the shallows are eating—there is no other reason they would stay so exposed. The more they eat, the greater the chance you have to stick a fly in their jaws. Also, fish get preoccupied when eating and are not as alert to danger, thus you can approach them easier and get a cast to them with less chance of spooking them. So although you can't jump into a river with abandon and begin casting and actually catch trout as you could in May or June, with a little stealth, a lighter fly line, and a longer leader, you may find that trout are easier under these conditions than you would suspect.

This is also one of the best times to fish a dry fly. In spring and early summer, trout have masses of insects on the bottom and drifting through the water column all day long, so they don't have to look to the surface to feed. In July through October, many of the aquatic insects have hatched, leaving the riffles a virtual desert compared to what they were in spring. Much of the food in summer comes from above in the form of terrestrial insects falling into the water. Even hatches of aquatic insects are easier to capture on the surface because in the clear water of summer, trout can see floating food coming to them from a lot farther away than they can food below the surface.

Fishing is more difficult in late summer and fall for another reason: Trout just don't eat as much, and as often, at that time of year. They are genetically programmed to eat ravenously when food is abundant and then slow their metabolisms down when food is not as abundant, and their growth is highest during the dense insect hatches of late spring and early summer, but slows down by midsummer. We see this empirically when we go fishing, but what we see is backed up by science. Biologists studying the growth rates of trout by looking at microscopic sections of their otoliths, or ear bones, see denser growth rings at this time of year, much the same as looking at growth rings on trees. You will read about trout packing on the food in late summer and fall to prepare for winter, but the science does not bear this out.

Late summer and early fall conditions are much the same, at least until the first prolonged cold spell changes conditions somewhat, and I will address these slight changes later in the chapter. I have also not singled out high- and low-water conditions in this period for a couple of reasons. One is that you typically don't have much high water during this period—it's the driest time of year for nearly every trout river in North America. Also, the techniques and flies you use for the rare high-water periods in late summer and fall don't differ to any degree, other than you just won't find as much activity in these

The flat, shallow tail of a pool like this is the perfect spot for night fishing, where trout can cruise for baitfish, crayfish, and large insects and trap them in the shallows. The tributary coming in against the far bank also offers a cold-water refuge during warm summer water temperatures in the main river.

In bright sunlight, agile little dace in shallow water can see trout coming and are able to evade them easily. But after dark, it's a different story. They can't see predators but a trout can find them by feeling their vibrations with its lateral line "hearing."

periods because trout are not feeding as aggressively as they would in spring and early summer. So if you fished a stretch of river in June and had a fish slam your streamer every dozen casts, don't expect the same results in early September. If you go into it with that philosophy, you won't be disappointed when you only move one or two fish—it's the conditions, not your technique, so hang in there.

NIGHT FISHING

You'll hear that large trout, over 16 inches, do all of their feeding at night, which is patently false. Fish well into the 20-inch range will gorge on aquatic insect hatches if the hatch is heavy enough, and especially if the insect is large, like the Eastern and Western Green Drakes, Brown Drakes, Hexes, and the giant stonefly called the Salmonfly. I have caught many trout over 20 inches long on size 18 Rusty Spinners when the spinner fall is heavy. Large trout will also feed heavily during the day when a rainstorm raises and dirties the water, even in the dead of summer.

It is true, however, that as the season progresses, large trout do more of their feeding at night. This is particularly true with brown trout, which are the main quarry when fishing at night. Large rainbows will also feed at night, but not to the extent brown trout do. I have found that brook trout and cutthroats stop feeding at dark, although I am sure there are some places where they can be caught at night. From what I have read on trout physiology, brown trout have better eyesight at night and better perception of vibrations in the water through their lateral line system. And we already know they have the dental work suited for capturing large prey.

I have seen studies that show that brown trout may feed at night any time the water temperature is warm enough for them to be active. They may feed at night in April, but I have never heard of anyone fishing for them at night successfully in early spring. Whether it is easier for us to catch them or perhaps because they really don't feed much at night other than summer, I'm not sure, and there is probably some room for exploration in this matter. I will leave it to someone else, though, because night fishing and warm summer nights just seem to go together.

Night fishing is not a high-volume proposition. With rare exceptions, there are just not that many large brown trout in any given stretch of river. And although I have not seen any peer-reviewed scientific studies on how often large trout feed, I suspect they don't feed every night. A crayfish or two, a few large chubs, or a mouse requires some time to digest—depending on water temperature, they could take a day or so. So not only do you need to find the hunting grounds of a large trout, you have to find that trout in a hungry mood.

Also, not all the trout you catch at night will be giant—I have caught brown trout as small as 10 inches long well past midnight. That is not the kind of trout you want to miss sleep and stumble around in the dark for, but on a good night you might catch a few fish between 14 and 18 inches and one monster over 20.

Location and Weather

Location and weather are important. My best night fishing, and also that of anyone I've ever talked to, is on still, warm, humid nights. Maybe it's because those nights are more pleasant on the river than sweating in a warm bedroom, but on cooler nights I've never found the fishing to be as productive.

There is also the question of moon. I have heard a few people say night fishing is better on a full moon, but I suspect that is more because it's easier to see what you are doing and what you might stumble into when there is some ambient light. Most serious night fishers prefer a dark night, either a new moon or when the moon is hidden behind the clouds. It seems to be the light level rather than moon phase, because I've had good night fishing while the moon is hidden by the clouds, only to have it shut off when the clouds break and the moon shines on the water. And I have had other nights when even under a half-moon, fishing is poor until it gets covered by clouds and then it picks up.

Location for night fishing is critical. For safety and to avoid the frustration of hanging up in trees at night, scout the location you plan to fish. Wade out a bit to determine the slipperiness of the rocks and to find out if there are any submerged logs you might trip on or large, slanted flat rocks that might slide you into a deep hole. A mishap that might be funny in the middle of the afternoon could end tragically after dark. I'm not going to preach to you and suggest fishing with a buddy—I often like to fish at night alone, as it adds to the adrenaline rush and makes you feel adventurous. It's also pretty spooky, bringing you back to your childhood, and I think that one of the reasons we enjoy fishing is that it turns us into 12-year-olds who are still afraid of the dark.

Pick your night-fishing spots based on what makes a good hunting ground and not necessarily where you suspect a large brown trout may live. A study of night-feeding trout in Michigan found that fish will rove up to a mile from their daytime resting sites in slower water near cover, returning to the same resting site after feeding. There was obviously something attractive about that feeding site a mile away, and most likely it was a piece of flat, shallow water—the kind of water where you would never suspect to find a brown trout feeding. But when you think of how these big fish feed, it makes total sense: In shallow water prey have only one dimension in which to escape, whereas in deeper water they have not only horizontal distance but also depth to use for evading capture. And most baitfish and crayfish, the primary foods of night-feeding trout, are more abundant in shallow water. In my experience, shallow tails of wide pools and shallow riffles with moderate current are the best places for night fishing, followed by large expanses of flat, shallow water.

Night fishing is better in large rivers than in small creeks. Larger rivers will likely hold more large trout, and because night fishing requires a relatively long retrieve through open water (otherwise trout don't have time to find and track your fly), small streams are very difficult to fish at night. The stream behind my house harbors a few relatively large brown trout that I never see during the day, but as it is barely 20 feet wide in most places, it is not easy to fish at night.

Don't ignore large rivers well downstream of what is considered prime trout water either. Large browns often drop downstream in search of the larger baitfish they can find in warmer water. Because they are not active during the day, they can survive warmer water temperatures, lying near submerged springs or cold tributaries during the day and hunting actively at night when the water is cooler. There they live among the smallmouth bass and carp, sleeping by day and not pestered by anglers until somebody does some fly fishing at night for smallmouths and ends up with a 23-inch brown trout instead.

Flies and Techniques

Night fishing, unlike most midsummer fishing, is not the place for light rods and fine tippets. Break out your bass rod if you need to. Rods for night fishing should be at least 6-weights and as heavy as 8-weights. You will likely be fishing large flies and heavy tippets, compounded by fighting a large fish in water you can't see, so the need to horse a fish at night to keep it away from unseen snags is critical. Use a floating line and a leader that breaks at between 15 and 20 pounds. Cutting a standard knotless tapered leader in half and using the heavy half is just about perfect. This is a floating line game—you're fishing shallow water and need to be able to pick up your line easily.

Occasionally, when there is a hatch of large nocturnal mayflies or the fish are feeding on big moths or stoneflies that fall into the water, you can fish a large dry fly. Unless there is any moon at all, this is strictly fishing by ear. You hear a rise, cast to where you think the fish rose, and strike to any splash you hear in the darkness. You can't see if your fly is dragging, but with large dries at night, the fish don't seem to be bothered by drag, so you might even want to swing your dry fly downstream and strike when you feel pressure on the line. Large Wulffs, Hex imitations, large foam-bodied hopper and stonefly imitations, and the famous Stimulator are all good dry flies for night fishing.

Fishing a floating mouse or frog in the darkness is not only effective, it's probably the most exciting way to fish for large browns at night. Ones made from deer hair are the most popular, but foam patterns, or combinations of foam and deer hair or rabbit fur, are also popular. Even surface lures normally used for largemouth bass will work. Whatever fly you use, make sure it is wide enough to push water, because the wake

Mouse flies can be cute and realistic like the two at the top, but all a mouse fly needs to do is gurgle on the surface and create a wake. The more impressionistic fly at the bottom, made from foam and fur but sans eyes and whiskers, will be just as effective—but not nearly as much fun to carry around in your fly box.

on the surface is quite visible to trout from below, even on dark nights, and wide flies also make vibrations in the water that brown trout hear.

Carry some large flies and some small ones, as you never know what the fish will respond to. Because of the heavy tippet, you won't break off many flies and you may want to stick with the same pattern the whole time, but if you go for an hour without hooking a fish, you may want to try a larger or smaller fly. But these fish are not selective—they are out prowling for mice or frogs or large insects falling into the water, so anything that looks alive will probably elicit a strike.

The actual fishing is not difficult. Begin by staying on shore if you can and cast 30 or 40 feet into the middle of the river. Cover this area walking up or down the bank, then wade carefully into the shallows and work as close to the far bank as you dare. Some people use flies with weed guards to lessen the chance of hanging up in brush, but remember with that heavy tippet, you should be able to pull your fly out of most snags without breaking your leader. The best cast is straight across-stream or angling a bit downstream. Just let the fly swing in the current. You will probably hear a big splash, but do not set the hook until you feel weight on the end, as sometimes fish will slash at a fly before actually inhaling it.

If you are fishing a wide, shallow flat, you might carefully wade into the middle of the river and cast to both sides. The fish you are hunting are not lying in wait for their prey as trout do during the day. They are most likely actively hunting, so a place that does not produce a strike now might be productive 10 minutes later. How much you move depends on how confident you are that there are fish feeding nearby (you may hear some splashes in the darkness) and how much real estate you have scouted beforehand. In a large river you can spend all night in one giant pool, but in smaller rivers you may want to try several spots.

The other technique, not as exciting but in my opinion more productive, is to use an unweighted streamer, fishing it just under the surface. Your fly should ride shallow because

This is a great fly for fishing subsurface, or just in the surface film, at night. Black is the most visible color against starlight at night, and the wide head made from spun deer hair creates a great wake in the water. The fluffy marabou and fur behind the head also give it great action in the slower water you might fish at night.

fish won't be able to find it as easily close to the bottom. They see objects against the skylight, so if your fly is too deep, they will only be able to find it with their lateral line sense. Your fly can ride shallow enough to create a wake if you use a pattern with a deer hair head like a Muddler Minnow, or ride just below the surface with something like an unweighted Woolly Bugger. But any unweighted streamer with a broad profile should produce if the fish are there and eating. You can experiment with colors, but it doesn't seem to be important. Black is the most visible color against the skylight, but I have had equally good luck with Muddler Minnows, which are pale brown, and black Woolly Buggers.

If you have enough current, with either surface flies or streamers the best course is to just let the fly swing in the current. Once the fly hangs straight downstream, let it hang there for five seconds or so and then strip it back to you, because sometimes trout will follow a fly across the river but won't attack it until it pauses in the shallows. In water without much current, slow, steady strips may help keep the fly moving enough to interest fish, but keep your strips slow and about 6 inches per strip.

FISHING TERRESTRIALS

Terrestrial insects are thought to be only a summer opportunity for both anglers and trout, but careful observation will show you that ants and beetles are some of the first insects to become active in the spring, even before many of our early aquatic insect hatches. So theoretically flies and strategies to imitate terrestrial insects can be used any time during the season, but actually they are more effective as the summer progresses for a number of reasons.

There are more varieties and a greater density of terrestrial insects during the summer, because as the weather gets warmer, more species hatch and become active as the vegetation they feed upon becomes more abundant. But even more important is that trout notice them more. In the spring, when water levels are higher and clarity is often lower, trout find out about surface insects by following the emerging adults to the surface. Here they find lots more insects, trapped in the surface film, that are even more helpless and thus easier prey than the emerging nymphs. If a bunch of ants fall into the water in May, trout are often not aware of this unless the water is very clear or they are already at the surface eating mayflies or caddisflies. They don't see the ants fall in and seldom notice them floating on the surface.

But with low, clear waters in summer and more abundant terrestrial insect life, trout see a lot more of the surface and look there more frequently because much of the food they have been eating below the surface has already hatched. And

By this photo of a single sweep with an insect net along the bank of a trout stream, you can see why trout are seldom selective when eating terrestrials. There is a wide variety of shapes, colors, and sizes, and the chances of a trout seeing lots of the same thing are not as likely as a fish seeing many different insects.

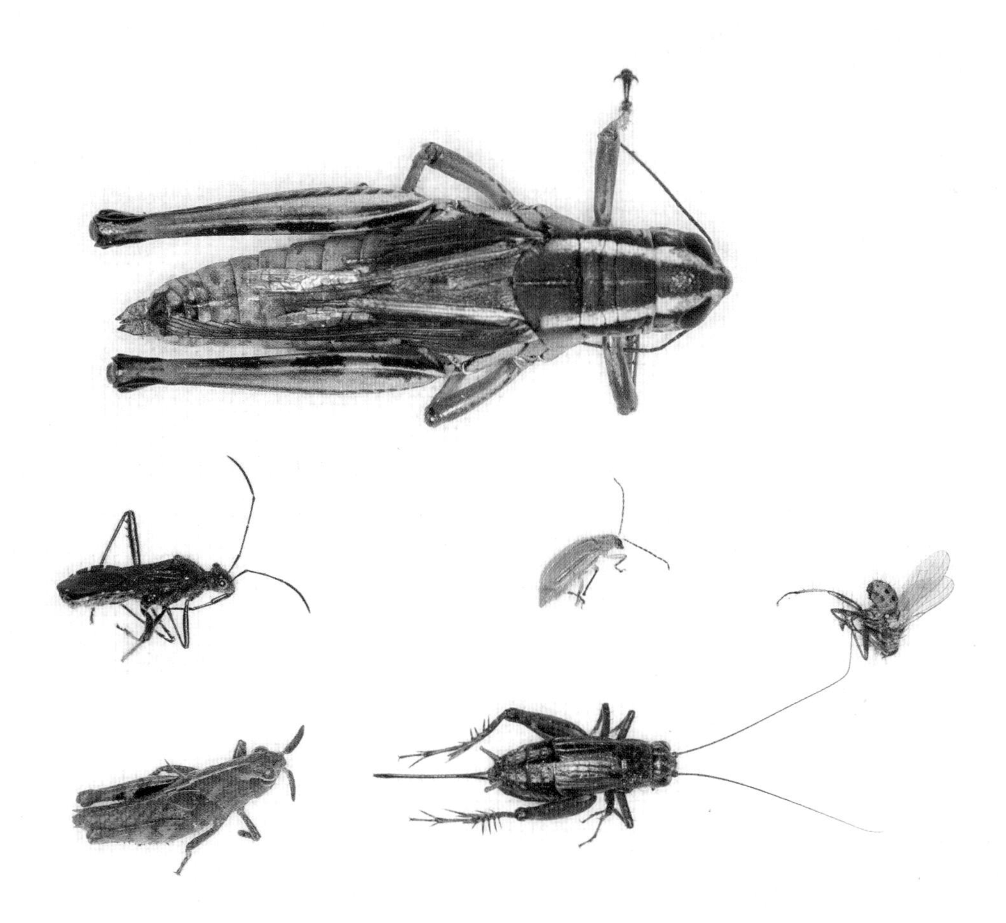

Grassy banks and overhanging foliage tell us the trout in here will eat a lot of terrestrials. But don't restrict your terrestrial flies just to this kind of water. Insects have wings, they get blown by the wind, and once they get into the water they can drift into the center of a big wide pool.

the variety of terrestrial insects is so diverse that most times trout are not very selective because they might see large beetles, small ants, medium-size moths, inchworms, grasshoppers, crickets, leafhoppers, house flies, wasps, and true bugs of all shapes and sizes and colors in the course of a day. As long as the fly you throw looks reasonably like some kind of terrestrial insect and not like a twig or piece of debris, and as long as it acts naturally and does not drag, a trout on the feed should eat it.

Terrestrial Strategies

Now that you are beginning to develop more knowledge about how trout feed and behave, get the idea out of your head that only trout lying along grassy banks eat terrestrials. It may be that a deep run along a bank is the best place for a trout to feed, and, yes, ants and beetles do fall into the water right along the bank. But most terrestrial insects also have wings. They fly into the water by mistake. They get blown into the water by the wind. And even if they fall into the water along the bank, the current eventually carries them to the center of a river. So just because you know trout live in a riffle 50 feet from shore does not mean they don't eat ants, beetles, and grasshoppers. By restricting your terrestrial fishing to grassy banks, you are really limiting your opportunities to catch trout in summer. Fish terrestrials any place you suspect trout live.

Because terrestrial fishing is almost always "blind" fishing (with rare exceptions, you don't see trout feeding regularly on terrestrials since they are targets of opportunity), your leader should be a minimum of 12 feet long, and for very clear water and spooky fish, 15 feet might be even better. Reduction of drag on your drift is even more important with terrestrials than with aquatic insects, because although most terrestrials might wiggle and struggle a bit, you can't imitate that by manipulating your line—any movements you make are too overt. We get the suggestion of the struggling of terrestrial insects by using materials like hackle and rubber legs to simulate movement.

There are exceptions to this suggestion. Larger insects like cicadas, grasshoppers, crickets, and moths do twitch and struggle, and these larger, stronger insects can swim a bit in the current, so the occasional twitch is not only acceptable, but it sometimes attracts trout. Just don't overdo it. Cast your fly, make a half-inch twitch with the tip of your rod, and then let the fly drift free. Maybe add another twitch

Larger terrestrials like grasshoppers do kick and struggle when they fall into the water, so an occasional subtle twitch may catch the attention of a trout. Just don't overdo it, because the amount of movement you can potentially create by twitching your rod is much more overt than the commotion a little insect can create.

as the fly begins to drag, because at that point it's going to move whether you like it or not. You can try a steady series of twitches if you want, but I have actually found that not moving flies like hoppers and moths is usually more effective than moving them at all.

If you don't try some of your terrestrial patterns sunk, you are probably also missing some opportunities, because terrestrial insects are not made for the aquatic life and don't stay on the surface for long. Trout are just as happy to eat them under the surface as they are plucking them from the film. Patterns like beetles and ants can be fished sunk merely by not adding any fly dressing to them, and then you just fish them as you would any nymph, dead-drift, with an indicator or not. A great way to fish them sunk is behind a larger terrestrial imitation like a grasshopper pattern or just one of the many variations of foam attractor flies. You catch the more aggressive trout on the large dry, and the trout with a little more reluctance to break the surface for a big ugly thing just might find a helpless sunken ant a great afternoon snack.

The bigger dries can be fished under the surface as well. Sunken hoppers have saved the day for me many times since I was shown this technique by my friend Steve Kenerk on the Popo Agie River in Wyoming. This stream runs through many grassy meadows, and the wind in Wyoming is invariably strong after 11 a.m. I could hear grasshopper wings ratcheting in the grass along the river, so I knew the trout would be on the lookout for them.

Steve and I separated to different parts of the river, and after an hour we got back together. I had gotten only a few half-hearted splashes at my hopper patterns, but Steve had hooked about a dozen. He crimped a couple of small split shot ahead of his hopper and had fished them under the surface. He didn't need any kind of strike indicator because the trout had taken the fly so firmly, there was no question of a strike. Now I will often fish a large floating hopper with a small Letort or Henry's Fork Hopper tied to the bend of the hook on the larger fly with 4X fluorocarbon and no floatant applied to the smaller fly. It's a deadly combination—not fun to cast with a light rod, but worth the effort.

Special Terrestrial Instances

Most times trout do not feed selectively when eating terrestrials. But there are rare instances when they do get picky, and it's always when you find large numbers of one particular insect on the water at once.

One obvious case is when grasshoppers are on the water. Different species of hoppers are abundant at different times throughout the summer, typically with small grasshoppers (often just immature versions of ones that will get bigger in late summer) more abundant in early and midsummer. By late summer, in some years we suffer through outbreaks of large numbers of grasshoppers that decimate agricultural crops, especially in the western United Sates. The only upside to these infestations is that trout gorge on the abundant food, and it's a good idea to have a grasshopper imitation that is close in size to the ones that are most abundant because a trout is more likely to recognize your artificial as food.

You don't often know what size grasshoppers you'll see, especially if you are on an extended fishing trip and traveling to a number of rivers, so it's a good idea to have a range of sizes from 4 through 10 in your box. The trout may not necessarily be selective to a larger hopper when locusts are raging through a river valley, but the larger fly probably gets noticed more than a smaller one would.

It's the same situation when periodic cicadas are abundant. Some species of cicadas hatch every year, but there are also species that live underground as nymphs for 13 or 17 years and then hatch in large numbers in certain years. However, you shouldn't plan a fishing trip to coincide with one of these hatches until you are certain the event will occur. Some years

A bunch of fresh cicada cases on the limbs and lower trunks of trees tips you off to the possibility of using a very large fly. It's easier to spot these cases than adult cicadas in the air, and because the adults are such big packets of protein, trout will move a long way to eat one.

a big emergence of 17-year cicadas is forecast and everyone gets all excited, but for reasons unknown to us they don't show up, or show up in disappointing numbers.

It's not so much that trout get selective to cicadas as it is that a cicada is such a huge bundle of protein that trout that won't move 8 inches to take a mayfly out of its feeding lane will move 6 feet if it hears the splat of a cicada on the water. This is one instance where expending a lot of energy on one bite is worth the additional effort. As a result, you can get pretty casual about where your fly lands and how it behaves because trout will go all out to get it and will throw most of their caution to the wind. The Green River in Utah is one stream with very reliable cicada hatches any time from mid-May throughout the summer, and throwing a large dry-fly pattern can get the attention of this river's brown and rainbow trout even if no fish are seen feeding on the surface.

Inchworms also exhibit periodic outbreaks, and although once again trout don't exactly feed selectively on them, inchworms fall into the water because they seem to prefer trees that overhang rivers. Fish stay on the lookout for these moth larvae even if they are not seen visibly surface feeding, because they know sooner or later a nice, juicy inchworm will make a mistake. So although it's not a matter of trout feeding selectively on them, by using a pattern that looks like an inchworm, you remove much suspicion from a trout rising to inspect your fly. And unlike most other terrestrial insects, which can be imitated quite well by standard trout flies, there are few patterns that look like an inchworm, so here you really do a need an inchworm-specific pattern.

One of the most exciting but challenging terrestrial opportunities is when swarms of flying ants or termites occur. Most ant colonies consist of a queen and wingless, sexually immature workers. Once a colony grows, the ants begin to raise sexually mature winged adults, which get pushed out of the colony to go on to form their own. Three to five days after a heavy rain, the winged ants swarm, mate, and all the males die and fall to the ground. Many of them fall in the water; in fact, for some reason they seem to be attracted to it. What makes these swarms so dense is that all the colonies in a given area seem to get the same cues at the same time, and as a result, many colonies in one area will swarm over a period of a few days.

Trout seem to relish flying ants—whether because of their abundance or because they taste good—and if you come upon a trout stream in late afternoon and find trout rising all over the place with no apparent insect hatch, you should immediately suspect flying ants. I often see them on the windshield of my truck or on my driveway. A swarm of flying ants is really not something you can predict. You happen on them by accident, but if you are near a trout stream and see scores of flying ants hitting your windshield, I highly suggest you drop everything and get to the river. It can be some of the best dry-fly fishing you will ever see at a time of year when heavy insect hatches of any kind are rare.

In the northeastern United States where I live, these swarms are most common from late July through early September, but I have talked to guides in the Southeastern states and in Western states who see swarms of flying ants as early as June. I suspect some of what we see is termites as opposed to ants, but again swarms of termites are not predictable, and although knowing whether a swarm is termites or ants might be important to you as a home owner, when you're fishing, I don't think you care.

This is the only terrestrial insect occurrence I know of that trout feed selectively upon. If you find yourself in the middle

Flying ants often cover the water but go unnoticed by anglers unless they look closely at the water's surface. Trout, however, seldom ignore them. For some reason, late afternoons two days after a late summer or early fall rain seem to bring them out.

This is the author's flying ant imitation, which also imitates many other small winged terrestrial insects. The name of the pattern is the General T, and it is simply a brown fur ant with a pair of pearl midge flash wings added. The midge flash imitates the transparent wings and also makes the fly easy to see on the water.

of an ant (or termite) swarm, often no type of standard dry-fly attractor or aquatic insect imitation will work. If you fish during the summer, it is always good insurance to have a few flying ant imitations in size 16 and 20 in your box, because sometimes you'll see swarms of larger ants and sometimes smaller ones, and sometimes two sizes at once. In my experience if both large and small ones are on the water, trout will eat the large one, which is a happy circumstance because the bigger ones are easier to see on the water. But if only small ants have swarmed and you don't have a small ant imitation, you could be in for some frustration.

I don't think the color is that important, and in a pinch you can get away with a standard ant pattern with no wings, but the nice thing about flying ant imitations is that they have white or pale gray wings that stick up, helping you track your fly on the water. If you don't have any ant imitations at all in your box, try the closest thing. A Griffith's Gnat, an adult midge pattern, and even a small Parachute Adams have all worked for me in a pinch—probably not as well as a flying ant pattern would have worked, but at least you won't go fishless!

Fly Patterns

With the exception of flying ant swarms and heavy grasshopper infestations, the exact terrestrial pattern you pick is less important than how and where you fish it. A size 16 black beetle of some type is a go-to pattern for many experienced anglers because most beetle patterns are made from foam and float better than other terrestrial flies. In addition, because beetles have wings, you can use a pattern that has something sticking up like a deer hair wing or small parachute post to help you see where your fly is drifting and whether it is dragging or not.

Equally important is that trout often eat terrestrial patterns with a very soft, almost imperceptible rise. These insects ride low in the surface film and trout know it is not getting away, so they can feed on them with the utmost of subtlety. You would be surprised—trout can even eat grasshoppers (and their imitations) with a soft rise that belies the size of the morsel they just inhaled.

If fish see a lot of grasshoppers with the typical tan coloration and red legs, a Dave's Hopper, with its more exacting features like red deer hair and knotted legs, might be the best way to fool the fish.

If an inspection of the streamside foliage turns up a large number of insects of one type or another, by all means try the closest terrestrial imitation you have in your box. The more familiar a food is to a trout, the more comfortable the fish is eating it. Pay attention to the time of day as well. Moths and beetles are more active early in the day than other terrestrial insects, so you might start out your day with either a beetle or an Elk Hair Caddis (a very fine moth imitation, by the way). Crickets and ants get more active later in the morning. Grasshoppers seem to need more warmth to get them going, and in most places they don't get active until almost noon. By that time the wind begins to blow on many trout streams, all the more reason trout may start eating grasshoppers.

All of these insects stay active through the evening hours. One of my favorite ways to kill some time before the evening hatch in summer is to fish a beetle imitation through riffles deep enough to hold trout. Most people don't think of fishing

Although the Elk Hair Caddis was designed to imitate an adult caddisfly, I also think it does a fine job of imitating moths or even tiny grasshoppers, so it is a good pattern to try if you think trout are eating terrestrials.

From underneath, a Royal Wulff might look like an ant or beetle to a trout. We may not think so, but we don't know exactly what a trout looks at when scrutinizing prey.

Even nymphs may be taken by trout because they look like a drowned beetle or ant. We think this bead-head Prince nymph is a stonefly imitation, but it sure works well in late summer when many drowned terrestrial insects drift down the currents.

terrestrial insects except in the middle of the day, but believe me, trout eat beetles whenever they can. I remember watching a lightning bug (actually a beetle) that had fallen into the water in a pool above me just at dark. I watched it float down the current: blink . . . blink . . . blink and then plunk! It disappeared into the substantial rise of a large trout.

Just don't get hung up on worrying about picking the right terrestrial pattern. I firmly believe that many of the large foam flies we use are taken because trout have been eating big grasshoppers or beetles or moths and are just accustomed to preying upon large, insect-looking things. I think even flies like the Royal Wulff, which to us looks nothing like anything in nature, may look like a beetle or ant to trout from underneath. Even the nymphs we fish, though we take great pains to imitate aquatic insects with them, may often be taken by a trout that has been eating sunken beetles. To a trout that gets only a brief glance at a submerged object that races by in the current, a Copper John or Prince nymph could look a lot like a sunken beetle or some other terrestrial bug.

SUMMER AND FALL NYMPHING

Summer and early fall nymphing are mostly low-water affairs, so you should adjust your tactics accordingly. One of the most important points is where you choose to nymph. You may know where trout are lying in a deep, slow pool, but your chances of success there are low. The first thing you should look for is some relatively fast water with a broken surface between 3 and 10 feet deep. Trout lie in these places because the broken surface keeps them protected from predators, as the distortion of the surface makes it hard for an osprey to see them from above. Don't take this point lightly—riffled water is as valuable for cover as a logjam.

A perfect nymphing opportunity—first light at the head of a pool with fast water. Most fish will be found on the seams at either side of the fast water.

Another important feature of faster water is that food is more limited at this time of year and the faster water brings food to trout at a quicker rate. Look for the bubble line, the place that brings the most food through the riffle. It is typically more apparent and more important in low water.

Drag will not be as much of a problem as earlier in the season because slower flows mean fewer conflicting currents. Don't get too casual about this, but realize that a spot that was not productive in May because the current had lots of squirrely currents may be a lot easier to fish. And you may be able to get a longer drift over productive water because of this.

One of the main modifications you should make is to your strike indicator, if you use them. Big plastic or cork indicators should only be used in the heaviest water. In shallower and more gentle riffles, switching to some kind of yarn indicator will make your casts land softer, and a small piece of fluffy yarn is a lot less disturbing to trout that have been fished over for six months than a pink plastic bubble. It just looks like a piece of cottonwood fluff or a bit of foam. And because it won't be as hard to follow your indicator, I prefer to use white ones, which are harder to see on some water but blend in better with natural stuff on the surface.

Early morning is the best time to fish nymphs in the summer, beginning as soon as it is light enough to see, before dawn, until about mid-morning. Fish are less spooky in low light, and any insects that are hatching are more likely to do so in the morning when the water is coolest. The daily nocturnal drift is also just ending, so fish will be on the lookout for drifting larvae.

In general, subsurface food is small at this time of year because the insects whose eggs hatched in the spring are tiny, plus many of the insects that hatch at this time of year are small. And don't rule out the fact that a small nymph is less likely to spook a trout when it hits the water. Small Pheasant Tails and their endless variations are good bets, as well as midge larvae and small, size 16 and 18, caddis pupae. But if you do get to the river at dawn, you might also consider trying a bigger nymph. Big stoneflies have multiple-year life cycles so there may be some big ones around, and tiny just-hatched crayfish are abundant and are a favorite food of trout. Size 10 stonefly imitations and larger general imitations like hare's ear nymphs do a good job at imitating both stoneflies and small crayfish.

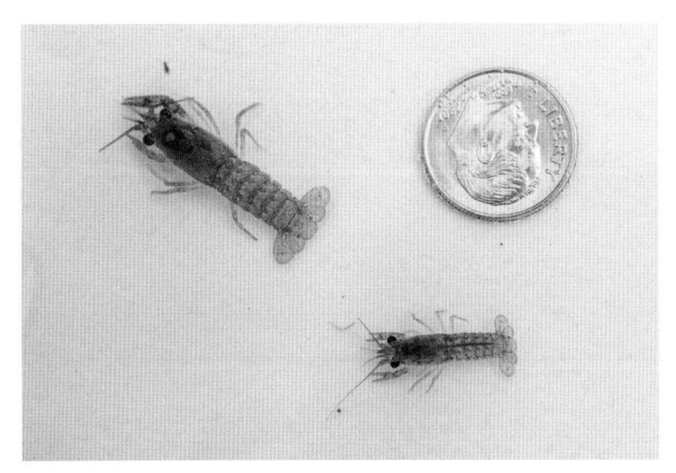

Tiny, just-hatched crayfish are a favorite of trout, because they are easier to capture and have not yet developed the big pincers of adults. A large stonefly or mayfly nymph can imitate these quite well.

Scuds and Sow Bugs

Besides crayfish, the other freshwater crustaceans favored by trout are scuds and sow bugs. These, of course, are entirely aquatic their entire lives, so they are abundant throughout the year. They are common only in richer waters with high calcium content, but if your river has any kind of weed growth in it, you can assume the presence of scuds and sow bugs. They are especially abundant in spring creeks and tailwaters, but are also common in freestone streams with weed growth. These critters can be at every level of the water column, since they live in weeds that might be along the bank or might stretch upwards into the current, and once they lose their grip, they are weak swimmers.

Most are shades of gray with hints of olive, tan, and brown, so any dull-colored fly with a little bit of fuzziness

Water with aquatic vegetation will host scuds and sow bugs 12 months a year, because they never hatch out of the water.

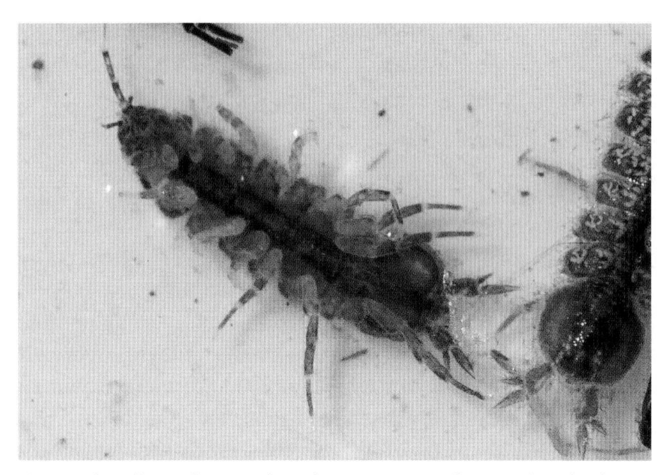

A couple of sow bugs taken from a stomach sample of a large trout in mid-summer.

to imitate their seven pairs of legs and one pair of antennae will work. They often curl up when disturbed, but they also drift with their bodies straight and uncurled. Although many imitations of them are tied with a curled shape, I have found that imitations with both straight and curled bodies seem to be equally effective. Sizes to imitate them range anywhere from 12 to 18, but I find the smaller sizes, like 16s and 18s, to be the most effective. Both of these little crustaceans turn orangish pink when dead, and trout may actually select the dead ones, because imitations tied with orange or pink seem to be very effective. I think that dead ones are especially common in tail-waters close to dams, as they live in the reservoirs above dams and may die when flushed through turbines.

SCAN TO WATCH VIDEO 011.

What to look for when trout are feeding under the surface.

Where they are common (and it's not hard to tell because a handful of aquatic weed will turn up hundreds if they are in a river), you can fish their imitations blind, as you would any other nymph, under an indicator, but the very best fishing is when you can spot trout eating them below the surface in clear, shallow water. Trout seem to prefer them just as the sun hits the water in the morning, and if you see a trout making downward spiral motions on a weedy streambed, or chomping a weed bed and then backing up, you can assume they are foraging for these little crustaceans.

If you can get close enough to trout feeding this way without spooking them, remember that our flies are seldom as deep as we think they are getting, so either an imitation with a bead embedded in the body or a tiny piece of weight on the leader a foot above the fly will be helpful. It's best to get across from a fish feeding like this if you can. You will often need to lead the fish 10 feet or more to get your fly to its level, so if you are fishing from a downstream position, you may not be able to get long enough lead on the fish without putting your fly line on top of it—a sure way to spook a trout.

In a case like this, it's best to watch the fish because you will seldom be able to see your fly. Lead the fish, trust in your planning, and when you see the fish open its mouth (a white flash often indicates this) or move quickly to one side or the other, gently tighten your line. If the fish has not taken your

If you see trout spiraling to the bottom and grubbing in the weeds, it's a pretty sure bet they are eating sow bugs or scuds—or both! Often I find both crustaceans in an individual trout's stomach.

This standard scud imitation has a bead embedded in its body to add weight and a little sparkle. Scud imitations should be fished close to the bottom, and you should avoid using a strike indicator or weight on the leader, if possible, to avoid spooking trout in clear tailwaters or spring creeks where scuds are most abundant.

fly, you won't spook it, and sometimes a slight upward movement of the fly will induce a strike.

I said you won't be able to see your fly, but I have a fly that lets you do this. Being able to see the position of your fly is, of course, a huge education because you can see where your fly drifts, if it's deep enough, and the reaction of a fish if the fly gets close. I recently experimented with an old English fly, the Killer Bug, invented by the creator of the Pheasant Tail nymph, Frank Sawyer, with my own modification. The traditional Killer Bug is merely a slightly weighted hook covered with a pinkish/grayish/tannish yarn. I added a bright orange tungsten bead to the head of this fly, both for added weight and to help me track it. Maybe the bright orange spot also got the fish to notice it.

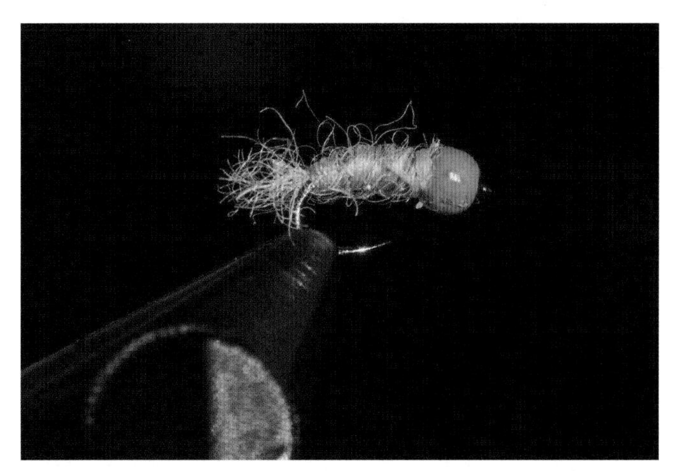

I added a hot orange tungsten bead to Frank Sawyer's simple Killer Bug pattern for extra weight and to give me a spot of color to follow under the surface when sight-fishing. The bright orange didn't seem to bother the trout; in fact, it may have increased its visibility to them even though it does not make a very realistic imitation of a scud.

On a spring creek I have fished for over 40 years, I was able for the first time to follow my fly nearly every drift. I was amazed at how far away from the fish my fly was when I would have thought it would drift right to the fish; how where currents looked uniform, there were tiny micro currents that would sometimes take my fly off course; and how sometimes what looked like a poor cast would be caught by these little currents and delivered right to the fish.

The first take with this fly was so subtle that the fish barely moved, and I was amazed to find myself connected to a trout, even though I could see my fly drift right into the trout's mouth. I watched other trout move off to the side to take the fly, in a typical manner. And I learned that if a trout moved for the fly but refused it at the last minute, no amount of subsequent casts would interest it and I would have to search for a new victim. The orange bead was probably so garish that it was either inhaled by the first cast that got close to the fish or ignored completely. Of course, you can use a very tiny indicator in this kind of fishing, but I find it much more satisfying to watch the fish and cast with just one tiny nymph on my leader.

General Summer Sight-Fishing with Nymphs

Trout are well camouflaged, and it's difficult to spot one 10 feet in front of you in clear water. In spring creeks and some tailwaters, where the water level is stable and clear for most of the year, you can see them any time of year, but in most freestone rivers the low, clear water of the late season is about the only time you can sight-fish nymphs. And it is every bit as visual and exciting as dry-fly fishing, with the added bonus that you get to watch a trout's behavior to your casting and its reaction to the fly. If you want to up your trout-fishing game at any time of year, being able to watch the whole drama is one of the best ways to learn.

First you need to find a place to do this. Not every spot in a river offers the chance. You need a relatively bright sunny day, the brighter the day the better, and, as in most late-summer fishing, I have found my best opportunities in mid-morning, when there is enough sun on the water to see fish but the water is cool enough for them to be eating aggressively. Places to look for visible trout are the shallow tails of pools, on the inside edges of bends in the river, along the banks, and in shallow riffles. Learn to trust your eyes, trust your instincts, and assume that everything that looks remotely like a trout is one. The worst that can happen is that you will feel foolish casting at a log or the edge of a stone for 10 minutes, but in late summer most of the crowds have left trout streams, so no one will see you do it.

You will seldom see the whole fish. Don't look for a fish shape; look for things that might be part of a fish and then slowly visualize the rest of it. Your brain will fill in a lot of the blanks—but also be aware that wishful thinking will fill in blanks that aren't there, and you will sometimes swear you can see fins and a tail materializing on the edge of a submerged stone! Here are some things to look for:

Tails. Even a relatively motionless trout will sway its tail from side to side to keep its position in the current. My friend

This brown trout's shadow will be easier to spot than the fish itself, so look for shadows that sway in the current.

Dave Jensen, perhaps the best trout spotter I have ever known, says to look for that flag waving in the current, which is an apt description.

Shadows. If the sun is right, a trout's body is well camouflaged but its shadow will show a distinct black shape.

Fins. Sometimes you will see the pectoral fins on a fish before you see the tail. They flare out when a trout is holding in the current and may show up if the tail is in the shade or otherwise difficult to see. Wild trout have distinct white edges on their fins, and in brook trout this is especially prominent

When spotting trout, you will probably notice the fins and wagging tail before you spot the entire fish.

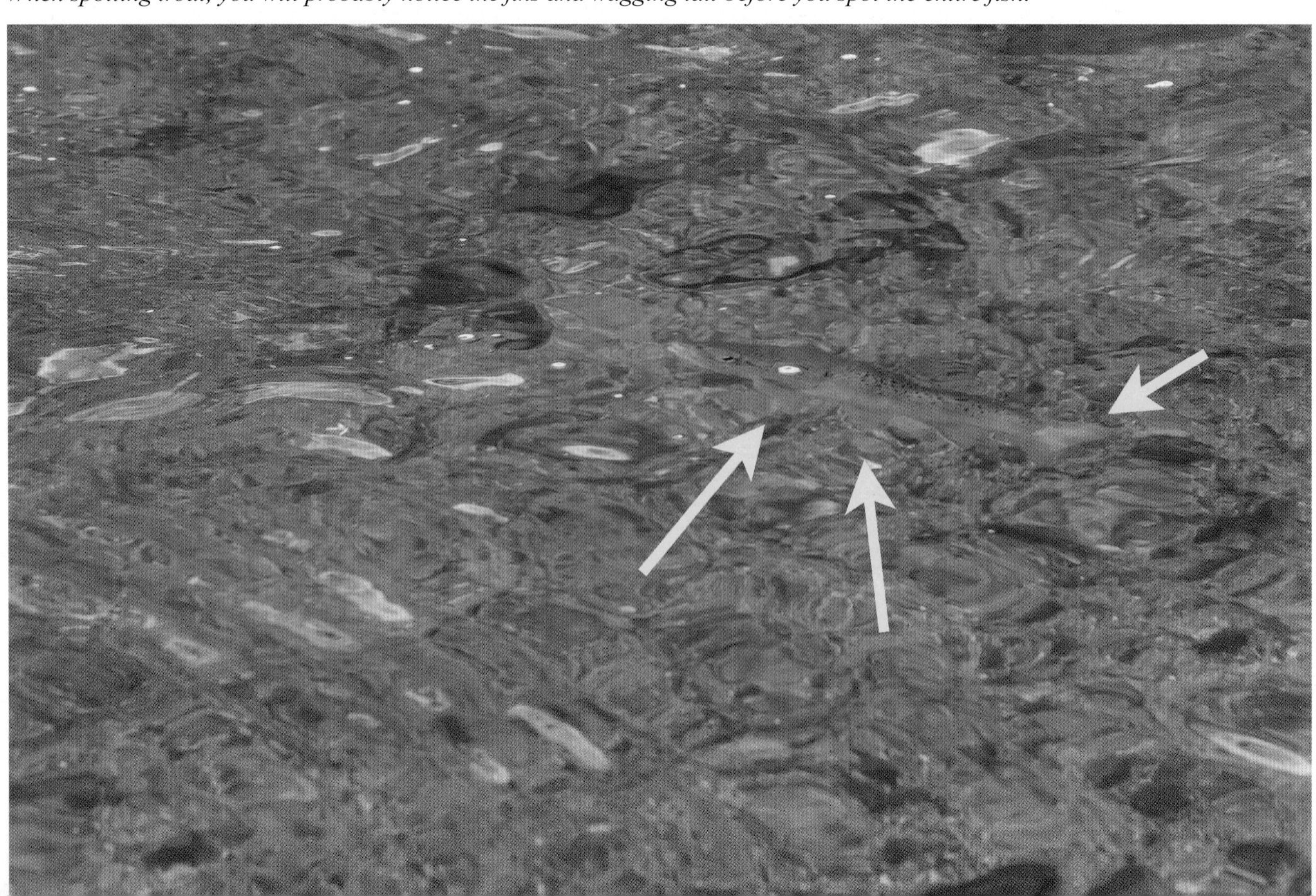

Fishing pressure is low in the fall, but drifting leaves in the water seem to put trout off the feed, so the pleasure of being alone on the water is sometimes tempered by slow fishing.

spinners fall, either hung under a small terrestrial or fished with a tiny strike indicator. And there are even more advantages to a heavy Trico spinner fall: Because the fish have been conditioned to look to the surface for their food, just prospecting with a small dry fly can be effective for the rest of the day.

LATE FALL

As I've mentioned before, the platitude that trout put on the feed bag in fall to fatten up for winter just does not hold up with scientific or anecdotal evidence. Although the fishing slows down in most places, rivers are seldom crowded and you can enjoy the wonders of fall foliage, whether it is the golden hues of aspens in the West of the riot of warm colors in the East.

There is a dividing line that most often happens with the cold, heavy rains of the fall equinox. Colder, higher water slows down the metabolism of trout, and the faster currents make them tougher to locate and can make it difficult to get your fly down to the fish. The other drawback is that where you have deciduous trees close to the river, the stronger winds of fall dump them into the water, and I have found that when the water is full of leaves, it puts trout off the feed. Trout that were feeding actively a few days before on a warm, still Indian summer day will suddenly seem to disappear. Dry flies don't seem to work well, nymphs get lost in all the debris below the surface, and streamers get hung up almost every cast, making it difficult to get a reasonable presentation.

If you are lucky enough to experience a warm, soft Indian summer day with light winds, you'll find fishing about the same as late summer. Tricos may still hatch (although trout sometimes stop responding to them later in the year for some reason), grasshoppers may warm up and get one last chance to chew grass and fall into the river, and there are some tiny (and I mean really tiny, size 26 through 30!) olive mayflies that hatch from September through November. A very large caddisfly, about a size 8 or 10, called the October Caddis also hatches on many rivers, although it's rare to see them in numbers dense enough to get trout to respond to them on the surface.

Nymphs will also work as long as there is not a lot of debris in the water. But fall is prime streamer time . . .

Spawners and Streamers

Brown and brook trout are fall spawners. Both spawn October through mid-December, and if both species occur in the same

There is perhaps nothing more spectacular in fresh water than a brook trout in fall spawning colors. At this time of year, they will be found in the upper reaches of rivers and in small tributaries, as they prefer to spawn in clean, shallow water with a lot of groundwater influence.

Streamers for fall should be showy, with lots of action to catch the attention of aggressive trout that may not be feeding but are inclined to slap things out of their way. This box full of big stuff contains both bright and natural-colored patterns because you never know what mood the trout may be in.

river, typically brook trout will spawn first. It's difficult to find spawning trout because some may spawn in the main channel of a river within yards of where they spent the rest of the year, while others will migrate many miles upstream. It all depends on where they were hatched, and trout, like salmon, are mostly faithful to the exact spot in a river or tributary. But there are various strains of trout in any river and some may spawn at different times than others, even within the same species.

Although the act of spawning takes only a few days, trout may begin to move more than a month before actually spawning, so in any given piece of water you may find trout moving slowly upstream. I have stood in the tails of pools as early as late September watching brown trout slide upstream, and they could only be on a spawning migration because there is no other reason they would be moving through a pool with such determination. Spawning trout don't feed much but they are aggressive, and they are particularly nasty to smaller fish because they are genetically programmed to protect their eggs from them, even well before they begin the act of spawning. Thus the effectiveness of streamers.

You may have to cover a lot of water to target trout on a spawning migration, because you never know exactly where

Because trout may be moving in the fall and won't be in their normal places, and because many of them will not be that interested in food, the best way to fish at this time of year is in a drift boat. This will let you cover lots of water with your streamer patterns.

they will be. They may not be in their usual haunts, close to cover or in places where it's easy to feed. Don't ignore the center of the river because just like steelhead and salmon, trout on a migration stay close to the main current threads, which they use as their highways. But don't overlook slower water close to cover either, because they might just as well decide to loll around in a pool for a few days or even a week, especially if the water gets low, waiting for enough water to navigate on their upstream journey.

The trout often have to navigate falls, and it is actually easier for them to get over falls in high water than low water, because sometimes they can get around the side of high falls if the water is flooded around the edges. They can also actually swim through falls—and the more water moving over a falls, the more room they have to swim, despite the faster current. This makes it a wise practice to fish either below or above sections of very fast water—to catch fish staging below the obstruction in preparation to navigate it, or just above because they need to rest after all the effort of getting over it.

In the fall, bigger streamers are better than smaller ones, and a slow retrieve is better than a faster one. You want a big fly, 3 to 6 inches long, so they notice it, and you want to keep the fly in front of them as much as possible because they aren't chasing a baitfish to eat it. You want to piss them off. This is one time of year when casting the same streamer to one place repeatedly is a good idea. A trout in May will either pounce on a fly and eat it or ignore it, but repeated casts when they are in a spawning mood might get them more aggressive with each repeated cast.

. . . and Eggs

Just like rainbows in the spring, brown trout eat their own eggs in the fall. Rainbows get their turn in the fall as well, because just as brown trout will follow spawning rainbows to eat their eggs in April, rainbows will follow browns to their spawning areas to eat their eggs in the fall. But it is not just in close proximity to their redds for either species. There is probably some sort of pheromone or other smell that tells both

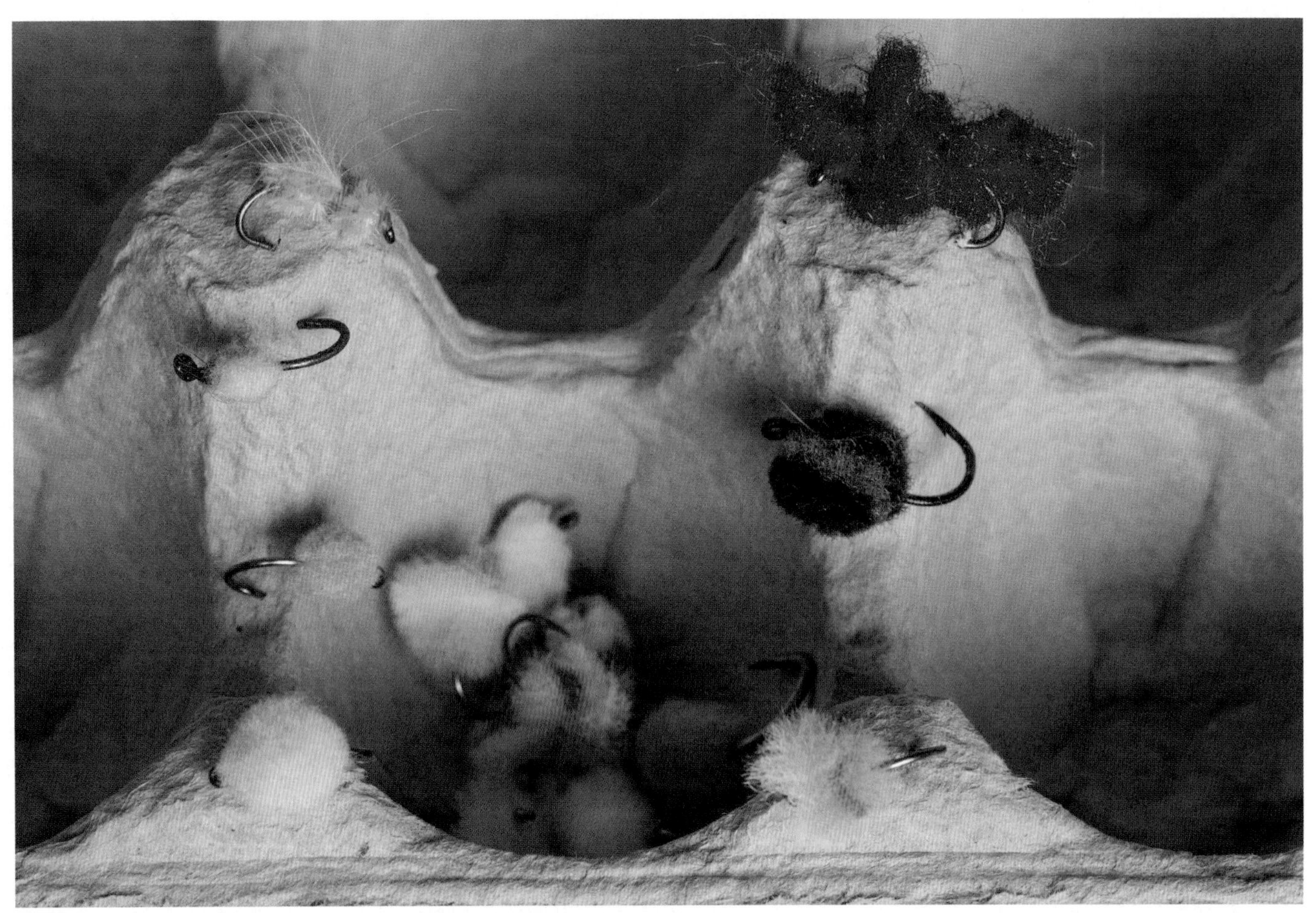

The simpler the better is probably a good rule for eggs flies—the simple profiles seem to imitate an egg rolling along the bottom better. And because these flies are fished deep, you lose a lot of them, so there is not much sense in spending much or taking a lot of time to create egg patterns.

species that spawning time is near, so even far from the actual locations of spawning, trout know to be on the lookout for eggs drifting in the current. If streamers don't work in the late fall, there is a good chance that an egg pattern, fished dead-drift close to the bottom, will interest a trout.

Whether you decide to fish for brown or brook trout when they are in the act of spawning is something you'll have to sort out for yourself. I've already gone into the reasons for and against fishing for them over redds, and if it's legal in your area, only you can decide if it's proper or not.

CHAPTER 9

At the End

All of what we discussed so far hopefully ends with a trout on the line. Sealing the deal is, for some people, the frosting on the cake, and the effort would not be complete without it. Playing the fish, feeling the muscular thumps on the end of the line, seeing a wild fish catapult into the air in a prism of spray, and finally holding that living creature you have captured in your hand brings us back to childhood wonder. It's as good as finally catching a bullfrog with your hands when you were seven years old, but even for people who grew up surrounded by concrete and neon, there is something fulfilling about the act. For others, just fooling the trout and hooking it is the end game, and for them a fish that is not landed is not a disappointment. At least they claim it isn't.

I often get questions like "I was fishing the other day and I kept losing the trout I hooked. What was I doing wrong?" There are too many variables in that equation to formulate a helpful answer, and probably only more time on the water can teach you how to finally bring a fish to hand. Of course, time

Even with many years of experience, sometimes just tying a simple knot can lead to frustration. We all have these days.

on the water also teaches you that these things happen, it's no big deal, and you chuckle or shrug or curse and move on.

Here is an account of a few hours one day from the person who has been fly fishing for 50 years, and is a supposed "expert." I was fishing a size 18 PMD on a river known for its big, finicky trout that probably see dozens of imitation PMDs in any given day. Several nice brown trout were rising within casting range. I needed to add a 6X tippet to my leader, so I pulled a piece of 6X tippet material off my spool, and while I was fiddling with the rest of the leader, I dropped my piece of 6X in the water and lost it.

I pulled another 4 feet of tippet from the spool and began to tie a five-turn blood knot, a knot I first tied when I was 10 years old. I probably tie thousands of them every season. For my first two attempts, I couldn't seem to leave a big enough gap between the two sides of material to poke the end through and had to start over. On the third attempt, a piece of loose skin on my thumb grabbed the end of the tippet and wouldn't let me pass the end through the knot cleanly, so I had to start over. On the fourth and fifth attempts, I again could not seem to leave that open V between the two pieces, couldn't pass the second end through the loop, and had to start over. On my sixth try, I managed to get both tag ends through the loop, but as I tightened the knot, one of them pulled out. I glanced up. Trout continued to feed. My frustration notched up.

I don't know how long this continued, but it must have been close to 10 attempts. Finally I managed to tie what seemed like a perfect blood knot. I wetted it, tightened it, clipped the tag ends, and tested it. With much less force than a knot with 6X should have withstood, the knot broke. I was glad I tested it, but now I was back to square one and getting more anxious to get my fly out to those fish. The wind also began blowing, which makes it much harder to tie knots because the ends get blown out of place and you have to put your back to the wind and hunch over to protect your working space. Finally, after a number of other mistakes, I was able to tie the knot, test it, and I was satisfied with its strength. I fished over those risers for 30 minutes and never managed to hook one.

What went wrong? It was late afternoon and I had been fishing constantly since sunrise, so I may have been fatigued. Maybe I didn't drink enough water. It could have been just a string of bad luck, because it often takes a couple of tries to get a knot right in small material but seldom as long as it took me that day. Maybe the moon phase was wrong. Never mind getting skunked, that happens all the time, but my inability to even tie a knot just shows you that it can happen to any of us, regardless of our experience. You will have frustrations. Get over it.

SETTING THE HOOK

Getting a good, consistent hook set is one of those things you expect to happen as you gain experience, but a lot can go wrong. Let's look at the basics. Trout flies are tied on fine wire, they are very sharp, and a trout's mouth seems to be made for getting a firm hook hold, because it is soft enough to make penetration easy but has lots of connective tissue that keeps a hook in place during the battle. Setting the hook is simple in theory: You tighten the line quickly until you feel pressure, then you gradually decrease pressure to prevent the tippet from breaking. Don't forget that force equals mass times acceleration, and even a 1-pound trout can break a 6-pound tippet if the trout takes the fly in a rush going away from you and you jerk viciously in the opposite direction.

What seems to take some novice anglers a while to recognize is that the amount of rod movement necessary varies based on how much line you have on the water and how much slack is in the line. They expect a formula, like "Raise your rod to the 10:45 position to set the hook." It does not work that way. If you are fishing to a trout 20 feet away with a straight line, the hook set might be only a few inches of lift. On the other hand, if the fish is 65 feet away and you have cast piles of slack on the water to help reduce drag, you might have to wrench the rod over your head and behind your back in order to feel contact with the fish.

You probably remember when you first began fishing how much trouble you had developing that quick reflex to set the hook. You would stare at the fly for a couple of seconds, realize what had happened, and by the time you reacted, the fish spit out your fly. Or you fished with a guide who might have to say "Set. Set. Set!" before you got the idea. At this point your muscle memory has probably developed to the point where you don't miss as many strikes, but sometimes the game changes, leaving you mystified. Seven-inch brook trout in fast water take a fly so quickly that it seems like you have to begin setting the hook even before you see the rise. Large Snake River cutthroats in slow water always get the best of me because they inhale a fly slower than any other trout I've experienced, and my reflexes are so ingrained for "ordinary" rises that I invariably set the hook while the fly is just on the outside of their jaws. So be thankful for your finely tuned reflexes, but recognize that you may need to modify them to suit conditions.

Hook-Setting Angles

In fish that are upstream of you or across from you in the current, hooking angles are firm and secure and seldom prevent consistent problems. Hooking a fish that is directly downstream of your position is tricky because when you tighten the line, there is a good chance you will pull the fly out of a trout's mouth. Understand that if conditions force you to cast directly downstream, as you would for a fish rising at the head of an impenetrable brush pile, or when you cast across-and-down and the trout seems to take the fly when it finishes its swing directly below you, you will hook fewer fish.

I once read in a magazine article that the solution to this problem is to set the hook off to one side so that the fly goes into the corner of a trout's mouth instead of being pulled out through open space. I went out to test that method, but I noticed that in practice, no matter how far off the one side you sweep your rod, there is more line in the water than in the air, and it follows the path of least resistance and slides straight upstream. Try it if you want, but it doesn't work for me.

About the best method I know in this situation is no hook set, or a much delayed one. It's common on English salmon

Often we miss fish because we don't strike quickly enough. But large Snake River cutthroats are notoriously slow risers, and if you have lightning-fast reflexes from fishing for smaller trout, you might strike too soon on these guys.

rivers for the gillie to suggest to the angler that he or she say "God save the Queen" before tightening the line, because salmon are notorious for taking a fly slowly, downstream of your position. The only way to get a firm set, in the corner of the mouth, is to let the fish take the fly and turn with it. Trout are quicker to reject a fly than salmon, so you can only hope that the fish does not feel the fake texture of your offering until it turns. Once you feel the pressure of the hook, you can then apply pressure of your own and the hook should be firmly set. Or not.

Fishing from a dock or high bank can also present problems, as your angle above the fish is much higher than it would be if you were wading or in a boat. I learned this painfully one year on a small brown trout stream in Alberta, which I happened to hit just right, with dull drizzly days, big *Hexagenia* mayflies hatching all afternoon, and large brown trout that were less cautious than they should have been. The stream in many places was too deep to wade but narrow, so in many spots we had to fish from a bank 4 or 5 feet above the water.

I kept losing fish that seemed to take my fly firmly, on a nice upstream angle, until guide Dave Jensen said, "You have tip sag." "I beg your pardon," I replied, thinking that Dave was making a snarky comment about my anatomy. But he explained that with a high rod tip, you lift the fly up into the air instead of into the jaws of fish, and that after casting I needed to keep my rod at as low a position as possible without ruining my drift, so that when I set the hook, it would be more in line with a trout's jaw. Not used to fishing so high on the bank, it took me some time to get used to that rod position, but since then I always concentrate more on my rod position when fishing from high banks.

Streamer Sets

You can hook trout on streamers using the standard upward lift of the rod tip, and this is the way many successful streamer anglers have been doing it for years. However, there is a better way, a more consistent method that borrows from saltwater fly fishing. If you have ever tried to hook a bonefish or tarpon with an upward lift of the rod, not only do you figure out that it seldom works, but you can also count on a guide muttering "trout set" in disgust. With a fish chasing a fly underwater, the most reliable way to set the hook is called a strip set, which is basically just a long, firm strip until you feel the solid pressure

When fishing from high banks, you are faced with a difficult angle for hooking trout. The best advice I ever got, from guide Dave Jensen (shown here netting a fish), is to keep your rod tip as low to the water as possible.

of a fish on the line. It has a number of advantages in streamer fishing as well.

First, the hook set is at a better angle for this type of fishing and results in hookups that hold better. Second, trout often bump or snap at a streamer before inhaling it, and if you lift your fly out of the water, you have no second chance. A fly that darts away, as a streamer will when you use the strip set, often elicits a more aggressive reaction from the trout and it may pounce on the fly. At least you have a chance. Finally, if trout chase your streamer in shallow water, they often boil behind the fly before actually taking it. Again, if you lift the fly from the water when you think a trout has taken it because of the boil, you lose any opportunity for the fish to keep following and connect.

This is, again, a hard reflex to break. I know because it took me years to develop a consistent strip set in saltwater, by concentration and repetition until it was finally reflexive. Of course, sometimes I return after long saltwater strips and strip set when fishing nymphs and dry flies. That does not work very well.

ONCE THE HOOK IS SET

You can learn a lot about problems in the first few seconds after you set the hook. In dry-fly fishing, if you have a good across-stream or upstream angle to the fish and you don't connect after setting the hook quickly, it's more likely the fish refused the fly at the last minute. A fish lying in 3 feet of water has to turn on the afterburner to intercept a fly on the surface. If the fish decides not to take the fly at the last microsecond, it keeps its mouth closed and its momentum carries it above the surface, looking very much like a rise. In the same light, if a trout is sipping gently, it is lying just under the surface, and if it suddenly takes your fly with a splash and you don't connect, it again means the fish decided something was wrong and it moved quickly to get out of the way. Trout do miss flies occasionally but it's the exception rather than the rule, so if you miss a few fish in a row, consider changing your fly or tactics.

If you set the hook and feel the weight of the fish, but it comes off the hook instantly or after a few seconds, suspect a bad hook point. Sometimes on very large trout the jaws are so bony that a hook won't connect, but that is relatively rare. It's much more likely the tip of your hook point is bent or broken. I nick them when my backcast goes too low and the fly connects with a rock on the bank. I also often bend the point after releasing a relatively large fish quickly without the benefit of forceps, and the hook point gets bent sideways as it slides of the trout's jaw. Sometimes a very large fish can bend a hook outward, which will also affect your hooking ability.

If you miss a fish after a brief connection, bring in your fly and look at the point. First make sure the point is straight and not bent. You can usually put a bent point right with a pair of forceps, after which you should resharpen the point. Bent hooks can also be put back into position by grabbing the bend with a pair of forceps and bending the hook until the point is on the same plane as the eye. Check the hook point—my test is to first make sure it grabs the skin on the end of my thumb, and then a final check is to drag the point against a fingernail. A very sharp hook will score the nail with a thin line.

Sharpening a hook is easy. You can use a diamond file, whetstone, emery board, or even a smooth rock you find on the bank. Work the sharpener against the point on both sides and the bottom until it passes my two tests.

SCAN TO WATCH VIDEO 013.
The proper way to play a trout.

FIGHTING AND LANDING TROUT

Trout should always be played as quickly as you can, which depends on the velocity of the water, the number of snags, and the strength of your tippet. One reason you should play trout quickly is that the longer you play a fish, the bigger the hole the hook makes in their jaw and the easier it can pull out. But an even more important reason is that trout played quickly are much more likely to survive. I can't give you a formula for how to determine how much pressure to put on the fish, other than having you tie on a fly, stick your fly into a tree, and yank on each tippet size you normally use until it breaks. Don't forget, though, that if a fish lunges away from you, much more pressure will be put on your knots than a static pull, so take that into account.

Once you set the hook, the fish will either sulk and thrash in one spot or take off swimming as fast as it can. Sulkers are easier to land because all you need to do is to apply steady pressure with your rod. With a fish that runs, don't try to stop it unless it is heading for a snag or an area of faster water that prevents you from chasing the fish. How do you know when to put the fish on the reel? You don't have much control over that. A fish that needs to be on the reel will pull all the line out of your hands and keep going. A fish that doesn't require the reel can be stripped in, which is the case with most fish under 12 inches long unless you fish very light tippets.

But this is probably review for you. With some trout under your belt at this point, what you probably want advice on is landing those larger trout that may have gotten away at this point in your career.

Always remember side pressure. A trout is good at pulling its head down because hydraulics give it help, so if you pull straight up on a trout, it will either tip its head down or turn away and use the current to its advantage. By fighting a large trout at a horizontal angle, you have a much better chance of leading it in any direction you want once its initial run is over.

Using side pressure to lead a trout in whatever direction you want it to go is one of the most important techniques for landing trout quickly. Vary the pressure from one side to another to disorient a fish, or use pressure to lead a fish into quieter water, where it will be easier to land.

A trout can only swim in the direction its head is pointing—it has no reverse gear.

A common situation is a trout that is across from you and bolting downstream. You don't want a large trout downstream of you, because it uses the current to its advantage. It does not have to fight the current, just ride with it, whereas a trout fighting upstream of you has to fight the current to get away from you. The best tactic to handle a trout running downstream is to turn the fish into you by placing horizontal pressure to force its head sideways.

Imagine a trout running downstream off to your right side. What you should do is move your rod to the left as hard as you dare to turn its head. Yes, the fish will briefly be broadside to the current and able to use the current to its advantage, but once you have the fish turned, move the rod upstream to bring the fish up against the current. This is not as difficult as it seems because a trout is so streamlined that once it is facing upstream, firm and steady pressure will move it in that direction.

Unless the fish lunges downstream again (at which point you have to let it run and repeat the process), keep leading it upstream until it is upstream of your position. Then turn it sideways again, let it run for a few feet, and then reverse your rod so it has to run in the opposite direction. If the fish stays upstream of you, it's possible to just tire it out by making it swim back and forth, or sometimes in circles around you, by maintaining firm pressure on it. And if the fish makes a run upstream, great—it will have to run against the current and you should be able to turn it once it stops running. Once it turns it may bolt downstream, and then you may have to reverse the process of turning it into you again.

Some trout run downstream so quickly and powerfully that you are unable to turn their head, in which case you have two choices: Follow the fish and get below it, or stand fast and hold on. I don't suggest the latter option because that fish may just keep going, so unless the water is too deep or treacherous below you, it's best to get to the bank or shallow water and bolt down below the fish. Sometimes the slack you develop as you race downstream will also confuse the fish when the pressure is released and make it swim back upstream. Either way, by moving you put yourself in a better position, with the fish upstream of you.

Standing in place when a fish runs past you is not a good option for a couple of reasons. The farther the fish runs below you, the harder you will have to work pulling it back against the current. Also, when a fish fights directly below you, its open mouth is facing you, and there is about a 50 percent chance that the hook will pull out if the tippet doesn't break from the weight of the fish combined with the force of the current. If you really can't follow a fish, try to at least turn its head before it runs down behind some rocks or in fast current below you. Or as a last resort, strip out about 20 feet of line quickly and give your line as much slack as possible. There is a chance the fish will move back upstream because if it thinks it is no longer hooked, it will try to return to its original position.

Often you're faced with a fish running for a nasty log or brush pile. Brown and brook trout are notorious for this, with rainbows and cutthroats less prone to jam into a sunken tree. If you can turn the fish or snub it, that's your best plan of attack, because once a large trout enters a sunken tangle of branches, it seems to have an innate sense of how to weave your leader back and forth among the branches as if it had taken knitting classes.

If a fish gets into brush and you can wade over to it, you may be able to free it or thread your rod through the tangle if the fish went out the other side. But typically they wrap the tippet around a branch, and with no stretch in the system because your stretchy fly line and rod aren't in the equation anymore, even a small fish can easily break a strong tippet by shaking its head. Then again, you could get lucky if the fish is hung up and for some reason the tippet doesn't break. This is always a judgment call that makes you cringe: Do you try to turn the fish even though it may break your leader, or do you hope to get the fish intact out of the tangle? I have better luck with the first approach.

On the other hand, fish that dive into a weed bed can often be landed. Once their heads gets covered with weeds, they seem to think they are safe, ostrichlike, even though half of their body might be waving in the current. This calms them so much that you can often wade over to the weed bed and scoop the fish up with your hands or with a net. I had one day on a tiny weed-filled spring creek in Wyoming when I was forced to use very light tippets and small flies over fat cutthroats that were all over 20 inches long. The first thing I would do was lead a hooked fish right into a pile of weeds, then stroll over to the spot and scoop up the fish with barely an inkling of a battle. Not elegant, but I got all my flies back.

You will lose many of the large fish you hook. Every battle is different, and unless you have a seasoned angler watching over your shoulder for advice and analysis, you may never know what went wrong but you will still probably learn something from it. I think the reason big ones appeal to us is that, unlike a 10-inch trout that you are sure to land, a 20-inch trout

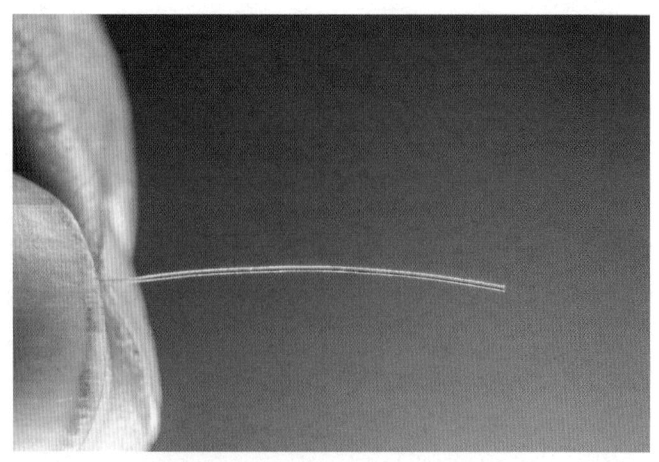

A clean break like this in your tippet means you just pushed your tippet to its limit, perhaps striking too hard or trying to put too much pressure on a fish that was swimming toward a snag. But this is an indication that your knots were tied properly.

gives the added suspense of not knowing if you will ever hold it in your hand.

GOOD CONNECTIONS

Some trout just get off the hook for no apparent reason. It's not something to agonize about. I have had some days where fish after fish seemed to be firmly hooked, and after the first run the hook would pop out even though I checked the point repeatedly and it was as sharp as it could be. The only thing I can blame it on is fish maybe not taking my fly confidently, not fully inhaling it, and just getting lightly hooked on the outside of the lip—or maybe it's just a run of bad luck.

Those kinds of losses are not preventable, so there is no need to berate yourself. When you do have the license for self-castigation is when a knot breaks, and especially when a broken leader comes back to you with a curlicue instead of a clean break, which means, sorry, you screwed up. Your knot was not tied or tightened properly because if your knots are good, your tippet will return with a clean break.

There are four places a leader commonly breaks, and each tells you something:

- If your entire tippet is missing, your tippet-to-leader knot was not as strong as the knot used to attach your fly.
- If your entire tippet comes back, the knot used to tie on your fly was weaker than your tippet knot.
- If you get back only a part of your tippet, you likely had a wind knot in your tippet. Most well-tied tippet knots are somewhere between 80 and 98 percent the break strength of the weaker strand, but a wind knot breaks at 40 to 60 percent of the tensile strength of your tippet.
- If most of your tippet except the last inch comes back, and the surface of the material is a little rough, you had too much abrasion on your tippet. This can happen if you fish nymphs deep along a rocky bottom, or if you repeatedly catch large fish. Under either of these circumstances, it's important to check your tippet regularly and retie the fly if you see even a hint of abrasion.

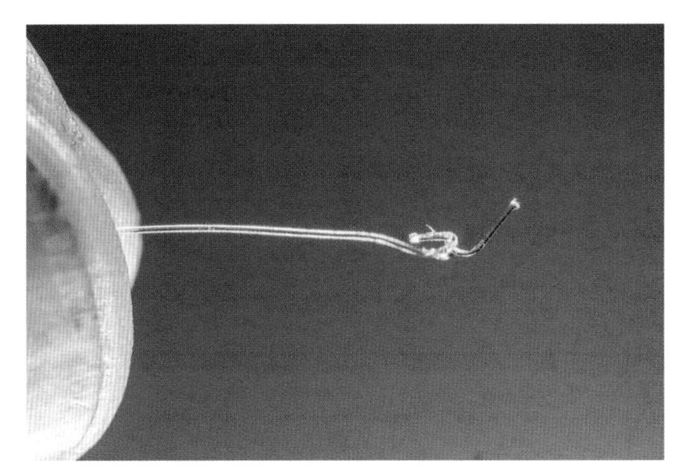

A tippet that breaks like this indicates a knot that was improperly tied. You may have tied the knot properly but not tightened it the right way. Failing to wet and tighten a knot with a smooth, quick pull is just as bad as failing to tie the knot properly.

If you repeatedly suspect wind knots, try to stop and correct any sloppy casting mistakes you could be making, shorten your tippet a bit, or open up your casting loop by making a longer arc when you cast. Wind knots are most often not wind knots at all and should be called casting knots. We call them wind knots to make us feel better.

If you break your tippet-to-leader knot and fly-to-tippet knot with equal frequency, you may be using too light of a tippet or playing fish with too heavy a hand. If one of these knots breaks nearly all the time, consider taking more time to tie that knot or try a different knot that serves the same purpose. If either knot comes back with a curlicue on the end, it's certain your knot was not tied properly because a good knot breaks cleanly.

A sophisticated Instron testing machine showed us that no matter how good you are at tying knots, there will always be variation in knot strength. Your best bet is to find knots you trust and can tie consistently, and accept that some attempts will be better than others—all the more reason to test your knots every time.

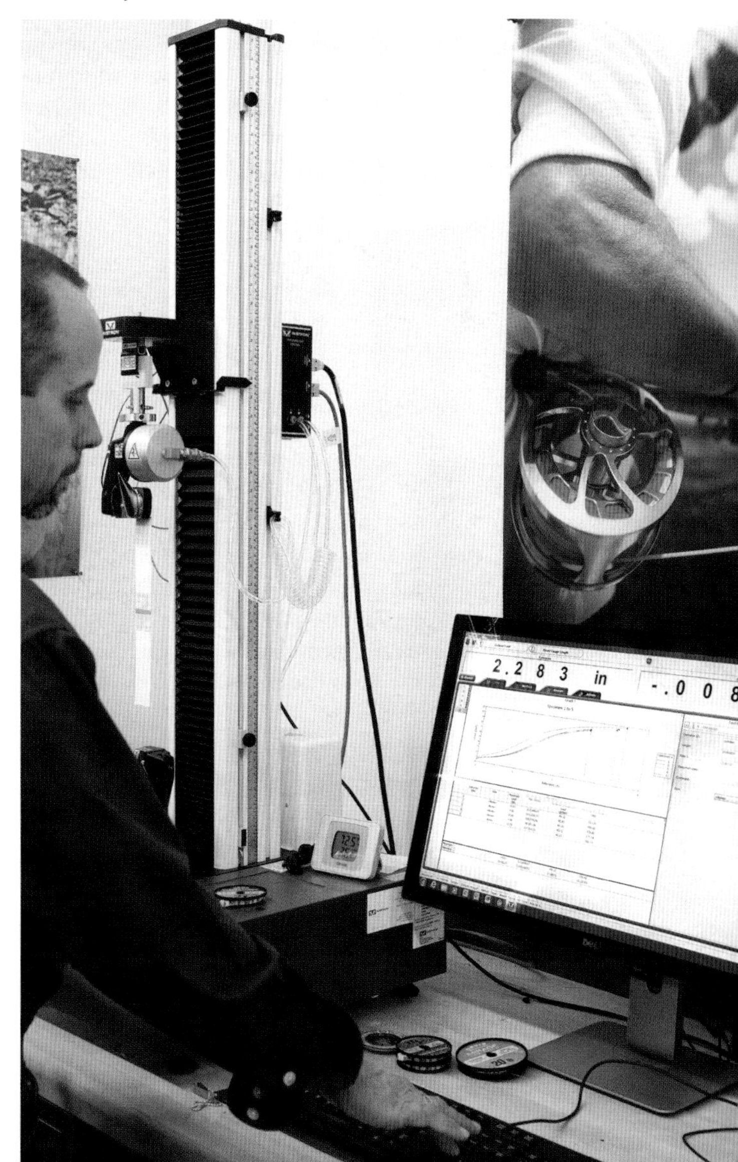

SCAN TO WATCH VIDEO 014.
Tying the Orvis knot for attaching a fly.

There are a myriad of knots used to tie your fly to the tippet and to tie your tippet to the rest of your leader. I am constantly asked which knot I use, or which knot is best. I honestly don't have the answer to that based on a test a bunch of fishing buddies and I performed on a sophisticated Instron testing machine we use at Orvis to test the strength of new tippet materials, fly line loops, wader seams, and other aspects of product development. We started out with the idea of testing the five-turn blood knot against the triple surgeon's knot to see which was the stronger knot for attaching a tippet to the rest of the leader. After that I wanted to test the improved clinch knot against the standard clinch knot, because testing I had done years ago suggested the improved was not as strong as the regular clinch in trout sizes.

What we found out blew us away. Each of us tied 10 knots, out of the same material, carefully in a nice well-lit room with no wind. We took our time to make sure each knot was properly tied and tightened, and, of course, each one was wetted before it was tightened to reduce heat from friction and to help the coils slide together smoothly. I must stress that all four of us are serious, sicko fly fishers whose lives revolve around fly fishing, and we are all knot geeks who sometimes play with knots at our desks for a break from typical 21st-century office work that puts you in front of a screen for eight hours a day if you are not careful. (Yes, even people in the fly-fishing business deal with the same issues most corporate employees do; we just spend more time on our vacations and free time on the water.)

Pete went first with an improved clinch knot, and to our surprise his knots, in a material with 12-pound break strength, broke anywhere from 11.9 to 6.2 pounds! They were all over the place. Next went Shawn—his improved clinch knots did slightly better, but his knots still ranged from close to 12 pounds to under 8. At this point I was rubbing my hands with glee, sure that my standard clinch knots would fare better. No such luck. I had similar spreads in my knot strength, as did the other Shawn who also tied standard clinch knots. If you averaged all 10 knots for each type, the improved clinch probably had a slight edge but not by much, and given the sample size, it was certainly not statistically significant.

SCAN TO WATCH VIDEO 015.
Tying the Orvis knot for attaching a tippet.

We repeated the same test with the blood knot versus surgeon's knot, but again the results were so varied that we had no confidence of getting a clear winner. What did we learn from this? First, we knew all of these knots were "good" knots going into the test because people have used them in nylon tippet since nylon was invented in the mid-20th century. If we had all tied hundreds of knots we would have perhaps learned which knot was truly better, but given the wide variation in such a small sample size, it probably doesn't matter. We tied each knot as best we could and were probably not going to get any better. What we did learn is that no matter how good your knots are tied, even a good knot can have a wide variation in break strength. So when someone tells you the Davey knot is better than a clinch knot, the most you can assume is that they had a good day tying their Davey knots.

What kind of practical use is this to you? Popular knots are popular for a reason: They hold reasonably well when tied properly, within that huge margin of error. My suggestion is that you learn one or two good knots for tying a tippet to the rest of your leader, one or two for attaching a fly to your tippet, and a couple for tying a fly to the tippet with a loop, which according to some people, gives a weighted fly better action. (I have never been convinced of this, except with a very heavy, stiff tippet.) Practice these knots whenever you can, and test each one and try to determine why the ones that were obviously weak failed. Did all the coils not tighten simultaneously? Did one end slip out?

You probably already use a particular knot to attach your tippet to the fly and the tippet to the intermediate sections of your leader. I assume you are happy with them. If you aren't, or if you want to add a second knot to your repertoire, I have been experimenting with the Orvis knot for attaching my fly to the tippet and the Orvis tippet knot for tying on tippets. Tests we have done with the Instron machine show that these knots are better and may be even more consistent than others. I have been using them for my trout fishing for quite a while, as have a number of fishing buddies who have switched over to them. Both knots are easy to tie and easy to tighten without any tricky moves. But, again, the superiority of these knots is only a guess, and in order to really find out, we'd have to test hundreds of knots, which would cut into our fishing time. And because we will all have variations in knot strength from one knot to the next, would it even matter?

THE FINAL MOMENTS

Once you get the trout you've worked so hard to capture alongside you in calm water, or in your net, you are responsible for that fish's well-being if you choose to release it. Catch-and-release is not a conservation tool, it's a social tool that stockpiles more trout for you or the next angler to catch this year or next, but it is nearly impossible to fish a wild trout population to extinction. Habitat protection and enhancement is the true path toward saving trout for future generations, and I urge you to join Trout Unlimited or at least a local club that is active in habitat projects or fighting for protection for our trout rivers. Climate change, and trying to reverse or at least maintain global temperatures, is one of the biggest threats to the future of trout fishing because they are so sensitive to water that warms even a few degrees.

Barbless Hooks

Handling time is one of the three stressors of released trout. Barbless hooks just make this easier, and it's a five-second project to crimp down the barb of a hook with forceps. I don't buy the idea that barbless hooks penetrate easier. The barbs on modern trout hooks are so low and smooth that I doubt if they offer any measureable resistance to penetration. You may not want to remove the barb from all of your flies. Perhaps you're fishing for a trout that you've worked on for over an hour and don't want to lose it, and if you use bead-head nymphs, their weight makes it easy for trout to throw them and you might want a trout for a photo.

There are a few places where I think barbless hooks should always be used:

Where they are required by law.

In streams where most of the trout you catch will be under 10 inches long. Small trout are not as tough as larger trout, and handling time with them is critical. In addition, their jaws are so delicate that you can easily yank off a piece of jaw if you are not careful. A large hook can also penetrate the eye or even brain of a tiny fish.

Where fishing pressure is high and fish are caught and released many times each season. There is nothing worse than landing a fine rainbow trout, only to find that its jaw looks like it went through a meat grinder from so many hooks carelessly ripped out of the fish.

Catch-and-Release Misconceptions

Sometimes people take catch-and-release fishing over the top, and the worst place this happens is when some self-made expert criticizes another angler's fish-handling techniques in print or on the web. Yes, the angler who squeezed a fish too hard is probably ignorant of proper trout handling, but a public forum is not the place to preach to someone. And often the angler making the criticism is just as ignorant as the accused.

Adult trout are tougher than most people think. During spawning migrations they repeatedly bash themselves against rocks trying to jump falls. Males rip and tear into each other fighting over females. They survive raging floods with a force enough to move boulders with very low mortality. You need to look no further than the real experts, fish biologists, if you doubt adult trout are tough.

Watching biologists sample trout populations gives you a good lesson on just how much handling trout can survive. I live on a small trout stream that supports wild brook, brown, and rainbow trout. Every year either the state or the US Forest Service (sometimes both in the same year) electroshock the stretch of river in my backyard. At first I was worried about this. After all, these are the trout I study and fish for more than any others. I did some research on electroshocking and called a few biologists I know in other parts of the country, and

SCAN TO WATCH VIDEO 016.
Biologists sampling a trout population.

could find no evidence of mortality due to electroshocking. Most sources said it was minimal, less than a few percent. Of course, you can imagine that every time they shock I am right there in the water with them, watching over "my" fish and hoping for some big surprises. I am typically quite accurate in my estimation of the density of the trout population and the maximum size of the fish, although a few years I have been stunned by very large brown trout that had been living under a logjam and under my nose with absolutely no indication of being there.

Here is the process: Four technicians or biologists get into the river. One holds the shocking probe, two net the fish, and one holds the bucket. Trout are stunned to the point that they

When the water temperature pushes 70 degrees, it's time to quit fishing because temperatures in this range put a great strain on a fish's respiration. Its metabolism increases, but warmer water holds less oxygen.

float belly up, then they are scooped by the netters and placed in the bucket. When the bucket gets too full, they are dumped in a holding cage in the river. Once they have completed their first pass, the biologists remove the trout from the holding cage and place them in buckets. The buckets go to shore and the stunned fish, which by now are revived, are further anesthetized by a few drops of clove oil placed into the bucket. Then each one is slapped on a board and measured. They are then laid on a dry scale for weight. Some years their stomachs are pumped to get an idea of what they have been eating. Next they are dumped in another bucket. When that bucket gets full, the fish are placed back in the wire holding cage in the river. Finally the fish are released back into the river.

This seems like rough treatment, but I can assure you I watch the river for weeks afterward and have never seen a dead fish. And dead fish would be visible, because the stream is shallow and clear and does not have much current. I once stupidly killed an 8-inch trout by hooking it deeply and then tossing it back into the river from about a 5-foot bank. That fish died and its body taunted my carelessness as it lay on the bottom, unmolested, for a week before it was finally washed away or grabbed by a mink or raccoon.

The Three Stressors of Released Fish

You definitely can kill a trout by careless handling. Scientific studies of adult trout have shown that three factors are involved.

Temperature: We already know what high water temperatures, above 70 degrees, do to trout. It increases their metabolism but the warmer water holds less oxygen, so fish can literally suffocate, particularly if they are physically stressed, which increases their metabolism even

Besides high water temperature and time out of water, the third stressor on a fish is playing it too long and exhausting it. Only play a fish long enough to get it into the net, where you can quickly remove the hook and get the fish back into the water without any extra handling time. Small fish especially should just be stripped in—don't waste time getting a small fish onto the reel.

If you plan on taking the classic hero shot with a trout totally out of the water, make sure that you keep it close to the water, and never hold it in the air for longer than 15 seconds—which is plenty of time to compose a photograph if you are prepared.

more. Trout can live in water up to about 75 degrees for a day or so, but 70 degrees is a safe number. In recent years, climate change has forced states like Montana to close rivers to fishing entirely or from 2 p.m. until midnight, because low flows that restrict habitat combined with high temperatures that stress trout make fishing a serious threat.

Playing Time: The burst of exercise used by trout to avoid capture places a great deal of stress on their physiological state. Studies have shown that plasma cortisol levels, an indication of the amount of stress placed on a trout's system, rise beyond base levels after two or three minutes of being played on a line. These levels increase dramatically in high water temperatures and if a fish has not fed recently.

Handling Time: The length of time a trout is held out of the water is the third way a trout can be stressed beyond recovery, which makes sense intuitively because while they are in the air, there can be no oxygen uptake through their gills. Mortality has been shown to shave off 20 percentage points when a trout is held out of water for 30 seconds, but 30 seconds is actually a long time. Most studies recommend a trout be returned to the water within 15 to 20 seconds, but that still leaves plenty of time to snap a quick picture.

All of these stressors work together, so if a trout is caught at 70 degrees, played for five minutes, and held out of the water for 30 seconds, its chance of survival is not good, even if it is carefully revived in clear water. But that's an extreme case, and for most situations you should not be overly concerned about the survival of trout if you keep these issues in mind. Some suggestions include:

Get ready for a photograph while still playing a fish. Keep your camera where it can be accessed with one hand if you fish alone, and if you fish with a friend, make sure the other person has the camera turned on, prefocused, at the right zoom level,

I think you can get a far better and less clichéd photograph of a nice fish you've caught by keeping its head in the water. It's much better for the fish because it can continue to breathe while you compose and take the photo.

and ready to go. If a friend uses your camera, make sure you give him or her a quick lesson before you even begin fishing.

Keep the fish in the water at all times if possible. Use a net if you fish tippets 5X or smaller. With heavier tippets you can usually just keep a trout tethered at your side and in the water by trapping it against your leg and holding on to the tippet.

Use barbless hooks and have your forceps where you can reach them with one hand. Barbless hooks definitely reduce handling time and often can be removed quickly with just your fingers. Forceps help to get a hook that is deeper, and my advice if you are fishing for brown trout is to always use forceps because the bigger ones have surprisingly sharp teeth.

Play trout quickly. An 8-inch trout can be brought to hand in about three seconds. A 16-inch trout in fast water can still be easily landed in a minute. Never use light tippets just to be "sporting." There is nothing sporting about playing a trout longer than necessary. There is a fallacy that light, limber rods make it tougher to land a fish quickly, but this is not true. A lighter rod protects tippets from breaking and with solid pressure can land trout as quickly as a stiffer rod.

Never fish for trout in water above 70 degrees.

If you follow the suggestions above, you will never even have to worry about reviving a trout, as a fish played quickly, handled for a few seconds, and kept in the water will jump from your hands fully ready to head back into heavy current. If a trout needs to be revived and held in moderate, clear water for more than a few seconds, you are most likely doing something wrong.

Bleeders

The one serious case, where trout have a good chance of not recovering, are fish that are hooked so deeply they bleed. Trout have few blood vessels in the outer parts of their mouths, but if a hook takes hold in their gills or farther down in their gullet, they will bleed profusely. There is really not much you can do, even if you use a barbless hook, other than to cut your tippet as close to the fly as possible and release the fish quickly. The fish has a much better chance of surviving if you leave the hook in it, and most times the hook will fall out in a few days. If you do like to eat trout and it's legal, you might consider taking a bleeding fish home for dinner.

Wet Hands

I don't know where the whole wet hands idea got started, but the common perception is that you should always handle a trout with wet hands because dry hands remove a protective mucus layer from their skin and opens them up to infections. Trout do have mucus on their skin, but there is no evidence

A trout's colors are so much more vibrant and interesting when shot from underwater. This image was shot with a pocket-size Olympus TG 2 camera.

that wet hands are any more protective than dry hands, no evidence that handling removes any of this mucus, and not even any suggestion in the scientific literature that a handled trout is at any more risk from infection than one that is not handled. If it makes you feel better, wet your hands before handling a trout, but if you do handle a trout with dry hands, don't lose any sleep over it.

Photographing Your Trophy

Think twice about taking a photo of every fish you catch, or even every big fish you catch. It's nice to have a memory, but do you really need a reminder of all the fish you caught? If you do, maybe you should start a fishing journal to remember them there. After all, they pretty much all look alike, unless a fish is truly huge or has unusually brilliant colors, or is the first individual of a particular species you've caught. Every time you take a photo you subject a trout to more handling time, leading to the expression "Facebook is the worst thing that ever happened to catch-and-release fishing."

I've found that I like pictures of trout half in and half out of the water better than grip-and-grin photos, especially when the trout's head is underwater. It adds more drama to the picture, shows the fish closer to its environment, and the flowing water adds more action to the photo or video. In fact, I think photos of trout taken from underwater show their lines and color so much better that most times if I really want a shot of a particularly attractive fish, I will shoot it underwater. You can now buy great pocket cameras that take brilliant underwater shots, with the added advantage that you never have to worry about a rainstorm or a quick spill in the river ruining your camera.

Improving the photographs you share is just one way of getting to the next level in fly fishing. Besides improving your skills on the water, taking care of the resource and showing respect for the fish reveal to yourself and others that you've reached the next level.

BIBLIOGRAPHY

Caucci, Al, and Bob Nastasi. *Hatches II*. New York: Lyons Press, 2004.

Daniel, George. *Dynamic Nymphing*. Harrisburg, PA: Stackpole Books, 2011.

———. *Strip Set*. Harrisburg, PA: Stackpole Books, 2015.

Gordon, Nancy, Thomas McMahon, Brian Finlayon, Christopher Gippel, and Roy Nathan. *Stream Hydrology: An Introduction for Ecologists*. Hoboken, NJ: Wiley, 2004.

Hafele, Rick, and Dave Hughes. *The Complete Book of Western Hatches: An Angler's Entomology and Fly Pattern Field Guide.* Portland, OR: Frank Amato Publications, 1981.

Humphreys, Joe. *Joe Humphreys's Trout Tactics: Updated and Expanded.* Harrisburg, PA: Stackpole Books, 1993.

Mosovsky, John. "Understanding Bioacoustics to Catch More Fish." Article in *The Lehigh River Report*, Issue 60. Trexlertown, PA: Lehigh River Stocking Association, March 2015.

Rosenbauer, Tom. *The Orvis Guide to Prospecting for Trout*. Guilford, CT: Lyons Press, 2008.

———. *The Orvis Guide to Reading Trout Streams*. Guilford, CT: Lyons Press, 1999.

Schnell, Judith, and Judith Stolz (editors). *Trout (Wildlife Series).* Harrisburg, PA: Stackpole Books, 1991.

Swisher, Doug, and Carl Richards. *Selective Trout*. New York: Lyons Press, 2001.

Willers, Bill. *Trout Biology*. New York: Lyons Press, 1991.

Wright, Leonard. *Fishing the Dry Fly as a Living Insect*. New York: E. P. Dutton, 1972.

Wyatt, Bob. *What Trout Want: The Educated Trout and Other Myths*. Harrisburg, PA: Stackpole/Headwater Books, 2013.

INDEX

Page numbers in italics indicate photographs.

ABOUT THE AUTHOR

PHOTO BY ROBIN KADET

Tom Rosenbauer has been with the Orvis Company for forty years, and, while there, has been a fishing-school instructor, copywriter, public relations director, merchandise manager, and editor of *The Orvis News* for ten years. He is currently marketing manager for Orvis Rod and Tackle. As merchandise manager, web merchandiser, and catalog director, the titles under his direction have won numerous Gold Medals in the *Multichannel Merchant* Awards.

Tom was awarded *Fly Rod & Reel*'s "Angler of the Year Award" for 2011 for his educational efforts through his books, magazine articles, and podcasts.

Tom has been a fly fisher for fifty years and was a commercial fly tier by age fourteen. He has fished extensively across North America and has also fished on Christmas Island, in the Bahamas, Belize, Kamchatka, Chile, and on the fabled English chalk streams. He is credited with bringing Bead-Head flies to North America, and is the inventor of the Big Eye hook, Magnetic Net Retriever, and tungsten beads for fly tying. He has about twenty fly fishing books in print, including *The Orvis Fly-Fishing Guide; Reading Trout Streams; Prospecting for Trout; Casting Illusions; Fly-Fishing in America; Approach and Presentation; Trout Foods and Their Imitations; Nymphing Techniques; Leaders, Knots, and Tippets; The Orvis Guide to Dry-Fly Techniques; The Orvis Fly Fishing Encyclopedia;* and *The Orvis Fly-Tying Guide,* which won a 2001 National Outdoor Book Award. His collaboration with photographer Andy Anderson, *Salt*, also won a National Outdoor Book Award in 2014. He has also been published in *Field & Stream, Outdoor Life, Catalog Age, Fly Fisherman, Gay's Sporting Journal, Sporting Classics, Fly Rod & Reel, Audubon, Men's Journal*, and others. His book *The Orvis Guide to Small Stream Fishing*, published in March 2011, is a spectacular book published by the prestigious Rizzoli International, world-renowned for their design and reproduction. Tom is the writer and narrator of "The Orvis Fly-Fishing Guide Podcast," one of the top outdoor podcasts on iTunes. He lives with his wife and son in southern Vermont on the banks of his favorite trout stream.